OAKLAND'S
Neighborhoods

Compiled by Erika Mailman

Made possible by a grant
from the
City of Oakland
Craft and Cultural Arts Department

Published by Mailman Press
Oakland, CA
November 2005
Second Printing, April 2006

ISBN 0-9768144-0-4
Library of Congress Catalog Card Number pending

Designed by Naomi Schiff/Seventeenth Street Studios
Oakland, California

For all general information, contact Mailman Press at:
P.O. Box 2791
Oakland, CA 94602

Introduction

OUR BEAUTIFUL and feisty city Oakland is dear to you, or else you wouldn't be reading this book. While we've had some pretty sharp heydays and are currently on the upswing, the history of Oakland is quite unsavory. From the native Huchiun peoples being pushed out of their land, missionary-ized or killed, to the Spanish government granting the entire East Bay to Don Luis Maria Peralta only to have squatters move in on it, to Horace Carpentier stealing the waterfront . . . it's been a tale told over and over again of land grabs.

But, reasons the little voice inside, who wouldn't want this land? Oakland has an incredible climate that allows us to enjoy being outside all year round, a profusion of interesting flora and fauna, spectacular views of the mountains and bay . . .

And today Oakland has a diversity other cities should strive for, an urban cityscape and yet some very rural locales. Oakland has multiple personalities in the best way possible.

As I began to look into the files at the Oakland History Room, the more fascinated I became. Who knew that a Civil War encampment for troops was clustered all the way west in Oakland? Or that early San Franciscans shipped their dirty laundry to the Oakland hills to be cleaned in a fresh-running creek? I marveled at the audacity of an 1800s developer who named a city after himself and advertised it with painted mules, and it perfectly illustrated the housing boom of the '20s to know that a contest led a man to build his own house in eight hours. Other intriguing tidbits were learning that Scientology grew out of observations its founder made in a hills hospital, that there was a legalized red light district for twenty years near the waterfront, that Lake Merritt was in danger of being filled in and used for a railroad station, and that it was hoped that MacArthur Boulevard would stretch all the way from Canada to Mexico. All of those stories, and many more, are here in this look at how our neighborhoods grew.

Researching was also an eye-opener in terms of the restrictions placed on subdivisions. I'd always heard about the racism, but until I actually saw the wording it wasn't real. There was no down-low on this; it was out in the open. Rather than slimy salesmen hedging that all the lots were already sold, the developers came right out with advertisements in newspapers that spelled out the horror. "These restrictions prohibit the sale of a lot to Chinese, Japanese, Hindus, Negroes or people of their type" reads a typical 1911 advertisement. Those racial covenants were in place until 1948, when a U.S. Supreme Court ruling overturned them. It is a testament to Oakland's resilience that we are such a multi-ethnic city today.

THE STORY STARTS THE SAME

The story of every Oakland neighborhood starts the same, before it splits off into 100 different stories. At one time, the entire range of the East Bay held small bands of Huchiun people living together along the profuse and various creeks that have been in large part now culverted. These groups were quite small, but there were many of them. One account names 96 different tribal groups living in the East Bay. Some people use the term Ohlone to describe the Huchiuns.

After the establishment of the Spanish missions, the padres launched an effort to convert the Huchiuns to Catholicism. Beginning in the 1780s, the Native Americans were baptized as Catholics, and the missionaries urged them into marriages that disregarded already-established polygamous bonds. Diseases which the Huchiuns were ill-prepared to fight beleaguered the missions, as did starvation and the sense that a culture was being lost. The missionaries did their work—within forty years of the Spaniards' arrival, the Native Americans had been assimilated or killed.

The second aspect of the story each Oakland neighborhood holds in common is that they were all once part of Don Luis Maria Peralta's lands. Peralta arrived in Northern California in 1776 as part of the Juan Bautista de Anza expedition, which rode up the peninsula to find sites for the Presidio and Mission of San Francisco. The group had started out from Tubac, Mexico, with 250 people and 1,000 cattle. While they were at it, the group explored the East Bay too.

Peralta was seventeen years old at the time, making the journey with his parents and three siblings. His family settled in Monterey, and when Peralta turned 21, he entered the Spanish military, protecting the various missions. In 1805, Native Americans attacked the priest and majordomo of Mission San Jose, and Peralta's hot pursuit and victory over the attackers fortified his prestige. He was 46 at the time. He continued to grow in rank until 1822, when Mexico became independent from Spain. But two years before that point, Peralta was given an unbelievable gift.

The Spanish government, pleased with his service, gave Peralta the entire East Bay.

It is mind-boggling to consider the scope of that gift given today's real estate prices. Although the beneficiary never actually lived in Oakland, his sons certainly did. Peralta had four of them, and in 1842 he divvied up the lands among them. The son named Antonio definitely got the sweet deal, with significantly more acreage than his brothers.

But the land proved too irresistible for others to simply let it lay. Squatters descended on the land and in turn sold it to gullible others. The Peralta brothers tried to keep track of their land, but the landholdings were so enormous as to render this nearly impossible. Antonio, for example, had over 15,000 acres to watch over. The Peraltas took their case to court, but litigation was protracted and even though they eventually won on paper, they had already lost on the turf.

After this, the story varies for Oakland's neighborhoods. Some land was part of a "lease" from Vicente Peralta to Horace Carpentier, Andrew Moon and Edson Adams. Some areas hosted lumbermen, ship's deserters or failed gold seekers, who left their mark on the land. Some parts remained bucolic, slowly-settled pasturelands, while others quickly bustled with immigrants who had heard the story of gold. And that is where this book begins.

> **WHICH BROTHER GOT WHAT**
>
> IGNACIO:
> From San Leandro Creek to Seminary Avenue
>
> DOMINGO:
> All of Berkeley, Albany, and part of North Oakland
>
> ANTONIO:
> Seminary Avenue to Lake Merritt
>
> VICENTE:
> Everything north and west of Lake Merritt, to about Alcatraz Avenue

THE BIG DISCLAIMER

Trying to identify crisp, clean boundaries for Oakland's neighborhoods is a complex task. There is amorphous fluidity to these borders, names that overlap the same plot of land, neighborhoods that seem to spread and even some that retract . . . . While I had lofty ideals of a comprehensive book that covered every single neighborhood and housing tract, drawing boundary lines for each with a definitive marker on the map, that soon became impracticable. I know with certainty that there are significant things I have overlooked, a disappointing inevitability with a project of this scope. I apologize in advance if you do not see mentioned in this book a part of this city that means something to you.

HOW THIS BOOK BEGAN

This book began with a grant proposal to the city of Oakland's Craft and Cultural Arts Department. A prerequisite of pride is knowing what it is you're aligned to. The goal of this book was to help residents become better acquainted with their own neighborhood, learning its history and identifying with the area that they live in.

The book, as my proposal read, would incorporate brief histories of the neighborhoods, historical photographs and creative writing by residents about their neighborhoods. The proposal also included holding several writing workshops at various library branches to get the word out about the book and invite submissions.

The creative writing workshops were a pleasure. Although they were only intended to be one-time events, I ended up returning to the Elmhurst Branch Library in a semi-regular fashion after the young writers there asked me at the end, "When are you coming back?" and I made a split-second decision to extend the workshops. I have the highest regard for those teens and younger children and was glad to get to know them in some small way.

Some of the Elmhurst students' poems appear here. Arising out of one of our writing games, the poems spell out the word Elmhurst at the beginning of each line. Writing along with them, I wrote one for my neighborhood Glenview, which also appears here.

Talking with Melinda Barnes of Mills College's Place for Writers led to yet another funded grant proposal, submitted by her to the Wallace

Although there is visible development in the background, this early undated photograph shows Temescal Creek as it might've appeared to the Huchiun people who hunted and fished along it in tule canoes.

Foundation, which stationed Mills graduate students in creative writing at six different Oakland library branches for free workshops.

Compiling creative writing from residents was an interesting task, and I thank Melinda Barnes and Gary Turchin for assisting me with screening the submissions.

And then I launched into the research. Steve Lavoie of the Oakland History Room of the Oakland Public Library, who had written a letter to the grant committee in support of the project, assisted me in compiling materials for this book, helped vet it, and then contributed two fine poems.

I made the decision not to footnote each reference or quotation but rather to quote generally in terms of "a 1921 newspaper article stated…" This book is not meant to be a scholarly reference but rather a personal look at the neighborhoods. If you wish to learn more about your neighborhood (and believe me, there is more available), I urge you to visit the Oakland History Room in the main library on 14th Street and ask to view materials on your neighborhood. The History Room is there for all of us to use, and you will look at your own neighborhood with fresh eyes once you know more about what used to happen there.

ACKNOWLEDGMENTS

I owe tremendous thanks to Betty Marvin, Gail Lombardi, Steve Lavoie and Dennis Evanosky for helping me try to corral these neighborhoods and for vetting the book. These people know Oakland's history backwards and forwards, and I am honored by their participation and assistance. Any errors that remain I take sole responsibility for.

I also want to thank organizations like the Oakland Public Library, which was so generous with its materials and meeting spaces; Oakland Cultural Heritage Survey, which has a treasurehouse of information on our city's buildings and homes; the Oakland Heritage Alliance, which publishes a thoughtful, scholarly quarterly and very actively advocates historic preservation; the city's Craft and Cultural Arts Department, which funded the project; and OCCUR, which created wonderful Neighborhood Profiles pamphlets.

I am also indebted to Beth Bagwell's *Oakland, the Story of a City,* which is an invaluable, beautifully-written reference.

Naomi Schiff of Seventeenth Street Studios designed the book. Seeing the book cover she designed was a huge impetus for the last push of getting this book to the printer.

Thanks to Mary Farrell and Patricia Richard of the Oakland Public Library as well as the other branch managers who helped me set up workshops.

I'd like to thank Dick Sparrer and the *Montclarion* newspaper for giving me the chance to become a history columnist. Since the first column in July 1999, I've appreciated the access to the Oakland History Room materials that this column afforded me as well as a good, solid reason to dig into the history of my adopted hometown.

And finally, thanks to all the contributors who took the time to send in their work!

Erika Mailman
September 2005
www.erikamailman.com

Contributors

Tracy Adamski

Bettina Alfred

Sissy Acton

Sanford Ames

Yolande Barial

Sophie Bennett

John Brennan

Susan Bryant

Yvonne Byron

Constance Callahan

Maria Cervantes

Steve Chow

Shemariae Bryanna Christian

Nicole Cooksey

Wendy Dutton

Anna Edmondson

Christina Eng

Alison Chokwadi Fletcher

Max Conneman

Ralph Fenno

Adelle Foley

Jack Foley

Edna Fong

Jesy Goldhammer

Rudy Gray

Haleh Hatami

Lorenzo Hearod

Dan Hess

Donovan Hoch

Zach Hofsteder

Natasha Horowitz

Alan Howard

Diana Iversen

Rosa Jimenez

Rhoda Johnson

My-Kell Jolly

Oktayveya Jones

Tobey Kaplan

Tisha Kennings

Jennifer King

Belinda Kling

Peter Kunka

Dana Lange

Steven Lavoie

Lin Lee

Manuel Lopez

Paradise FreeJah Love

Rose Mark

Alison McLean

Charlie Melville

Jack Miller

Sam Milston

Nancy Mattison

Rachel Medanic

Clarissa Mettica

• **X** •

Sara Moore

Thomas Nash

Kathy Nguyen

Judith Offer

Harsha Patel

Chi Phan

Darla Pritsky

Mark Rauzon

Mona Reich

Phillip Richards

Mark Rogers

Floyd Salas

Mertis Shekeloff

Gentian Smith

Margarita Soares

Mark States

Jan Steckel

Robert Steele

Phillina Sun

Samantha Tigsdale

Hanh Tran

Brian Tso

Gary Turchin

D'Jos Upton

Lenore Weiss

Magda White

Lois Wills

Russell Yee

Andrena Zawinski

Jhian Zhong

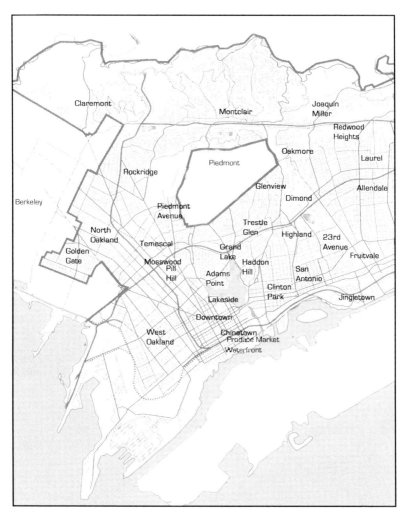

Claremont

Montclair

Joaquin
Miller

Redwood
Heights

Oakmore

Laurel

Piedmont

Rockridge

Glenview

Allendale

Berkeley

Dimond

Piedmont
Avenue

North
Oakland

Trestle
Glen

Highland

23rd
Avenue

Temescal

Grand
Lake

Fruitvale

Golden
Gate

Mosswood
Pill
Hill

Haddon
Hill

San
Antonio

Adams
Point

Clinton
Park

Jingletown

Lakeside

Downtown

West
Oakland

Chinatown
Produce Market
Waterfront

1 MILE

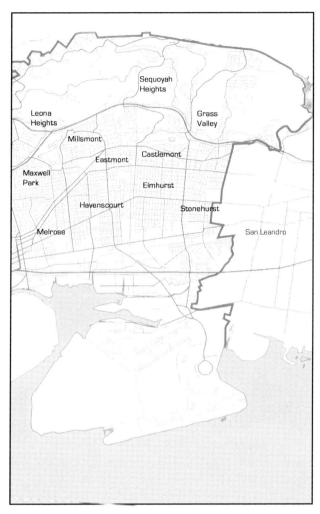

This map is based on a 1994 City of Oakland Map from the Office
of Planning and Building, which credited a 1993 CSAA Street Base Map

ADAMS POINT

WHERE: *The area bounded by the lake, Harrison Street/Oakland Avenue, Grand Avenue and MacArthur Boulevard.*

THIS NEIGHBORHOOD is named for pioneer Edson Adams, who settled the north end of the lake in the 1850s. One newspaper article calls him "Oakland's first real estate man." He was one of three men who squatted on land belonging to Don Vicente Peralta, the son of Don Luis Maria Peralta—the lucky soldier who received the entire East Bay as a gift from Spain in 1822 and dispensed it among his four sons in 1842. Adams' squatting mates were Horace Carpentier and Andrew Moon—those three men's "holdings" constituted the original city of Oakland. Adams Point is composed of several tracts, the oldest of which was an 1869 subdivision.

Due to a large refugee camp established in 1906 for those fleeing the burning rubble of San Francisco, the area began settling heavily after that time as some people decided to stay. The refugee camp housed thousands. A June 21, 1906 newspaper article—the earthquake was April 18—reported the closure of the Adams Point Camp: "There they were,

A 1930s view of Adams Point

The white tents of the 1906 refugee camp on the shores of the lake can be seen in the distance.

the silent people, packing their scant worldly belongings, a mattress, blankets, a dress or two and the little trifles which they had collected . . . . Those who were going to San Francisco had their things piled on the freight cars which took them to the steamer *Caroline* awaiting them at First Street and Broadway."

But many people who moved to Adams Point were already Oaklanders, including John McElroy. The 1911 fountain in Lakeside Park was erected in his honor after he died suddenly of pneumonia. He was city attorney, known for fighting the Southern Pacific railroad to get back Oakland's waterfront. He is also responsible for the bond issue that created Lakeside Park, releasing Lake Merritt and its grounds from private ownership and opening it to the entire city. His house on Lee Street was a 1907 Julia Morgan design.

The Bellevue-Staten is another landmark in the neighborhood. Built in 1928–29 by the Lakeview Building Company as cooperative housing, today it is condominiums. The gorgeous high-rise on the edge of the lake provides a distinctive silhouette, with its multi-tiered roofing with Art Deco detailing.

Around that time, women created the nearby Women's Athletic Club at 525 Bellevue Avenue, a place for them to meet, dine, and sleep. Its

French-style architecture now houses a still-active club for men and women, known as the Bellevue Club.

Also in the neighborhood, people frolicked in water heated by the steam engine that drove the cables for the streetcars at the Piedmont Baths at Bay Place and Vernon Street. They could also marvel at plants in the 75-foot glass Harmon Conservatory, where the Veterans Memorial Building is now. The baths and the conservatory are gone.

"Adams Point was a mysterious, a romantic spot. Masses of old live oaks with all sorts of wild flowers underneath them . . . . It was quite a long row across the boulevard-less lake in our old white boat the Lady of the Lake . . . The streets were only sandy lanes wandering among huge live oaks in the 1860s." This was from a 1942 letter in the Oakland History Room written by Mrs. E.K. Tompkins, whose father was a friend of Dr. Samuel Merritt and bought land in Oakland in 1861. Her uncle was Governor Henry Haight, and her older brother was one of Oakland's first schoolchildren.

Several Adams Point residents were prestigious men. George Perkins was a senator and California governor. Victor Metcalf was a Congressman and presidential cabinet man. Together, they were largely responsible for bringing President Theodore Roosevelt to Oakland for his 1903 visit of . . . a whopping hour and a half. After the 1906 earthquake, Metcalf was Roosevelt's special representative, sent to San Francisco to assess damage and report back. Mayor Frank Mott was also an Adams Point resident.

For information on Lake Merritt itself, see the listing for Lakeside.

The Sounds of Home

BY RACHEL MEDANIC

*". . . down his nose. Greasy fingers smearing shabby
clothes. Heeey Aqualung. Drying in the cold sun. Watching all the pretty pennies run. Haaa*

*yyyy . . . Aqualung. Feeling like a dead duck, spitting out
pieces of his broken luck. Heeey Aqualung."*

The Doppler effect grips Ian Anderson pouring out from the topless,
cherry red Chrysler Sebring roaring up Perkins Street. Convertibles in
November? Welcome. Welcome to California. In fact, welcome to Oakland. Here in my home, you're just as likely to hear something like this as
you are to hear the deep throb of a loaded, battle-worn Cadillac or
Oldsmobile Cutlass Supreme as the metal of its back end pulses and
vibrates to the merciless bass of the stereo thrust into its front end. One
sunny day, I had an opportunity to ask a fellow Oaklander who was trying to hit on me what it meant.

"What is it with the stereo thing and having the bass at so many deci-
bels so the poor car vibrates and trembles?"

"It's totally a guy thing—totally. It's not even about getting the ladies
to look. It's guys getting the attention of other guys. The bigger the
sound, the bigger the message 'Hey, I got the biggest sound around.'"

Sound. Another vehicle for testosterone? Why yes, even Nature can
verify that. In the quiet moments, when no cars are speeding by, you can
hear the scratchy throated chirping call of some hummingbird throwing
his sound around. Chirping out unspecific yet "within earshot" (ear?)
warnings to some hapless Western Jay or an out-of-line Chickadee. What
kind of music would the male hummingbirds play if they had access to
souped-up Oldsmobiles to drive (fly?) around?

Here, during California's supple November weather, the soft clickety-
clack of half-downed, muted tone yellow and red leaves tremble in
pointed wind that can sometimes turn vicious, suddenly aware that it is
winter, and it'd better start blowing like it! Some of the trees that have

been watered all summer have these resilient leaves—able to hang on in the generally amenable climate. Humans drive convertibles, humming-birds are present all year and the leaves just hang on, hanging around until they are pushed away by the buds of spring. Nature's eviction process . . . or is it gentrification?

"Don't walk so close, bitch," attacks a tall girl of about 15 as I have to angle nearer to her to walk past because of a jogger approaching head on.

I can see her point of view, sort of. How many people have stood or put their shopping carts practically up against me in line at the grocery store? But the oncoming jogger had forced me to get within about six inches.

"I'm just walking."

"What'd you say?!" she screeches in rage.

She increases her walking pace to catch up with me, mustering a vibe to intimidate me in support of her misplaced cause. What could she be on? The emerald grass from the park behind her glistens as we proceed down Grand Avenue, now beginning to interact. My steps slow to address her hostility. I can't avoid the look of consternation on my face. But I can't run either.

"What'd you say, white bitch?"

"I said, I'm just walking."

"You say anything an' I'm gon' murdur yor shit, Cuz!"

The Black English Vernacular is drifting somewhere over my head. The implied threat hasn't fully resonated with me and she knows it. She can see it floating . . . several inches over my head as I deconstruct her sentence. I am an immigrant to Oakland, an invader. I know that. I knew that when I came here in 2000. But can't I make it up in love for the place, in respect, in being involved with the community? I begin to shake my head sadly

I walk onward, turning away from her. Not sure she'll follow. She's making like she's after me at first, but peripherally, I see her rage has sub-sided because her threat, while duly felt, has been in another language. It hasn't affected me as fully as she'd hoped. The roots of Oakland most certainly do have conflict in them. It's conflict between classes—which in America often translates to race. I took six inches more than she could afford to give me without protest. But this is one of the things that I love about Oakland; I noticed the variety of people when I first came in 2000 to Adams Point. We have every color under the racial rainbow and that is a source of great pride for me. I'm disappointed by her, but not undaunted in my mission to continue being. Sometimes, all the sounds a place makes aren't joyous.

But they can be mysterious and ironic. Like the bellowing foghorn offshore near the Port of Oakland in the summer, when the fog gets so thick you have a hard time associating the month of July with anything as far south as Northern California. Or the joy and gratitude I felt the first time I saw the Oakland Interfaith Gospel choir at Christmas. A Korean man with the most gorgeous African-American voice singing "I Stood on the River Jordan." Paul Kim, the choir's Assistant Director. Mystery—of course, we must choose to ingest it into our lives. There's not much occurring naturally any more. During the dot-com boom, I would flee my cubicle for the soft, quiet utterances of my yoga teacher Robert. His vivid, instructive descriptions of *exactly* what happens and where resistance will crop up in a body performing Iyengar yoga positions are meditative, unforgettable and sacred.

"Root the belly back and into the earth through your legs. Feel the earth through your legs and connect with the seasons and the cycles of birth and death that are happening. Let what is in your mind now fall away and become less important."

But sometimes, it is a wonder why some sounds do get retained in memory. The unassuming, beep, beep, beep of the elevator at the Scottish Rite Temple as it climbs its way up to the fourth floor, for instance. All I can hear is the submarine from *20,000 Leagues Under the Sea* as each floor passes. Every December, there are joyous sounds brought to this theater. The shuffle of feet on the rug, moving clothing and shoe steps on a wooden stage as hundreds of people dance in snake patterns, connected hand to hand and moving around the theater, into the lobby and up on stage in celebration of the returning light of the Winter Solstice and the Shortest Day. As they dance, slightly incorrect lyrics to the refrain of *The Lord of the Dance* are sung,

"Dance, dance wherever you may be. I am the Lord of the Dance said he. And I'll lead you all, wherever you may be. And I'll lead you all in the dance said he." One word gets sung wrong year after year. The actual lyrics are, "Dance, *then*, wherever you may be . . ."

There simply is no place to dance like at home in the living room. Since I came to Oakland, I've made my threshold in three places—all within .2 miles of each other. With each apartment, I've pushed the limits of my "desired criteria" list ever further, always reaching for the right blend of charm, space, light, ventilation, price, access to green space and amenities. My current apartment suffers from lack of space and sunlight but excels in late evenings on summer nights when, if you listen very closely, you can actually hear the quiet sweet pulsation of crickets that reside in the thick brush of an abutting yard. It's a lot to ask, to be able to walk to a fabulous café or restaurant *and* to hear crickets at night.

Oakland is a community that both asks and gives a lot. Every Saturday, I volunteer at Oakland Animal Services because it gives me hope and joy. My work there helps validate where and how I can make a difference in my own back yard.

"How long have you been doing the veterinary technician stuff?" I ask our Community Outreach Program Manager as we inspect a homeless kitten.

"Since June."

"Why haven't they hired a replacement?"

"It's political. The City Council wanted to have another Executive Director on board before they hired a replacement."

The health, welfare and operational (volunteer) support for a facility with hundreds of animals is in her hands. I remember reading about the Executive Director giving notice to move on in the late Fall. She has been doing two huge jobs ever since. In my mail a few weeks ago, I received an invitation to Councilmember Nancy Nadel's holiday party for the community. I wonder what percentage of local politics are actually significantly influenced at parties or social gatherings.

But Oakland does respond if an issue is threatening enough. You don't always know what will fire up the community's ideology, but when it is aroused it is an obstacle to be reckoned with. The Lakeshore Avenue church is filled with hundreds of people—crying babies, children, strollers and all on a weeknight. It is the public's chance to meet Mr. Hahn, an African-American owner of the ancient Kwikway burger joint on Lake Park. He wants to sell his land to McDonald's so they can put in a drive-through. At the microphone, Mr. Hahn tells us that he didn't expect so many people to attend, but that he *too* is a "family man" with children of his own. He tells us he cares about what happens to Oakland and to the community, but that he also has a right to pursue free enterprise. Muttered, scornful retorts pepper the pews around me. Community members are invited up to the microphone at the podium to publicly share their concerns.

"I grew up in East Oakland and I've lived here all my life. And you should all be glad that you have the ability to come together to fight this. Where I grew up, we didn't have no way to keep McDonald's out of our neighborhood."

Others share their concerns at the microphone with varying degrees of decorum: an elementary school is nearby and the children will be the customers (victims); pedestrian walk patterns already jeopardized by existing traffic volume (Kwikway sits one block between on and off ramps to the freeway) will face further threats from a drive-through; cars driving through will reduce air quality and increase trash. But one simple comment hits the nail on the head.

"This is about brothers taking advantage of brothers," says an African-American man at the microphone.

These are the sounds of my home. A place where I am proud to have a chance to honor the diversity around me and "act locally" to be the change I want to see in the world.

Achimar

BY NICOLE COOKSEY

once upon a time, say last night, there was this girl. and she was a very funny girl, she was very silly and light, flippant some would say. would they be right? perhaps. but that's really not the point. anyway, this girl, this day, or night as it were, this night she was drunk. she was roasted. lit. fired. filled to the rim with the richness of brim. she was done. she had gone out for her friend's going away party and instead of taking a ride home, she decided to walk. and honestly, she really liked walking home alone at night, for whatever reason. it wasn't a smart thing to do, she knew that, that hadn't completely missed her, but she liked to do it nonetheless. it gave her a charge, a certain verve. it's weird how you have to be on the edge sometimes to realize how peaceful it is in the middle, you know? does that make sense?

anyway, so this drunk girl walking home late sounds like a story you read in the newspaper underneath the headline "body found," but joy-fully, that's not the way this story ends, though there are moments of doubt. as she walks and weaves this boy comes up behind her, this whistling boy. this whistling boy is walking just over her left shoulder and she's thinking of walking faster, thinking of the headline "body found" because she doesn't know the end of the story yet. she jumps this low stone wall, a move she's always proud of whenever she does it, it just makes her feel happy and athletic. strong. she jumps the wall in a skirt, no less, a long dark skirt with deep slits down the sides. and she thinks to herself, "i bet he didn't think i'd do that, i bet he didn't think i could do that. i can do anything. i can do everything" because that's how little drunk girls think. and they're not completely wrong.

so the boy behind her keeps whistling and he gives a long whistle when he sees her jump the wall and after the jump he catches up to her and he says, "hello hello" and he has a very thick accent, as it turns out. he's egyptian he says which is fun for the girl because she's never met an egyptian before and at the time she was thinking, "it's weird he's so light," but in retrospect, that's silly because not all people from africa are black and egypt is actually closer to the middle east where the people are not black but tan, light-ish but mostly she just thought it was cool to meet someone who was egyptian. she really liked other countries and meeting people from different countries and she often thought she should learn to speak more languages because she was really good at them.

"hello hello what is your name?" he says first and she laughs to herself because this happens to her often, these people that call out to her on the street. it's weird because the boys she would really like to call out to her never do but the other ones just pipe up all the time, they can't seem to let her past without dropping something at her feet. some word, a name, a dirty thought that she can't wash off, just anything. but none of it works, generally, and she wonders why they do this, she wonders what they hope will come of these cast lines but then again, maybe each of them have stories like this.

so she laughs and gives her stock false name, "michelle, my name is michelle" which is not her name but is often a name she is mistakenly called. maybe she looks like a michelle, but really she doesn't think she does. "o michelle, how are you doing tonight? where are you going?" he is trying to keep up with her though she's walking very fast. "i'm going home, i've got to get home" she says with a smile and doesn't turn around. "i am going home too" he says "i will walk you, i walk to you, no, with you, i will walk with you" and this endears him to her because she loves helping people and watching people learn and he is learning english so she slows down. "i live on oakland" she is looking at him now and enunciating her words, exaggerating her lips so he can see how words are pronounced, so he can read her lips "i live on oakland too, me too, 407" which technically is just a few blocks ahead of her but for some reason he never makes it to 407 oakland.

he has headphones and a cd player, that's what he was whistling. "it's egyptian music" he says but pronounces it much different, his e's are much longer than hers, she doesn't know why. he puts the headphones on her and pushes play and she listens to egyptian music walking down the dark street with the boy she doesn't know but she likes the music, it's like dance music like house but there is a wailing in the background like is it indian music where there is wailing in the background? if it is then that's what this was, that's what it sounded like. "i like it. it's good, like dance music, it's very good, who is it?" "amour deenib" is what it sounds like he says. she stops and reads the cd he shows her, amar dnab, though she thinks she won't remember it later and he says to her, "you drink? you drinking you?" and she smiles and sways "yes, yes, i've been drinking" and he makes a face. "drink is bad, is bad to be drinking. muslim" he points to his chest "muslim like me: no drink, drinking very bad, to drink and to pig ermmm pork? is bad, drink and pork bad" and he reduces years of faith, bitter jihads, the pharisees and moses, to two command-ments: thou shalt not drink, thou shalt not pork.

well, none of this is going over well with the girl. she really has a prob-lem with authority and she really really has a problem with people telling her what to do and she really really really has a problem with stupid boys who've just met her and think they can attribute their stupid faiths and traditions to her obviously american, drunk, bent self. "that's good for you" she smiles, slithers "you shouldn't drink, it's bad for you" and she walks away faster. really though she thinks, "who does he think he is telling me what's right and what's not? this from a man who covers his women, who hides them from themselves, why would i ever listen to any-thing he has to say?" and she asks him, "isn't it weird to see me?" "weird?" he echoes and gestures with his hands in a shrug and she mimes being covered up, wearing a burqa, "i should be covered" she says, "should i be covered?" and he smiles and says, "no it's good not to be covered, it's good to walk, walk down the street" he says "but it's bad to drink" he adds, covering well trod territory. "you are christian?" he says and she nods, sure, christian sounds good. she believes in God, maybe that's not entirely the same thing but she can't figure out how she'd mime the dif-ference between religion and spirituality and isn't it just a weird night to be walking down the street having a religious argument with some ran-dom egyptian boy who is trying to get her to stop drinking, a feat even her mother can't perform. "good christians, they don't drink. christians don't drink, drink is bad" he says with a smile as if his thoughts are going to change her world "yes" she says and agrees "i am a bad christian" she says with a smile, she says it simply though in truth it makes her sad because she really does believe and she fears often she is going to hell and if she were stronger she probably would stop drinking but she's not.

he reaches for her and strokes her chin kind of like reaching up and picking fruit off a tree, a peach, gently because you don't want to squeeze the juice. no one has touched her in a very long time and no one has ever stroked her chin like that, like she was ripe, like she was smooth and firm and ready. and she likes it. she likes that such intimate things can happen with strangers. "you are not bad" he says and absolves her like a priest "you are not bad" and he starts to walk with her again and he doesn't notice how she tilts her head so the tears run down her far cheek.

"i would to kiss to you" he says on the next block and it was just that sudden. it came out of nowhere. honestly, it had probably been in the air the whole time. it's rare that a boy starts talking to a random girl, drunk, under the cover of night without wanting, waiting to kiss her. but honestly she forgot there was a game in play. she forgot that she had a role here and there was something to be gained or lost. "kiss you here" and he touches her lips "kiss" she says "you can't kiss me" she smiles "good muslims don't kiss girls they don't know" and he stops her and holds her hips "i am bad, kiss me" and it's funny because minutes ago he was a prophet and now he has aligned himself with evil to taste her. "no, it's bad to kiss" she says, teasing and funny though part of her is reading tomorrow's headline and beginning to be a little concerned. she moves around him.

"once" he says, dogging her steps, "kiss you once" and she relents because she's . . . well, many things: bored stupid tired drunk randy thoughtful spiritual ridiculous and she kisses him and really he has very soft lips. it's been a long time between kisses and she's forgotten how soft they are, how they fold and smooth, shape and she uses her lips to encircle his top lip and she sucks at it slightly she pulls on it and then she strokes it with her teeth she nips at it and she's really glad that a) he has a really dry mouth. there are lots of people that are really spitty kissers and b) he's not a bad kisser, he doesn't cram her full of tongue, their teeth don't bump, he doesn't breathe into her mouth though she does notice that he smells lightly like garlic but it's not a bad smell it just smells like he works in a kitchen (which he actually does, this story has been edited for size) and she's always liked kitchens because they're warm. she stops eventually, she stops kissing him in the middle of the sidewalk, three blocks down from her house. she pushes him back and his eyes shine. "wait, again" he says like a child with a new toy, "once more" he says and she starts to worry now if this boy is going to follow her all the way home "no, because it's bad" she says but she doesn't really believe that. she thinks it's fun and funny. she thinks it's something that no one else will believe she's done. she thinks it's funny because she spends each day standing up straight and thinking that people would never think she does the things she does like when she pees in back alleys or not even back alleys but front yards and mailboxes and wherever else she can get to; like when she shoplifts from the store, the eyeliners and the lipsticks and the hand lotions and really these are silly things these are junior high things and why does she like these small stupid things why does she like doing them?

she walks away from him now while he is grabbing at her hand and he holds on and comes around front, "please once more" he says, "again" and he holds her arms and she doesn't like that, she doesn't like how he holds her and she starts wondering if she can take him but she's still not really scared because she's a stupid girl two blocks from her house and she's drunk and for some reason she just believes herself invincible and honestly, if God could interject, he would probably say all the same things but maybe he would give reasons for why he's spared her life so often because he has, he's saved her a lot and it doesn't make sense but maybe it doesn't have to so she kisses him again and she still likes the feel of his lips and how he crushes her against him and he has stubble that is scratching at her chin and lower, farther down he is rubbing into her hip, the Him of he, the It, that is growing, that is growling, that is moving on its own and it really is. it must be so weird to have a part of your body that does its own thing, that you're not really in control of, it's like if for some reason your ears just took to wiggling or your nose just chose to move down your face. really bizarre. i don't know if it's really like that but that's what it seems like but i'm sure this is not what anyone really wants to hear about.

she pushes him away again "bye" she says and keeps walking but he follows her again and maybe this is why he seems so harmless how he follows like a puppy, how he runs after her and waits and hopes and begs and it's interesting how cruel all this makes her sound isn't it? cheap and easy and mean, like cruella de vil on spanish fly, like joan crawford in mommie dearest but honestly it didn't feel like that at the time, it was more sort of thrilling without going off the edge, it was walking the line and tipping ever so slightly tipping which is exactly what she was doing walking drunk down the street away from the boy who followed still and said "again again please" as they had become his new favorite english words and it's weird that before they had managed to talk about so many things without him even knowing the language, he had told her about his job and she had told him about hers ("you know computers?" "computers?" blank stare "the internet?" "yes, internet!" "i work with computers" "yes, computers" "a database" "data . . ." "nevermind") and he had told her about egypt and his family and they had had a whole freakin' argument about faith and now all he could say was "please" and "again" like he was three like it was the only thing he could ever think to say ever again. "how do you say it in egyptian?" she says to buy time and because she does like languages, it's always good to know these things, you'll never know when you'll need them. "say it in egyptian: one more" "achimar" he smiles with his shiny eyes "achimar" he says with a tilty head like he's asked for a cookie, like he's asked for allowance. "achimar" she says and holds up a finger so he knows for sure she's said it in her language she's said it in his language she's said it in the universal language (which is math, by the way, not love) "achimar" because she's close to her house now and she's afraid he'll follow her in, follow her in and demand all of it, do something to her roommate and her kitchenware. because if one kiss could make him forget he's a good teetotalling muslim what would two do? what would three do? and come to think of it, she doesn't know his age, she doesn't know has he done this before, has he kissed anyone before? do they allow kisses in egypt? can the women uncover their mouths without fear?

and he reaches in for her and his hands crush her back and he bunches up her shirt in his hands which is a shame because she just ironed it and she licks his lips like a cat like ice cream the pointy little parts and if they were anywhere else this would actually be sweet it's sweet to be so wanted so desired that people are chucking out faith that they are tossing mohammed from windows that allah's shoved off the balcony like so much dirt or pine needles but she has to remember, she starts to remember that she doesn't know him that she's not special to him that she could be any girl she's just the girl that let a boy she doesn't know kiss her while walking home from the bart station. she licks the inside of his lips she nips with her teeth she presses her lips full against his and she pulls back to quick small pecks before she licks again and presses full and all the while he is pressing, pressing against her pressing into her willing himself inside of her. he touches her skin where her shirt has come up and he sighs and holds on tight.

she crosses her hands in front of her chest and pushes him back and he moves back, he's so easy. she's sure someone else would have raped her by now. standing in the forest island that divides her one way street from another she could be taken in back of the tree he could ball his fist and knock her in the eye he could slap her hard so she falls and fall on her then and press her down with his weight rip her skirt drive his knee between her thighs oh he could be horrible he could be horrible he could be horrible . . .

"achimar" he says, pleading, he pleads with her, he begs "achimar" he says in a whine and his eyes are shining still and she looks at him there under the street lamp and he truly glows he is light and so she says no "no" she says "i am bad and i will make you bad" "achimar" "no" and she walks away from him "please wait" he says standing still for once "wait your number" he says "phone number" he says "michelle" and it's sad because he doesn't know that the thing she likes best is walking away from someone who wants her.

ALLENDALE

WHERE: *Roughly bounded by Foothill and MacArthur boulevards, between the Fruitvale neighborhood and Maxwell Park*

LIKE A lot of Oakland neighborhoods, Allendale began as its own settlement. It was annexed to Oakland in 1909.

In 1895, the little village had only four cottages, but five years later 60 families lived there. The 1906 earthquake brought over a fair number of San Franciscans. They settled into the small town of Allendale, which now had a Methodist church, a bakery, a butcher shop, a hardware store, a community hall and a saloon—all located on Allendale Avenue.

A year later, talk of annexation to Oakland began. The *Fruitvale Progress* reported in 1907 on an annexation meeting: "Attorney Hufacker, in a long speech, stated that Allendale was populated by a very bad lot of people; that policemen were the most needed thing in Allendale, to drive undesirable characters away." Another complaint at the meeting was that there was a bad smell due to the lack of sewers. The 45

This 1911 photograph is labeled "Joe's barn on High Street."

OAKLAND HISTORY ROOM OF THE OAKLAND PUBLIC LIBRARY

This undated photo shows the streetcar and, in the distance, the lighted sign for the Allendale Theatre.

citizens present planned to take a straw ballot to show Oakland Mayor Frank Mott that they were in favor of annexation. Two years later, Allendale was folded into Oakland.

Around the time Allendale joined Oakland, the streetcar line arrived. A huge celebratory barbecue was held on the vacant lot at Liese (today, 38th) and Allendale avenues.

The neat neighborhood of bungalows was praised in the *Fruitvale Progress*: "To be sure, they are not palaces, but they are 'homes,' built by hard working men, endowed with pride and pluck to secure a home for their loved ones."

The Allendale Improvement Club had 250 members in 1910 and worked to make the district better. The executive board's initiation that year involved board members riding goats, to "create more interest in the work of the club," according to the newspaper.

But soon people began reminiscing about the old Allendale days. A 1915 article ran with the headline, "Old-Timers Working Hard to Keep Name in Popular Usage." Apparently some people wanted the district to be called Brookdale, and to add insult to injury, they had asked the City Council to change the name of Allendale Avenue to Fairweather Avenue (W.D. Fairweather worked in the construction department of the Oakland, Antioch and Eastern railroad.) Neither suggestion panned out.

The Allendale Theatre was built in 1927 and seated 800. This art deco structure still stands, now in a new use as Theater Apartments, at 3116 Liese Ave. Most of Liese is now 38th Avenue except that one short stretch. Egyptian "papyrus" columns frame the entrance with goddess statues holding instruments. It closed as a theater in 1941.

35th Avenue Ladybug

BY JAN STECKEL

Ladybug, ladybug,
go fly away home.
Your house is on fire,
and the whole neighborhood
has turned out to watch.
The popsicle guy rolls
his Delicias de Michoacan cart over.
They're selling refrescos
and chicharrones
on the pavement outside,
cuz this is East Oakland, bug!
Who knows when the fuck
that fire truck
is ever gonna arrive?

Allendale up and over

BY ROSA JIMENEZ

Sideways, Allendale, that's
the way it goes, up and over
through the avenue

I'm no stranger to the danger
I'm no pipsqueak for the earthquake

The land just rolls over and over
and all we say is counting up to 35th
and counting down to come back

through
the avenue

CASTLEMONT

WHERE: *In the vicinity of Castlemont High School*

THE NEIGHBORHOOD gets its name from Castlemont High School, which was originally named the East Oakland High School. Located at Foothill and 84th Avenue, a November 1929 article said it was "designated the most beautiful school of common brick construction in the United States in a competition sponsored by the Common Brick Manufacturer's Association of America." Since the school looks like a medieval English castle, the name evolved to Castlemont.

The architects who created Castlemont High School were Chester H. Miller and Carl I. Warneke of Oakland. They also designed the Hill Castle Apartments (continuing the castle theme), the Malonga Casquelord Arts Center (originally the Women's City Club) and the main library on 14th Street, all near Lake Merritt.

This undated postcard shows the castle-like architecture of the school that gave the district its name.

This longer shot from 1934 shows the nature of the surrounding neighborhood.

This area was originally part of the larger Elmhurst settlement of the late 1800s (see Elmhurst listing.)

Castlemont Gardens rental housing project was opened in 1948. It nestled in a natural canyon on the edge of the Arroyo Viejo Creek. This development was at the time the largest in Oakland, sitting on a nine-acre tract off MacArthur Boulevard between Golf Links Road and Seneca Avenue. The land on which it sat was formerly the Holy Redeemer College.

Welcome To Oakland

BY ALISON CHOKWADI FLETCHER

Great grandma Eunice
Half African American
Half Native . . . American
When she was young she looked more
Indigenous
As long black braids swept her shoulders
And unsmiling lips
Faced the camera
When she was old she looked more African
A sun-dyed woman
With hair whitened by time
And curled by lineage

Around the turn of the 20th century
She left Kansas with Great Grandpa
And headed west to California

They arrived safe and sound
With a handful of children in the back of the wagon
She tilled Stockton's soil
He worked the shipyards along the coast
Then they purchased their own home
In East Oakland

One day, a man came knocking
Sayin,
"This here is a petition signed by all the good white
folks of the community.
We feel it our duty
To ask y'all
To leave"
Well,
Great grandma had a little somethin of her own to tell
him
And a little somethin more
Up her sleeve
She said, while pointing the pistol at his head,
"Get the hell off my porch"

Daddy said he hardly heard her say
Two sentences his whole life
Yet she said something that day
She staked her claim
And claimed her rights

The man
with the petition
backed his way down the steps
And as it went
My family stayed in that house
For the next
thirty years

83rd Sunrise

BY ALISON CHOKWADI FLETCHER

Grandma woke up early one mornin and started us
breakfast: eggs, bacon and toast. Then poured
herself a cup of instant coffee, Yu-ban.

The sun, hardly up yet peepin over a horizon turnin
pink yellow and orange as it did, shone in our sleepy
faces.

Mr. Rooster in the yard behind ours crowed "Cock a
doodle doo!" and all the children on the block stirred,
fightin morning, fightin cold, clingin to dreams of
tearin up and down the block while grandpa kept watch.
Kept half an eye on us cuz he could hardly see out of
it and none a'tall out the other one.

So, we ran in circles. We ran after each other. We
ran in backyards and in back streets. Across railroad
tracks, through housing projects and over freshly
manicured lawns.

We leapt fences made of two-by-fours, iron, wire and
mesh. Challenged each other at Tic Tac Toe, Chinese
Checkers and Jacks.

Called out rhymes like Little Sally Walker sitting in
a saucer, rise Sally rise, wipe your weepin eyes and
put your hand on your hip and let your backbone slip!
Aaaaw . . .

We played Hide and Go Seek coverin our eyes without
takin a peek!   We said, 5, 10, 15, 20, 25, 30, 35,
40 . . .

We found mystery and mischief in everything we did.
Then we ran and we ran and we ran some more!   So far
away grandpa's half- eye couldn't track us.   So far
away his hearing became deaf to us.

We left miles and miles between ourselves and grandpa
'til "Trouble" and "Mess" became our middle names.   We
played like children do, like children should.

You see, we, were the kids of the 83rd Avenue hood!

CHINATOWN

WHERE: *The region centered around
9th and Webster streets downtown*

OAKLAND'S CHINATOWN is today fairly grounded in a specific area, but
at different points in our city's history there were several different China-
towns, as Chinese settled and then were pushed out as the city expanded.

The Chinese first worked in the redwood lumber industry in the
Oakland hills in the 1840s, and some became farmers. Since they were
not allowed to own real estate, they leased land from white landlords.
Many migrated to California as Gold Rushers, and then later as laborers
for the transcontinental railroad. They also came to escape droughts,
floods and the peasant uprisings of the T'ai-p'ing Rebellion. In 1868,
Chinese helped construct the Temescal Dam, which created Lake
Temescal. Workers removed heavy, wet clay by the ton and then dug
even deeper for bedrock.

China Town   Oakland, Cal.

*Based on the date, this 1910 postcard must depict the present-day Chinatown
centered at 9th and Webster, which was forming by 1880.*

There was much racism against the Chinese, especially when jobs were few and people blamed the shortage on the cheap labor Chinese provided. In the 1870s, Denis Kearney incited the Sand Lot Riots in San Francisco, so named because meetings were held in vacant lots to plan attacks against immigrants from China. (Kearney was himself an Irish immigrant, only coming to the U.S. nine years before the riots, but that irony apparently didn't dawn on him.) These attacks lasted for days, and anyone who looked Asian was mauled.

That anger passed over the bay to Oakland, where in 1877 violence was promised to the railroad if it didn't fire its Chinese laborers. Several other industries that hired Chinese were threatened to be burned to the ground. Mayor Enoch Pardee formed a Committee of Safety with 900 volunteers to make sure the railroad and Chinatown stayed intact—which it did.

But foul play was certainly suspected in various fires that afflicted the Chinese settlements. The first official Chinatown was on the east side of today's Telegraph Avenue between 16th and 17th streets. At that time, Broadway dead-ended at 14th Street, and if it were to be extended Chinatown would have to be moved. In 1867 the settlement, which probably consisted of a row of wooden structures, burned to the ground . . . curiously.

The displaced residents were prevented from rebuilding by city authorities. They instead moved to today's San Pablo Avenue, but only temporarily. Creation of other streets—such as 19th and 20th—required forcible removal of residents by the City Marshall, who paid $1 as "compensation" for each surrendered property. Current archeological digging in this area could provide some information on this iteration of Chinatown. Residents then scattered to two locales. Some moved in 1872 to Second Street, while others went north to what is today Grand Avenue. The Grand Avenue location was dismantled for expansion of the business district, but it's not clear what happened to the Second Street Chinatown. There were several other Chinatown locales in Oakland, such as one at the foot of Castro Street and one in West Oakland.

Our present-day Chinatown, centered at 9th and Webster, was forming by 1880. Soon after, the federal government passed the Chinese Exclusion Act, which put a ten-year halt to Chinese immigration—which was extended and finally made permanent in 1902. The preamble of this 1882 act read, "In the opinion of the Government of the United States the coming of Chinese laborers to this country endangers the good order of certain localities within the territory thereof." The act wasn't repealed until 1943 when Chinese were finally able to apply for U.S. citizenship.

One of the cruel laws enacted in Oakland was the Pure Air ordinance, which assumed unsanitary conditions accompanied the small shacks where several Chinese would live together. In accordance with this was the law that all Chinese in the City Jail must have their hair cut, which disregarded cultural tradition about the queue, or braid. A peculiar 1880

OAKLAND HISTORY ROOM OF THE OAKLAND PUBLIC LIBRARY

A Chinese parade held in Oakland sometime before 1906.

ordinance abolished opium dens only if operating as a business. If, however, Chinese smoked in their own homes or stores for pure pleasure, they were fine.

In 1904, a huge conflagration "swept over three quarters of the block bounded by Webster, Ninth, Franklin and Eighth streets," according to an April 1904 newspaper. The story ran under the compassionate headline, "Two bodies burned to a crisp in last night's fire disaster—Forty Thousand Dollar Blaze Wipes out Chinatown." The blaze was punctuated by the explosion of two million firecrackers, as one of the establishments that burned was a firecracker store.

After the 1906 earthquake, a destroyed San Francisco Chinatown sent many Chinese to Oakland. (See Lakeside listing for more.)

Decades after the Committee of Safety was formed, there was still a cold eye cast on Chinese laborers. A 1919 issue of the *Alameda County Union Labor Record* contained a jarring combination of racial slur and admiration, "The average union man could take a leaf from the book of the knowledge from the chinks."

On the more pleasant side, conditions appeared to be very neighborly within Chinatown itself. A nice story was told to the newspaper in 1955 of Chinatown's early days. At Franklin and Ninth lived a man who loved his canary, heartbroken when it escaped. His neighbor was kind enough to put her canary's cage out to hang on a tree branch, telling the gentleman to hang his empty cage next to it. Her bird sang sweetly enough to lure the other bird, which due to habit flew right back into its cage.

Today's Legendary Palace restaurant at Seventh and Franklin streets dates to 1924, when it opened as the Pekin-Low Restaurant. A December 1924 article on the building states, "The building reflects the true Chinese atmosphere in all respects. The Chinese dragon plays an important part in the architectural entity and the color scheme has been carried out along strict Oriental lines." The builder told the newspaper he had undertaken a "thorough study of Chinese architecture"—he was not Chinese.

In 1977, bilingual street signs were erected in Chinatown, marking street names in both English and Chinese.

Oakland no. 27

BY CHRISTINA ENG

i have tried
to write about the city
in a series of poems

to give it
the respect it deserves

all i have talked about
            is myself

Chopsticks

BY LIN LEE

It is funny when someone asks for a fork.
I roll my eyes.

To me, the chopsticks are a perfect extension
of my fingers.

When they are plucking, I am plucking
a piece of chicken, a water chestnut.

And when they support a hunk of rice,
it is as if I hold rice in the palm of my hand.

CLAREMONT

WHERE: *The environs of the Claremont Hotel on Ashby Avenue*

THIS LOVELY area with spectacular views was once part of Vicente Peralta's lands, given to him by his father in 1842.

The Claremont Heights subdivision was on Tunnel Road just above the Claremont Hotel. "You will want one of these broad, deep lots. It may be flat, gently sloping or steep; you may choose one with the oak, bay and eucalyptus trees that add so much to the beauty of the entire tract," read a February 1924 advertisement from the Claremont Heights Syndicate.

Another subdivision was Claremont Estates. "Central location and proximity to San Francisco transportation make this district desirable to business executives of San Francisco as well as the Eastbay. The new homes and building sites are attracting hundreds of visitors from both sides of the bay each Sunday. . . . Claremont Estates is reached by driving up the old Tunnel Road past the Claremont Hotel to Alvarado Road,

An early view of Claremont shows the beginning development in the fold of the hillside.

which leads directly to the property," stated an April 1936 advertisement.

The reigning landmark of Claremont is the Claremont Hotel. It was originally built to show its dark, half-timbered wood, emphasizing its European look. The half-timbering is still there, just covered with a coat of white paint. The streetcar used to come right up to the hotel's front

This 1908 postcard shows the original, darker look of the Claremont Hotel, as well as the pastureland it once presided over.

door. The building was designed by architects Dickey and Reed for Borax Smith and Frank Havens of the Realty Syndicate. Famous musicians played here for appreciative audiences, including Count Basie, Louis Armstrong and Tommy Dorsey.

Various financial problems delayed the hotel's construction, so while it was begun in 1906 it wasn't completed until 1915—just in time to house attendees of the Panama-Pacific Exposition in San Francisco. All that effort was worth it. The landmark provides such a strongly visual symbol of Oakland that firefighters in 1991 made an especial effort to save it.

Hotel Monolithia

BY DANA LANGE

The effervescent rich scuttle off to Europe
with hundreds of gestures,
and the rich of elsewhere come here
to the monolithic hotel on the hill.

A shallow ruckus in each guest room;
they make love carelessly.

Morning spits back noise—
Ashby Avenue popping with traffic.
Cold spots in the hallway
where someone broke her heart
fifty years ago. But that's no matter;
she paid up and left.

It is strange to have so many rooms
and walls and blankness.

My neighborhood

BY LOIS WILLS

I love this place,
my view. I won't be guilty
because I'm not wasting it—
I eat it up every day, all day
on my deck, just looking

I use up every bit of it
like the Eskimo with the whale
I use the trees
I use the view of water
I use the hillside
and at night the twinkling lights

I love it
and it's part of me
as if the landscape looks back
and also enjoys
we are mirrors for each other
I am Oakland
It is me

CLINTON PARK

WHERE: *The area bounded by the channel, the estuary, 14th Avenue and E. 18th Street*

ALTHOUGH THE neighborhood is called Clinton Park today, the original settlement was just known as Clinton. Like nearby San Antonio and Lynn, it was settled by the very first immigrants to the area. In 1849, a disillusioned prospector named Moses Chase pitched a tent and hunkered down for the winter, looking for warmer climes on his doctor's recommendation since he was showing symptoms of tuberculosis. Some sources in the Oakland History Room say his tent was at the very foot of Broadway; some report that he was stationed in San Antonio, east of the slough that is today Lake Merritt.

Regardless, he was rescued by three other pioneers, the Patten brothers of the northeast who had also given up on goldmining. Apparently, they popped their heads into his tent, savvied the situation and nursed him back to health. The Pattens bought 600 acres from Antonio Peralta

This 1939 view of Lakeshore Avenue, met by E. 18th Street, shows traffic patterns that flow a little differently today. According to some reports, Moses Chase pitched his tent not far from this spot.

OAKLAND HISTORY ROOM OF THE OAKLAND PUBLIC LIBRARY

to grow grain. Chase helped them grow it. The Pattens built a cabin at present-day 3rd Avenue and East 9th Street, and Chase built a wood-frame house at 4th Avenue and E. 8th Street. Chase's house was said to be the first frame house in Oakland, built of redwood timbers from a sawmill on the Palo Seco Creek in the Oakland hills and demolished in 1948. The Laney College campus is sited where his home was.

So where does the Clinton part come in? Well, not only was Chase unhappy about his lack of gold-finding skills and his poor health, but his intended fiancee back in Massachusetts died just as he swung back into town to collect her. She was buried in what would have been her wedding dress. And her name was . . . Ellen Clinton or Mary Ellen Clinton, depending on the source you consult.

So those of you who live in Clinton Park, you're on a morose, heart-broken plot of land. But hey! You're close to the lake.

The subdivision entitled Clinton was established in 1854. In 1868, the 12th Street dam was constructed, connecting Clinton and San Antonio to Oakland on the other side of the lake. This saved travelers the time of going all the way around or rowing across. It also was a welcome alternative to an earlier bridge where benevolent Horace Carpentier charged tolls.

By 1897, the area was so well settled residents were already complaining about a nicety of city life, the town square: which in this case is known as Clinton Square. A letter to the editor of the *Oakland Enquirer* complained about the planting of border shrubs and the lawn's overtaking by dandelions and a fountain. About the latter the writer said, "The less said about . . . the curly-haired and blistered Indian maiden in the center, who supports a huge wire bird cage affair on her head, the better." A conservatory was being built and that displeased the letter writer as well.

The famous Tubbs Hotel was situated on E. 12th Street between 4th and 5th avenues. It operated between 1871 and 1893, and was home to Gertrude Stein and her family for a year. With 200 rooms and spacious grounds, it was one of the city's largest employers of African-Americans until a huge fire brought it to the ground. In 1902, a saw mill was erected in the middle of the block to raise family homes. Sixteen houses were built.

In 1955, Clinton Park was chosen as the first federal urban renewal project west of the Mississippi. One hundred buildings were torn down, including some homes built before the 1890s, and 50 new apartment buildings were built. According to an Oakland Heritage Alliance pamphlet for the area, "Federal housing policy throughout the '60s and '70s

This October 1948 aerial view shows Clinton Park's connection both to the lake and to the estuary.

continued to favor large apartment complexes, and the high cost of bringing older houses up to code reportedly drove a large number of established homeowners out of the neighborhood."

One of the true delights of Clinton Park is the 5th Avenue waterfront area. This funky artisans' cove has roughly 100 people living amidst the tools of their trade.

Names east of the lake can be confusing. The same area seems to be referred to interchangeably as Eastlake, Brooklyn and Clinton Park. It helps a little to know that many Oakland districts or neighborhoods were once separate towns with fairly distinct borders. Clinton joined with San Antonio and Lynn to become Brooklyn, which was then annexed to Oakland in 1872. Why the name Brooklyn? After the ship that brought Mormons from New York to San Francisco in 1846.

Storm in Clinton Park

BY NANCY MATTISON

How do I come to you?
Talking too softly
so you bend
for words
already past.
You are surrounded
by this landscape.
Every possible road
leads to water.
Other things
demand your attention.
Already your head
turning for the tide,
flushing in from the estuary,
my hands dropping.
Thunder should start now
and I will cower
in your footprints,
step by step to the house
that looks like nothing.
Far from the windows,
dead center of the room,
I'll begin again. You will
listen until lightning
cuts out the lights.

Eastlake

BY D'JOS UPTON

Eastlake they say Eastlake
they said it
Eastlake for all your life
Eastlake I get it

Eastlake it is for me
and Eastlake it's home
for my sweet, sweet hood
I wrote a poem

DIMOND

*Where: Between the Glenview and Laurel neighborhoods,
with a commercial district centered at Fruitvale Avenue
and MacArthur Boulevard*

DIMOND IS named for Gold Rusher Hugh Dimond. The Irish immigrant arrived in California a 20-year-old with three children and in 1867 purchased the acreage that included the area now called Dimond Park.

Before Dimond's time, the land was part of the Peralta family's ranch. Antonio Peralta's 1821 adobe, described in the book *Oakland Parks and Playgrounds* as the "first substantial house built in Oakland," was built outside of Dimond, at Coolidge and Davis, where the present Peralta Hacienda is. That adobe fell into disrepair when it was abandoned in favor of a newer, 1840 adobe. Dimond's son Dennis carted some of its bricks over to what is today Dimond Park, where in 1897 he incorporated them into a small cottage. That structure was later used as a scout hut (more on the scouts further down) starting in 1924 until part of it

OAKLAND HISTORY ROOM OF THE OAKLAND PUBLIC LIBRARY

A picnic at Dimond Park, undated.

burned in 1954. Today's utility building shows the stone arch of the Dimond cottage and, to the side, some of the 1821 adobe bricks that were so well-formed that they have survived nearly 200 years of weather. Next to the building is the Dimond Oak, a sturdy, gnarled tree that dates back 200 years, and an 1896 bell which originally hung in a streetcar barn which later became the headquarters for the Dimond Volunteer Fire Department.

After the Peraltas and before Dimond was Henderson Lewelling. This North Carolina-born man of Welsh descent (many have placed him as

being German) planted 700 Bing cherry trees here in 1856 and named the plot Fruit Vale (a large area that encompasses today's neighborhoods of Dimond and Fruitvale). Lewelling was a Quaker leader when he lived at one point in Salem, Iowa. He formed an abolitionist group there, and his Salem home may have been a stop on the Underground Railroad. When he decided to head west, initially to Oregon, he brought 700 living grafted fruit trees with him. Members of his wagon train fought him over the

The massive Dimond Oak hovers over the 1897 Dimond cottage, a portion of which remains today in Dimond Park.

load, believing it would kill the cattle, but he was determined to bring them. It is said that the Native Americans did not attack Lewelling's wagon train, as they had others at the same time, because they saw the trees being transported and believed them to be sacred. (Salem, Oregon is so named because of the Salem, Iowa wagon train.)

Another major landholder in the area was Frederick Rhoda, who planted orchards in 1859.

OAKLAND HISTORY ROOM OF THE OAKLAND PUBLIC LIBRARY

In 1917, the city purchased 12 acres at Fruitvale and Lyman streets from the Dimond estate for $24,000—today's present park.

The Oakland Park Department set out wide fireplaces to encourage picnicking, and according to *Oakland Parks and Playgrounds*, Sausal Creek was so clean that "breathless children leave their games to quench their thirsts at clear, cool springs."

In the 1940s, Dimond Park missed its chance to hook up with Joaquin Miller Park and become a behemoth park, replete with a manmade lake twice the size of Lake Temescal. According to a 1946 newspaper article, plans called for construction of a dam above Leimert Bridge which would create "Inspiration Lake," a sandy-shored lake with six acres of water surface. The design also included space for stores and a theater. "Thanks to the 20-year park improvement plan of William Penn Mott, Jr., Oakland's curves and contours are to be corseted and girdled to make her the most theatrical and glamorous park city in the world," said the *Post-Enquirer*.

It went on to rave, "Oakland's great mountain park-to-be will dwarf in size and scope San Francisco's Golden Gate." The area planners hoped would be the site for the lake is today the Montclair golf course and driving range.

Intense residential development in the Dimond began in the 1920s, with the picnicker and hiker's haven becoming everybody's front yard.

A 1921 Realty Syndicate advertisement for a subdivision called Dimond Park 1/4 Acres read, "This is the only 1/4 acre tract ever offered for sale where skeptical purchasers have been unable to find any faults with the property. Practically everyone that attended our opening sale last week purchased either a 1/4 acre or 1/2 acre homesite." That quarter-acre price-tag? $550.

The homes went up quickly, and so did a certain amount of attitude. The ad continued, "Your children can play and go to school with other nice refined children." Now, you have to wonder how they screened for "nice" and "refined," don't you? Although, if it was like other subdivisions of that era, that phrase was probably a way of saying that minorities were not allowed to purchase property. The advertisement also mentioned that roads were presently being graded. "You can build right now," coached the ad. "Buy your lumber tomorrow and fool your landlord."

At the corner of Fruitvale and Hopkins (now MacArthur) was a fancy hotel with a French restaurant, the Hermitage. Legend says that city officials came out to Dimond for their lunches . . . and a little extra. French prostitutes worked the upstairs rooms at the hotel. A bit down the block, where today's post office stands, was a German biergarten, one of several in the neighborhood.

One landowner at the intersection was William Montgomery, who hoped to use his 15 acres as a rehabilitation center for San Quentin convicts, but after neighbors protested he dropped the plan. It is unknown when this idea arose, but San Quentin was built 1852–54 so it might've been quite early.

And finally, Dimond Park history has a fair amount to do with those varminty bad-news kids . . . the Boy Scouts.

Guess which city had the very first Boy Scout troop in the entire western United States? It was Oakland, in 1909, according to *Oakland Parks and Playgrounds*. Among the members at the first meeting was Harry Butters, the first American killed in World War I.

Although the Boy Scouts used Dimond Park proper, 28 acres in Montclair were purchased in 1918 in Dimond Canyon to establish a Boy Scout camp. In Camp Dimond's first year, 150 boys attended. By 1934, that number had jumped to 3,700.

The boys had been used to sleeping in 8-man tents, but in 1922, they were given 27 permanent cabins and a 500-person mess hall. The camp was free to any Oakland Boy Scout, although they had to pay for meals.

In the late 1940s, the Oakland School Board took over the 28 acres and today two schools sit on the former Camp Dimond site: Joaquin Miller School and Montera Middle School. The rest of the area is residential.

And now you know why Montclair's Scout Road is called Scout Road.

Friends of Sausal Creek

BY MARK J. RAUZON

In 1995, a few neighbors got together to talk about the health of our local creek. Out of this gathering grew the Friends of Sausal Creek (FOSC), a grassroots, volunteer-based nonprofit organization. Our mission is to promote awareness and protection of the Sausal Creek watershed, both as a community and natural resource. We strive to promote an appreciation that, even in urban Oakland, there are wild places worth visiting, restoring and preserving.

The soul of Sausal Creek resides in an ancient oak in the Dimond Park. This venerable oak tree lives next to the scout hut near the pool. Perhaps the oldest and largest oak in Oakland, this battered behemoth is a survivor of another era. It saw the original residents of Sausal canyon come and go. Who knows? Maybe a grizzly bear sharpened his claws on the tree; it's old enough to have been a substantial oak even 200 years ago. That tree must be 500 years old with a dbh (diameter at breast height) just shy of 15 feet. A sacred tree indeed, as Gary Snyder the poet/wilderness writer suggests. Why not dedicate the life of this witness of hundreds of years of canyon life to the restoration of the wellspring that waters its roots, shelters the birds in its branches and binds a community together?

The scout hut itself is rich with local history; the kind future generations will search for in strip malls without success. The next time you visit our garden, pause and read the plaque on the hut. The Dimond cottage was first built in 1897 as a playhouse for the Dimond boys and was in use until 1954 when it was destroyed by fire. The adobe walls and stone arch are all that's left. The 1893 bell hung in the headquarters of the Dimond Volunteer Fire Dept. and "serves as a reminder of the unflinching sacrifice of volunteer firemen." The new building was dedicated in 1955. Adobe bricks reputed to be from the original Peralta homestead have been incorporated into the scout hut's walls that face north. The old oak literally thrives in the dust of the past. The scout hut has launched the many projects that the Friends of Sausal Creek do.

Our tools are stored here. With them and our volunteers, the "tragedy of the commons" has been averted here. Instead, FOSC volunteers maintain the commons for a variety of user groups who may not even be aware of FOSC, the oak or the power of restoration. The commons are reclaimed and still the Dimond Oak watches in patient regard, holding together the living center of the watershed. The next time you pass her, reflect a moment on this grand living being and wonder how much water has flowed down Sausal Creek since she was an acorn.

Workday: This bird has flown. The Old Slav never left his name, just words of encouragement in broken English. He and his ridgeback were daily users of the Sausal Creek trail. He always stopped to chat on workdays in the canyon. He would talk to anyone that listened, offering advice and complaining about the rascals who destroyed our fences. Today, I expect him at any time, and slowly it dawns on me I have not seen him in a while. I then remember his gait, gauntness and complaint of ill health. He left a hollowness. What happens when the present becomes absent, when the shadow disappears and the void is filled? Anyone working in the canyon soon knows the regulars; these are our neighbors and village elders, and those that have time to exchange pleasantries are rare birds indeed.

Winter 1999: Yuletide in the canyon, and there are tiny evergreens festooned with ornaments. Tiny orange hemispheres, some with black dots, drip from these small Christmas trees. Certainly there's the feminine touch present—indeed, Mother Nature is at play. Here ladybugs are gathered in the horsetails.

It's a hibernacula of sorts, the ladies in waiting together for safety. They're conserving energy all together in a body pile. And in the warmer weather, they party! A beetle mating orgy occurs in spring. Soon they disperse into the hills from whence they came. Maybe to return next year again, some time, some place. Not unheard of. Another orange and black relative does the same thing in the Pacific Groves of Eucalyptus. We have our ladybirds to fly away home. "Hey, didn't I spot you last year at the Millennium Party?"

Spring 2002: End of winter, and the white winter light filters through the oaks as the treetops are tossed by winds. The raggedy call of the woodpecker carries over the bubbling stream, but the skies roar and the land sighs. I'm sitting in the green glen of Dimond Canyon, cool and damp in the hollow where a seep trickles soundlessly, with fresh fungus and sprouts everywhere. A Steller's jay in a blue pullover, with peaked black hood, hops to the ground. Up close I see its cerulean blue eye and stripes on its forehead. A varied thrush looking like a gigantic Black-burian warbler is fossicking in the earth, an easily spooked bird, soon to wing its way north. The spotted towhee shares the same bit of ground, scratching for bugs in the leaf litter. It looks like the black-headed gros-beak, soon to be here on its summering grounds. I can hardly wait for the new waves of migrant birds and the winter to melt into full spring. Already the mockingbird sings of spring, and its excitement is conta-gious. If it would only stop imitating that car alarm, I could embrace the hope of spring in the face of war.

Summer: All's not as it seems at Sausal Creek. Near the demonstration garden, I see a silver object swimming in the water. A fish? No! A mole (Townsend's mole) with air trapped in its fur. Out of its element, it's swimming through a small rapids trying to reach the other side. Unfor-tunately, a low cement wall blocks its exit and it has to turn tail and swim back for cover. Later on the Bridgeview Trail, I find another animal out of its element. A shiny pecan-sized water beetle colored like a roasted coffee bean crawls along the path looking for what the mole had found. Both critters negotiated their challenges with versatility and maybe they just were taking a walk on the wild side for a change.

Fall 1999: The sparrow sits on the fat black pipe, now almost hidden by this year's new growth of willows and nine-bark. I don't have my binos, but I swear it's a Lincoln's Sparrow. No beard or top hat, just the typical hunched posture and secretive nature give it away. When it hops down into the deciduous vegetation, I feel like shouting Eureka! A Lin-coln's Sparrow is proof positive that the Friends are creating bird habitat and attracting new species. I was intrigued when earlier this summer a white-crowned sparrow chose to nest near here instead of migrate. Now here's a migrant who's chosen our patch of new willows for a respite on its long, solitary night journey when most birds migrate. A night in this Lincoln's bedroom doesn't require a huge donation to the Democrats, only a moderate donation to the Friends.

The topsy-turvy construction of the summer is over. The creek side was literally turned upside down, but now the dust has settled. Stroll down the trail now and you'll see more willow and nine-bark cuttings in the newly-sculpted banks of Sausal Creek. Imagine in a few sunny years a riparian corridor with enough habitats for many Lincoln Sparrows and that other presidential bird of the watershed—the Wilson's warbler. Just imagine!

Winter 2004: The shortest day of the year, death of summer past, the promise of the return of the sun. All these things are the meanings of solstice. And the canyon is not about to let us forget that. Once one tunes into the seasons and pays attention to the lessons at hand, the opportunities are endless. For example, we are planting a new slope for the future growing season when we are reminded of the glorious past. A bright yellow parakeet lies dead on the ground. Perhaps frozen in a cold snap, the lifeless bird is a visitor that experienced freedom, albeit briefly. Now it is dead and a reminder of all the fallen leaves and flowers that jewel the ground. We tuck its wings around it and dig a shallow grave next to the council oak, a sapling first fertilized with the flesh of a Sausal Creek trout. The council oak will now carry the carbon of the bird and fish into the glorious future that we are planting. As we also bury the roots of new plants, we speak for the future of Dimond Canyon. Happy Winter Solstice!

In Dimond Park

BY NATASHA HOROWITZ

I swear to God I saw this: he threw a Frisbee to no one and ran choppily after it. For a good half hour.

I sat smoking the Camels I had made my boyfriend quit and wanted to write letters to all my friends. This is what they do in California! Singles Frisbee!

Early that day at a library I fought with an unkind librarian. She guarded her meager books and wouldn't let them circulate. Up flights, through stacks, I vexed myself into a frenzy and who wants to read these obscure poets anyway. Let them ferment like cheese or wine. In fifty years, I'll be back to marvel at the claret spine, the Boston typograph. In the meantime you'll find me playing partners Frisbee

or maybe dodging the disk, because goddamit he almost hit me! (I would say in the letter) Apparently he couldn't run hard enough.

Now it's getting dark while I wait for said smokeless boyfriend and maybe he was waiting too, because a girl steps off a bike, holds his hand and while he backs up she throws the damn thing. With accuracy. Out of nowhere a dog leaps up and bites the prize plate.

I decide it would be better to write a poem than a letter.

DOWNTOWN

WHERE: *Centered at Broadway and 14th Street and radiating outwards*

TODAY S DOWNTOWN was really "the country" when Oakland was first settling, since growth first began at the waterfront. But as more and more people arrived and began setting up shop, growth proceeded up Broadway.

In 1871, Oakland's first official City Hall was built at 14th and Washington streets—two previous Council meeting places were in other structures. When it burned down in 1877, another was built in its place. While that one still stood, today's version began construction in 1911. Our City Hall was the first one in the United States to be built as a skyscraper!

This January 1912 photograph shows men doing a test of the 4-inch floor slab. This slab will hold weight for the floors above the first floor of the new skyscraper City Hall.

Early Oaklanders called it Mayor Mott's wedding cake, understandably enough with its white "icing" and decorative furbelows on the tower—and the fact that Mott got married the year construction began. Once it was completed, its predecessor, still sadly standing next to its newer, brighter successor, was demolished. The 1989 earthquake severely damaged City Hall, enough that there was talk of bringing it down. Today, it glides around on seismic pads in the basement so it can hopefully ride out the next big one a little better.

The plaza surrounding City Hall is named for Frank Ogawa, an influential city councilman. He was the first Japanese-American council member in a major city in the continental United States, and he held that position for 28 years until he died. Ogawa experienced the ugliness of the Japanese internment camps during World War II, but turned the experience upside down by organizing people and beginning to practice his unique style of leadership and representation.

Near City Hall is the place where the University of California was born before the half-grown child was moved to Berkeley. Henry Durant arrived in Oakland in 1853 and set up a school in a former fandango house (music hall) at the corner of 5th Street and Broadway. Here's evidence of the man's need to pour himself into his work: he arrived May 1 and by June 6 the Contra Costa Academy was open for business! He only had three students, but given that Oakland's population at this time was only several hundred, he was doing all right. Soon he purchased a site at the four blocks bounded by 12th, 14th, Harrison and Franklin streets. The school was then called the College School.

By 1855, the institution was incorporated as the College of California, but the College School continued to operate until 1861, since it took five years to get a freshman class together. Reverend Samuel Willey provided much capital and is recognized as one of its founders. What began as just a handful of buildings steadily grew until eventually there were 13 buildings on the site, including dormitories, a chapel, a cow barn and the like. In 1868, the state legislature passed a law organizing a state university, which started in the Oakland buildings with 10 faculty and 25 students. Those students, the first graduating class of the University of California, graduated from the Oakland campus in 1873. By September of that year, operations were transferred to the Berkeley site. Today, the site of the origins of one of the nation's best-known schools is a parking garage—but a parking garage with an historic plaque!

Nearby on 13th Street is the historic Oakland Tribune building. It started life in 1906 as the John Breuner Company, a furniture store built by a San Francisco earthquake evacuee. It was taken over by the *Tribune* in 1918; the newspaper had been housed in five previous locations since its establishment in 1874. The tower came later. Before that, steel framework on top of the Breuner Building supported the clock and the neon lettering that spells out "Tribune." After the tower was constructed, the

Construction of the skyscraper City Hall continues. Next to it is the sturdy but tiny City Hall it will replace, facing a different orientation. Note the San Pablo streetcars.

clock face and lettering were moved to its top, with the clock placed above the neon rather than below as it was before. In 1923, Harry Houdini hung upside down in a straitjacket from the tower's construction framework as several thousand cheered him on. A 500,000 candlepower searchlight once emanated from the tower. The clock's minute hand is nearly 8 feet long.

The *Tribune* was owned by the Knowland family from 1915 to 1977. Robert Maynard became the first African-American to own a major city newspaper when he bought it in 1983 from Gannett. Ten years later, former editor Pearl Stewart was the first African American woman editor of a major city newspaper, serving under ANG's ownership, which continues today.

In walking distance from City Hall is the Pardee Home. This Italianate home was built in 1868-69 by Enoch Pardee, a Gold Rusher who was a gold miner, eye doctor, mayor of Oakland and state senator. He passed along some of his predilections to his son George, who was also an eye doctor and mayor, but more importantly George served as California governor at the time of the 1906 earthquake. George was roundly praised for his reaction to the disaster. As mayor, he worked to get Oakland's waterfront back into the public hands and then served as one of the first Port of Oakland commissioners when that body was created in 1927. Never one to let moss grow, George was also the founder of our water utility, EBMUD, and the Pardee Dam is named for him. The dam still provides most of the water for this area. The home was inhabited by Pardee family members until in 1981 George's last child died. Since George's wife was an avid traveler and collector, and the children —even when grown up—did not want to disturb her displays, the museum in the house today shows very vividly how one eclectic and important family lived in the 1800s and early 1900s.

Further up Broadway from City Hall is the Uptown neighborhood. Here, two theaters' histories are linked in an ironic story where the theater that helped the other succeed has now been closed for 40 years. The Fox Oakland Theater opened in 1928 as a vaudeville and movie house, and it is said that its initial success at filling its 3,500 seats led to the nearby Paramount Theatre's construction in 1931. The Fox was the first sound theater west of Chicago, screening the "talkies" that had fairly recently arrived on the scene. Yet both theaters had rough times; the Fox closed in 1965 and the Paramount in 1970. However, the Paramount got a full, loving restoration in 1973 and is a gorgeous Art Deco destination. As of this writing, the Fox had a new marquee and blade sign to brighten its sad façade—and plans are underway to partially restore it for use as a live entertainment venue, with a charter school occupying the office spaces.

VJ Day

BY FLOYD SALAS

"Whooooooooooooooooooooooooooooooooooooooooo!" the air-raid siren goes off on the Oakland Tribune Tower and everybody freezes in the doctor's office, but the spot of blood pops up on my thumb and the nurse quickly flips a drop of it onto the glass slide and wipes the blood off with a dab of cotton and drops it in the wastebasket and stands up and runs to the window with me as the siren keeps blasting, blasting, blasting, a long, deep hoot that won't stop blasting: "Whooooooooooooooooooooooooooooooooooo!"

But it isn't an air-raid, because everybody else is at their office windows too and dumping paper out the windows down onto the people running out of the stores and restaurants and bars and onto the sidewalk and the street, and everybody's yelling and shouting, "The War's over! The War's over!"

Horns honk and cars and streetcars stop right where they are in the middle of the street, and the drivers and passengers jump out of their cars and run up and hug each other and kiss each other and spin each other in circles and dance and shout and scream. Broadway, the main street of town, suddenly becomes a river of people, currents of people, whirlpools of people, splashes of people, torrents of people running and mingling and turning and churning in all different directions like some giant New Year's Eve in the middle of a hot summer day!

I run out of the office where I went to get a blood test for my tonsil operation the coming week that the doctor says will help me grow, because I've barely grown since Mom died. I run down the four flights of stairs to Thirteenth Street and right to the corner of Broadway, where I plunge into the crowd and scream and yell with everybody else because it's over and Evan will be coming home from the Pacific and Manny will be coming home from Texas and all my cousins will be coming home and no more Americans will die in the War, and we'll have a family again. My family, I think, and the thought brings tears to my eyes.

I move with the crowd as it forms a spontaneous parade of people marching on the sidewalks and riding on car bumpers and roofs and truck beds and the backs of streetcars. I join it as it moves up Broadway where I see freckle-faced Jack Soots standing by Compton's Donut Shop.

Jack waves, says, "Come on," and runs into the street and leaps up onto a truckbed full of young men and women, and I leap on, too, and shout and yell with Jack, and soon Greg Jones appears and Gato and Warner and Irv Brill, too, my buddy who lives across the street, and it seems like everybody in Oakland has come uptown for a great big party.

Everybody's celebrating, breaking bottles open out on the truckbed, and sailors are kissing all the young women, and I wish I was older and bigger so I could kiss them all, too. But I'm happy and I stay on the truck with all my buddies and wave to Mona when the parade moves past the corner of Kress's Five and Dime where she stands out on the sidewalk and she waves and smiles at me. I want to jump down from the truck and run up and kiss her because I know she secretly likes me, but I'm afraid everybody will look at me, and I only wave back and lose sight of her pretty face in a quarter of a block.

Then I join Jack and Warner and Gato and Greg and Irv when they jump off the truck and leap onto a car, climb onto its running board and bumper and up onto its top as it moves up Broadway. I scream and shout and want to do something to show how I feel, want to do something heroic. I wish I had a trumpet and could play like Jack and Benny, that I could blow a beautiful song from the top of the car to show how good I feel, how good I really feel, now that my brothers will be coming home. We'll have a family again! We'll have a family again!

"Hooray! Hooray! Hooray!" I shout and lift my fist up at the people in the buildings above us. I shout and scream and squeeze everybody's hand who will let me, who will touch me back. We all shout and scream, scream and shout, "Hooray! Hooray! Hooray! . . . Hooray! Hooray! Hooray!"

* * *

I'm standing so close to Gene Krupa up on the bandstand at night, I can see the sweat popping out in little beads all over the thumping, drumming, pop-pop-popping, famous drummer's face. He looks like Manny. He looks a lot like Manny. Manny, who won't die now. It's the end of the war. It's VJ Day. And Krupa's filled the block-size auditorium with his thumping, jumping, big beat, big band, boogie-woogie sound.

The place is packed on VJ Day night. Soldiers and sailors and Marines by the thousands. Packed with young people in their new fancy war-bought clothes. The men in suits and ties. All the women in fancy dresses and high heels. And lipstick and mascara. And pretty hairdos and pompadours. For VJ Day. VJ Day!

Everybody dancing in small circles, so little room. Here and there a circle forming, clearing a space to watch dancers jitterbugging it up, daring to break apart and dirty-boogie and snap their hips at each other with each pounding beat. Shimmying and shaking. Doing every kind of mating dance in tune, in time to the rocking beat, the thumping beat.

I stand next to the bandstand with my buddies in the mass of people, thrilled by what I see. An army of Napoleon after a great battle. When there's no more death. Drunk and dancing with the girls. I'm present at a great historical spectacle. Just like in the biography of Napoleon I've just read.

Then the band suddenly hits it hard again with a loud blast of trumpets and a roll of drums, and it looks like everybody in the whole place starts jitterbugging. We form a circle around a girl from our neighborhood who's dancing right next to us with a soldier from the neighborhood, too. She can really dance.

Everyone stands around them, grinning, and claps in time to the jumping sound, grinning, watching her curvy ass in the knee-length skirt shimmy and shake away in rocking time as she breaks apart from her partner and backs up to do the dirty boogie. She doesn't see me and bumps into me with her butt.

"Hey, Baby!" I say and shake my butt, too.

"Dance!" she says and grabs my hand and jerks me out into the circle, and I grab her and spin her and twist and turn and skip under my arm and under hers and twirl her around and clasp hands and meet her and skip back and stamp my feet and then break apart from her and wiggle my shoulders and flutter my hands and rock my head and shuffle my feet all in time to the boogie woogie sound.

She gasps and claps her hand over her mouth and flutters her eyelashes and wiggles her eyebrows and shakes her butt and her shoulders and her head and sands her feet in her pointed high heels, and quivers her whole body in pulsing rhythm as we move around and around inside the circle, around and around, keeping the motion in perfect beat.

I swing to the big band, the dirty-boogie woogie, come-and-get-me-baby sound. It goes on and on and on and on to a great big band climax, and the pretty young girl and I stop in perfect time, frozen in motion for just that final second of sound.

* * *

Stuffed with hot dogs, about two o'clock in the morning when it seems like the celebration has been going on for days already, I walk with my buddies away from the Oakland Auditorium where Krupa wailed with his band and see a teenage kid picking the pockets of a drunken sailor lying in the darkness under a small tree.

The kid touches him carefully, slowly, but doesn't even bother to glance over at me and my buddies, all dressed in our drape slacks, with baggy knees and tight cuffs, sport shirts and sweaters, and fingertip length sport coats.

We say nothing. We keep moving. We only stop to watch when two young sailors suddenly start fighting on the sidewalk right across from Lake Merritt and one knocks the other down and kicks him in the face, not real hard but enough to make him shout, "I quit! I quit!"

We move on and keep moving, only stare when we hear a siren and see a fire truck come swinging down next to the lake, shoot past us in front of the auditorium, because it must be the hundredth fire truck we've seen come rushing by, going nowhere but to a false alarm today. Fire alarm boxes with the glass broken and the little doors hanging open on them are on every other corner. We watch without any real interest as it rumbles and screams by us, and keep walking down the broad sidewalk toward town again, still looking for something to do, but heading generally in the direction of our neighborhood on the other side of downtown.

"Look!" I say, and everybody turns to see a sailor running fast down the street toward us, a skinny little guy with his black navy raincoat unbuttoned and flapping at his heels.

When he runs past us, I notice his smooth pink face and the round sailor's cap pulled down low over his head clear to his ears, not shaped like a cute little rowboat perched on the top of his forehead like a sharp sailor from our neighborhood would wear it. He looks comic with his black coat flapping in the wind behind him, a little like Laurel, the skinny little sissy sidekick of Hardy, the fat man in the comedy team of Laurel and Hardy.

We idly walk along in the same direction behind him as he runs off up the street toward downtown and disappears from sight on the other side of the courthouse. We're all tired, finally, after hours and hours and hours of celebration, and not very interested in the sailor, when, glancing back, I see a big husky sailor, a lumbering heavyweight, come running from the same direction as the little sailor. He's running hard, but slow and panting, panting, his face red and sweating, and grunting with each breath.

"Say! What's up?" I ask.

"Hu-hu-hu-hu-" the big sailor pants, running toward us. "You, hu-hu, catch, hu-hu, that sailor and I'll, hu-hu, give you a buck apiece, hu-hu-hu-hu-hu."

"Let's go, you guys," I say, and we start running.

Refreshed by the excitement, we run up the small rise, but see the sailor still a block ahead, and I say, "Catch up to him, Warner, and slow him down."

Warner, all five foot eight and a hundred and thirty-five pounds, sails down the sidewalk, seeming to barely touch the concrete, and catches up with the sailor in two blocks, bumps into him, blocks his way, hampers him, and slows him down to a walking trot until the others and I can catch up.

Noticing how the skinny little sailor is barely moving now and how his pink cheeks, glistening with sweat and puffing in and out with his short breaths, make him look so much like a sissy, a little momma's boy, I say, "Hey! That big sailor told us he'd give us a dollar apiece if we caught you for him."

"Oh, no! Oh, no!" the pink-cheeked sailor cries, and slaps his hand over his mouth like a girl. "I'll, I'll give you a dollar apiece if you let me go! I will! Here! Here!" he cries and reaches into his breast pocket, pulls out his black wallet, digs into the bills there and hands me a dollar.

Then all the guys crowd around him and get in front of him and stop him to get their dollars, too, and I hold out my hand again and he gives me another dollar. But when he puts his wallet back in his pocket and tries to run, I stick my foot out, catch my toe on his ankle, and trip him, drop him flat on his face, his black coat spread out like bat's wings. Then when he jumps up to run, all the guys jump in front of him and block his path.

"Oh, no! Oh, no! Oh, no!" he cries as the big sailor comes running up and tackles him, knocks him flat on his face again, straddles his back like a horse, holds him down, then pulls out his wallet, gives each of us a dollar, says, "Okay, blow!" and waves us off.

As we walk away, he grabs the little sailor by the back of his neck and says, "Got you, you sonofabitch! Got you! Got you, you little sonofabitch!"

* * *

The house looks all dark when I let myself into the big hall. I start to go up the stairs to my room when I notice a crack of light under the dining room door, and thinking Dad might still be up, I go back to wish him a happy V-J Day, a Victory in Japan Day, since I haven't even seen him in three days.

But no one's in the kitchen where the light is on, only an empty whiskey bottle and several small glasses on the table. I don't feel bad, though, because Dad doesn't get drunk too much anymore. But when I glance into the dark bedroom and see him lying on his stomach with one arm hanging off the bed, his mouth in a pillow and snorting as if he's having trouble breathing, I get worried and hurry into the room and up to the bed to see if he's okay. I try to roll the big fat man over on his back so he can breathe, but can't, it's like trying to turn over a giant boulder and I say, "Daddy! Daddy! Are you okay?"

"Huh? Huh? Huh? What?" Dad asks and opens one eye, stares at me blindly with a glazed eyeball. Then it suddenly focuses and he grabs my wrist and jerks me onto the bed as he rolls over on his back and hugs me, saying, "My poor little boy! My poor little boy! It's over! It's over! Your brothers will be coming home! They'll be coming home! And I've got you here with me! My little boy! My poor little boy! His brothers will be coming home!"

Then he starts kissing me on the cheek. He kisses me and kisses me and kisses me and mumbles, "My poor little boy! My poor little boy! He's safe! He's safe! He'll never have to go to war! My little boy! My poor little boy!"

Then he starts french-kissing me on the cheek, tonguing my cheek, kissing me all over my cheek, slobbering my face.

I try to break away. I throw my feet off the bed, and try to pull out of his strong grip, saying, "Daddy! Hey, Daddy! Please, Daddy! Hey, Daddy! Please, Daddy!"

I feel embarrassed, then—when he won't let go, and won't stop kissing me—silly, and I finally grin, then chuckle, and then, as he keeps on kissing my cheek, break out laughing, saying, "You're right, Daddy! Evan and Manny are coming home! They're coming home!"

And I keep laughing and laughing and laughing.

Pink Pile

BY STEVEN LAVOIE

another bent-over old man night
the disabled list an inevitable result
of no couch
the pink pile gone from the window
of the store where James Brown bought
his beds, for lease, for years
neck cracks with every step along Broadway
green suits bearing logos
empty garbage & drive on
a line forms painlessly for French fries
no sense with this ache standing
I grab a bus
for comfort in the back
with the monty & the mystic tape

EASTMONT

WHERE: *Around 73rd Avenue*
and MacArthur Boulevard

LIKE MANY Oakland neighborhoods, this one was largely developed in the 1920s. Before the housing boom, this was part of the old Peralta rancho: farm land and grazing land. It was taken over by several early families for use as country homes: the Durant, Hellman, Heron, Talbot and King families.

Much of the settling of Eastmont had to do with the Chevrolet factory, which was built in 1916 where the Eastmont Mall is today (73rd and MacArthur). Factory workers settled the area in droves, creating the Eastmont and Havenscourt neighborhoods. Small farms initially surrounded the highly-industrial plant, but residential and commercial growth quickly took the farms' place.

At one time, the Chevrolet plant was the West Coast's largest. During World War II, the factory was leased to the Army, but other than

This shows what would become the Electric Loop Tract, in the area of 73rd Avenue and Foothill Boulevard. The photo was taken around 1910.

that, it continuously built cars and trucks between 1916 and 1963. In the beginning, the facility produced 45 cars a day with 250 employees, but by the time of closing was producing 55 vehicles an hour with 3,550 employees.

By 1963, GM moved the plant to Fremont, and the mall was built on its site in 1965. The Oakland Unified School District had hoped to build a high school on the site but lost out in the bidding process.

One of the subdivisions in the neighborhood was Columbian Park (not to be confused with the Columbian Gardens neighborhood by the airport). A 1926 advertisement of the Minney Company, one of the real

OAKLAND HISTORY ROOM OF THE OAKLAND PUBLIC LIBRARY

In 1917, they could sure put out a lot of shiny "Tin Lizzies" (Lizzie used to be a common horse name). Here is a day's output at the Chevrolet factory where the Eastmont Mall is now.

estate developers, called Eastmont "The Piedmont of East Oakland: a beautiful, restricted home section in the Country Club district." The country club reference was to the nearby Sequoyah Country Club, still in existence today. The Realty Syndicate, another developer, advertised that Columbian Park home lots could be had for $25 down ("less than a month's rent," reads the advertisement) and that it would provide free lumber "to build a small, neat home. The lumber will be on the ground Monday. Get your friends to help you put it up."

It's amazing to think that only 80 years ago, regular people were equipped to build their own homes. The Realty Syndicate provided a

$25 prize to the person who could built their house the quickest: the winner and his friends were able to throw up a home with only eight hours of labor. They competed with 54 other builders furiously framing and constructing. The winner, of course with beautiful timing, finished on July 4, 1922, and told the newspaper, "I'll tell the world that this is a real Independence Day for me. I own this home and I'm through with landlords."

The Columbian Park area was once known as a poultry district. A 1922 Realty Syndicate advertisement ran under the heading "Chickens Pay at Columbian Park" and extolled the virtues of having "your very own rich-soiled little farm" to grow "vegetables, berries, chickens, rabbits or fruit . . . . If you want a one-man farm—unusually rich soil—in the city, but not of the city—HERE IT IS."

Another area was known as the Electric Loop Tract, sitting west of Foothill and nestling up against the Chevrolet plant. This area, "flanked on all sides by industry and built-up residential districts," was held off the market until a large sale in May 1922, an ad states, when "every lot [was] sacrificed at wholesale prices." The name referred to the large loop the electric streetcars made around the neighborhood.

A good road

BY MAX CONNEMAN

I'd like to say a few words about 73rd Avenue
which later on becomes Hegenberger
and around about that time exposes
its truly glory: it is the road to the A's!!

I love the Edwards exit off 580,
the nice right turn where already traffic
can be gathering, and the rolling curves
past the donut place, all those neat but tired
houses, and then becoming flatlands near the
Eastmont Mall. Everyone's got an A's sticker
on their car and we all think This is the year.

Thank you 73rd for so easily bringing me there.
I love this stretch of road like no other.
Even in off season I still get the mighty feeling.

It has not escaped our attention that '73
(your number too) is the second time of three
consecutive years that the A's went all the way,
World Series Champions!!!!!!!!!!!!!!!!!

Eastmont's heyday

BY RHODA JOHNSON

Heyday is a funny word
like you're saying "Hey!"

It was the day of saying "Hey,
that's cool!" of things
that are
no longer
cool

They used to make
cars out of where
the Eastmont Mall is
beautiful glossy
automobiles
boxy and sturdy
that was when
they would say
Hey!

but now it is
hard to say
hey

not a heyday
but it could be someday

ELMHURST

WHERE: *The area bounded by 73rd Avenue,*
MacArthur Boulevard, San Leandro city limits
and the Nimitz Freeway

ELMHURST IS one of those Oakland neighborhoods which was once its own town, albeit not incorporated. It was established due to the power and car houses of the electric railway system that ran between Oakland and Hayward. With several hundred people settling there, a small community soon grew, with stores, churches, schools, a weekly newspaper and electrically lighted thoroughfares, according to a 1910 report in the Oakland History Room.

It had a post office as of 1892, the same year that the first tract maps were filed for Elmhurst.

One of Elmhurst's primary residents was Andrew Jones, whose time on the land predated the electric railway. He was a farmer, producing vegetables for the area's canneries and pickle factories. He began with 35

Horses and streetcars share the road in this early 1900s photograph of Elmhurst.

acres and added 29, and then 15 more, lamenting the fact that crops went to waste each year for lack of men to harvest his huge output of tomatoes, cucumbers, peas, squash and peppers.

Jones Avenue is named for him—and the settlement itself almost was. But rather than Jonestown, the humble Jones suggested Hurst Town, in honor of one of the other residents, Ed Hurst. That didn't go over well, but someone at the meeting that had been called specifically to name the town suggested that it carry the name of the elm trees Jones had planted. A compromise was made, and Elmhurst was named for the trees and the man.

In 1909, Elmhurst was annexed to the city of Oakland, along with Fruitvale, Melrose, Fitchburg (now Lockwood), and Claremont.

By 1910, an improvement society had been formed: "Their work is beginning to tell. Where wooden sidewalks or no sidewalks at all were formerly the rule, stone walks are taking their places. Where formerly weeds grew, lawns have been substituted, and where the people cared little or nothing for civic pride, they are now beautifying both their homes and their home surroundings," said the 1910 report. The little settlement of Elmhurst was then considered a 20-minute ride from Oakland, and was at that time beginning to subdivide. Its climate was stated as so favorable that San Francisco's "sick children of the poor" were sent to Elmhurst's Toy Memorial Home to recuperate.

The Kenwood Park subdivision in 1913 was "enjoying one of the most successful campaigns that has ever been launched by any real estate firm," according to a newspaper article. It was located at the East 14th Street streetcar line, "one and a half blocks from the new Southern Pacific Melrose extension." The timing of this settlement had much to do with the Panama-Pacific Exposition in San Francisco, organized to commemorate the opening of the Panama Canal in 1915. "The unusual demand for Oakland property by non-residents gives one a good idea of the fact that Oakland will receive her share of growth in population in direct consequence of the coming exposition, which is only twenty-four months off, and opening of the Panama Canal in October of this year," reported the newspaper.

In 1926, Elmhurst hosted a 10-day Seventh Day Adventist camp meeting, which drew 7,000 people to the tent city erected for that purpose. The huge religious revival was record-breaking for its attendance. A big

A bird's-eye view of Elmhurst, circa 1907.

draw was a former Fiji cannibal chief who spoke about his life of cannibalism before converting to Christianity.

Brookfield Village can also be folded into this neighborhood, where homes were built in the 1940s specifically for workers in the war industries. The history of Elmhurst includes many factories: canneries, glass manufacturing plants and . . . thank goodness . . . Mother's Cookies. Many plants shut down in the 1960s, leaving the neighborhood to fight unemployment and poverty.

Elmhurst

BY MY-KELL JOLLY

Evenings spent outside
Listening to the
Mockingbirds sing
Helps me to wait
Until I
Receive the
Songs that
Teach us how mockingbirds sing.

Elmhurst

BY LORENZO HEAROD

Elmhurst students
Low in academic achievement
More fights every day
Higher it increases
Until it all stops. But it won't. It'll
Remain that way for years
So don't call the cops
The terminator's here

Birch Street song

BY SHEMARIAE BRYANNA CHRISTIAN

Bringing violence
Into the street to
Review something bad might
Catch me and I see
How that something might happen.

Walking Slow

BY YOLANDE BARIAL

I started to think how our kids walk across the street
Walking so slow —can it be they have no place to go?

Living in this place called 'hood appears
to take away dreams of children far too early

Waking up to the siren's blue wails, the moans of red engines, guns
popping, flames flickering, monuments to dead kids on garbage
incrusted corners emblazoned with candles, empty 40's
and metallic balloons

Seeing men who don't live in this 'hood,
Men who don't care at all about my neighbors

For these men uniformed in blue and black and yellow, walking so
slow is an impediment to their 4-wheel progress running
to and from incident and accident and then racing away
to areas where kids can run to the "well-lit" Albertson's or Safeway,
to the deli round the corner, to the library, to the park uncluttered
with 40's and needles and mattresses
and the smell of urine on a nice hot day

Walking so slow allows one to view the existence of young men whose
dreams have been snuffed out by hard liquor, hard nights, cigarettes
pulled on so tightly one can see bones imprinted on skin exposed with
each inhalation, teeth stained with a hint of yellow
not sun-drenched but drenched with an image of sun's burnt rays, of
'no escape right now or ever my brother'

Young men who hang onto street corners at 10 a.m.,
3 p.m. or 11 o'clock at night

No real jobs, no real nothing else better to do
You know, they say we run in packs in this soft hood

I agree. Now that I am here I see packs of boys who so desperately
want to be men, want to be seen as valuable as some bodies to any
body that they sell poison to their own progeny
and sell their amazing ability to speak their image
of truths lyrically and musically in vulgar expletives which denigrate
their own identity knowing that embellishment, using their image
of a life where walking slow is all there is, will get them played
or at least listened to for a little while

Everyone wants to be a millionaire but don't want to do
what a millionaire can do:
Think it through, have a plan, implement the plan and work the plan
If they only knew that if God guides you to it
he will guide you through it.

What must a life lived vision-less do to a little boy whose God-given
birthright is to lead? What must it be like to be a little boy who comes
into his own to realize that his vision has no support, no roots on
which to grab on to, no strong branch from which to swing and see
the tops of the trees, branches outstretched to see possibility and
imagery and life . . .
This soft hood mentality of having it all NOW
Robs little girls from their "each-ness," that spark we see
when they are 3, 5 and 8
as they play with Barbies and sing songs in imagined microphones
wearing ballerina shoes, telling grand stories about what
their mommas or daddies did and when was the last time
they saw that dinosaur walk down the street.
Their pupils dance as brown-ness dilates
and light dances playfully in their eyes

Soon, their skips turn into struts that turn into walking slow
so everyone can see their beautifully defined thighs and butts and hips
and breasts through clothes fused on to them because our so-called
enlightened culture sells g-strings, matching bra
and panties and teddies with more lace and see-through fabric
than any 13-year-old little girl should be allowed to wear
Keep in mind that they wear it—but we the enlightened masses of
adults buy it and what's worse we buy into it. Our little girls are

"microwaved" women way before their time walking slowly in this soft
hood. Seeing older "cooked" women parading around selling and
showing pieces and parts of their "them-ness" to whomever is drooling
and willing to pay for it regardless of age, ability to hold
a conversation or even if they are deodorant challenged

Girls who've became microwaved lay on back seats, bent over in back
alleys, just to be able to afford
another day's living to wake up to begin
that strut all over again.

Little girls being abused by men who've had babies on top of babies.
Little girls raising them all alone, scared and broke doing the best they
can in this soft hood because her image of male is viewed as she passes
by grown men sitting on milk crates, old dirty couches, broke chairs
and broken down cars with flat tires and dented fenders
drinking out of brown bags, talking loud and yelling at this fused
frame they see

Brown and yellow families running businesses in this soft hood
Where in order for them to enter during certain "curfew" times of the
day "only two students are allowed in store" and "no bathrooms."
Cigarettes are sold one at a time as singles, stamps are sold
for 55 cents each and milk cost $5.00 a gallon,
speaking to us behind bulletproof glass and locked doors as soon as
the sun goes down.

Places where yellow sisters cater to every whim a girl can ask for
whether long or short or colored or frenched, manicured
and pedicured. All manner of design
and the latest embedded stud is placed, but either due to lack of
respect for clientele or I'd hope
it is ignorance, these same yellow and brown sisters refuse
to speak to each other in English but use only their native tongues
as if to say to us that we know you will patronize us
because vanity and "look good" is what we are all about anyway.
Yellow sisters know—the microwave generation.

Punishment is such a part of life that it is acceptable whether it be in
nail salons or behind bullet proof glass and even in the mighty blue
and red machines that protect us

Flamboyance on the outside only masks the lack on the inside.
We punish ourselves.

You see, we are so used to abuse we have no room for the brother or
sister who possesses the entrepreneurial spirit.
This spirit is seen in hair salons and barbershops where
young sisters and brothers are doing their best to make it work.
Oftentimes being successful and realizing that walking slow is a luxury
of time that business does not have.
This idea causes dissention, causes unrest amongst those who walk slow

Must we all be crabs?

Living in this soft hood I can understand why our kids walk slow
cause they have nothing better to do

The views of what they see is really all they know,
which becomes their base line
for a belief system that has to be bound up in lies

They subconsciously understand that with each and every step they
must enjoy every minute because it is not promised to them.

So they imbibe and inhale and shoot up to forget, talk loud, destroy
their minds with the beat
and rubberstamp the stereotypical imagery of lazy

To bury the skeleton of dreams not lived and dreams not nourished
and not accepted
and of course never revealed.

Walking slow because they have no place to go.

Talkin Story

BY MARK STATES

On a clear day—you can smell it a block away—
fresh cut daily.
Not those dehydrated then rehydrated
then jammed through a play-do grinder and coming out
looking like albino carrot sticks—
but REAL french fried potatoes
fresh cut daily at Kwikway Hamburgers in Oakland.

And one Saturday around six
I was getting my high cholesterol fix when
Dude at the front of the line
poked his head through the window and hollered:
"Hey! Where's my order, I been here 15 minutes!"
He turns around and explains to us that he'd just
gotten out
of Highland Hospital and wanted to take his dinner home
before his Vicadin kicked in.
We saw his arm in a cast from elbow to knuckles—
he said some dude had come up on him talking smack
so he had to put him in check.
The second man in line said, "I feel ya dawg"
and turned around & pulled up his tee shirt
to show off the bullet wound in his back,
which kinda looked like his belly button got tired of
the view
from the front of his fat self and migrated.

Then they looked at me, the third man in line.

Now I coulda shown off my battle scars but I didn't
because that's not the point—
the point is
there's too many warriors walking our streets
and none of us play basketball for Golden State,
too many of us on the streets of Oakland
killing each other over street corners we don't own,
over women we only think we own
and dirty looks!

I doubt when Marcus Garvey said "Buy Black"
that he meant
     money to the Black dealer
so when he gets capped there's
     money to the Black undertaker

Why are us men killing each other? So we can get
money for fast cars and faster women
money for hundred dollar tennis shoes?
For that Foster Grants and we are strapped?

The point is

there are too many of us men dying on the streets of
Oakland

the point is

there are too many of us killing other men
on the streets of Oakland, and for what?

There's nothing redeeming in sirens shrieking
and car tires screeching and women screaming
while the air is reeking of gunpowder,

there's nothing glorious in the talking BS stories
that us men do about
"I dropped im where he stood" and "Yeah I did ten in
the pen
for icing someone and I would do it again . . ."

So, there we were, three men
(two Black, one White) at six o'clock on a Saturday night
at Kwikways in East Oakland
talkin story about our lives on these streets.
And I said
funny thing about knives:
you swear you can feel the coldness of the blade
before the burning heat when the blade's pulled out . . .

Cruising

BY MARK STATES

Sean & me
are old friends from East Oakland
and tonight—on Memorial Day weekend—
we debate for 15 minutes whether to drive
to Operation Impact checkpoint at 98th Ave.
and #%!!! with the cops
cuz we are Black and White cruising on a Friday night.

We roll up on the 580
around about 9:18
past Lakeshore to Park Boulevard
Fruitvale, High Street
listening to the beats of D12 World
returning to Oakland streets at MacArthur/Mills College

Sean & me
waving our arms to ghetto beats
turning right onto 73rd
the world of drug deals in "The Killing Fields"
well every coupla blocks there's some cops
pulling people's cars over and layin batons across
their shoulders
Sean says, "I pray we not next!"
as he crosses his chest.

Cruising
left turn where we slow our roll on Sunnyside
when I tap Sean & say "Dayam she tight!"
Baby got back—and top and bottom—
red mini skirt v-cut blouse and fur over her
shoulders and I bet her calves
are strong enough to cut a man in half!

I roll down the window to appreciate the show
and she gives us the "What the #%!!! You Lookin At?"
scowl— well I just throw her one last smile
and we move on cruising turning right and then left
up International to about 90th
when Sean sees his old lady's number on the cell
and says Oh Hell—What Now?

While they talk we u-turn past two teenage girls with
a gang of backside
on a questionable late night stroll
and wake up a pile of tattered clothes leaning on a
bus pole
he looks perturbed when we pull up to the curb
near International & 83rd
to a store I ain't never heard of let alone been in
being a kid from 35th and 60th.
Sean hands me a few dollars & says
"Get my boys some soda and pork skins from the store"
the moment I step through the door
three chins hit the floor—
God, ain't they seen a whiteboy before?

Rolling to his crib for home-cooking and videos,
Sean pokes me in the ribs—
"Man the cops is EVERYWHERE!"
"Well Sean aren't you glad I chopped off my hair?"
"Man—they can't see your hair
under that hood, dawg"
and we laugh our X%!!!es off
cuz we know if the coppers gonna stop us
it don't matter if I'm a skinhead or a hippie
they'll STILL be tripping:
Black and White cruising together on a Friday night
oh they MUST be up to no good!

THIS NEIGHBORHOOD is the one where the Peralta family influence is best felt. Although at one time the four Peralta brothers built over a dozen homes here on Rancho San Antonio, the only one still standing in Oakland is the 1870 wood-frame house known as Peralta Hacienda. On the site of the present-day home, Antonio built an adobe in 1821, the first substantial house built in Oakland. Later structures housed family members, Native Americans, cattlehands who handled the 8,000-plus cattle, horsemen for the 2,000 horses, and visitors—at one point, there were 20 guesthouses on the property.

Here, celebrations could last for weeks, with horse races, rodeos, games and fandangos (parties with dancing). The Peraltas shipped their cattle hides and tallow (animal fat used to make candles, soap and the like) from a wharf they built on the bay.

Peralta Ave. Fruitvale, Cal.

OAKLAND HISTORY ROOM OF THE OAKLAND PUBLIC LIBRARY

A circa 1910 postcard of Peralta Avenue, today Coolidge Avenue.

So how did this area transform from Rancho San Antonio to Fruitvale? The answer is the fruit: In 1856, Henderson Lewelling planted 700 Bing cherry trees, giving rise to the name (for more, see Dimond listing). Fruitvale was initially spelled Fruit Vale, and that extra space emphasizes the "vale," which means valley. In the area was also the first California commercial rose garden. After Lewelling came Frederick Rhoda, who also planted orchards in 1859.

The historic Cohen-Bray House falls under this district, at 1440 29th Ave. Built in 1884, this Stick Eastlake has been untouched by time and contains complete intact interiors. It now operates as a house museum.

The neighborhood was once so lush and blissful that a 1903 newspaper article read, "It is said that when a distinguished preacher's sermon

OAKLAND HISTORY ROOM OF THE OAKLAND PUBLIC LIBRARY

The Eagle Carnival in 1910, at East 14th Street and Fruitvale Avenue.

on 'Heaven' failed to arouse much enthusiasm in Fruitvale the reason was explained to the speaker by an ancient citizen of the place. Said he: 'Doctor, you certainly painted the heavenly glories in a splendid way, and you gave the region in the sky a good "send-off," but if you preached a hundred years Fruitvale people could hardly be convinced that heaven is a nicer place to live in than is their own town.'"

Known at the time to be affluent, Fruitvale was described in the same article as being the place with "homes on every side that speak of wealth and culture and good taste." Its accessibility to transit was also eloquently noted: "Electric cars whirl one to the place in so short a time that distance seems to be annihilated." Fruitvale had yet to be incorporated at this time.

In 1909, Fruitvale annexed to the city of Oakland. The Key System's expanded streetcar line aided in development, as did the 1906 earthquake which brought many stranded San Franciscans. In the 1930s, Mexican immigrants began arriving, largely to work in fruit canning operations. In the 1940s, African Americans began arriving to work in wartime shipyards.

Fruitvale has gotten attention more recently for its Transit Village begun around the Fruitvale BART station in 1993. The Dia de los Muertos (Day of the Dead) and Cinco de Mayo (Fifth of May) festivals always bring out crowds of people.

Altares
for all the Altaristas

BY ANDRENA ZAWINSKI

Children empty the mother's house of her,
muscles aching from the weight of her loss
held in their arms so close to their hearts.
Light a candle for them.

Neighbors bemoan an old man lost
just blocks from his home.
No one ever reported him missing.
Pray on beads for them.

Strangers, heads darting this way and that,
circle a young man on the tracks who slipped
into a heap crossing the street.
Petition the saints for them.

Light candles for them.

Light a candle for girls who gave birth
in the dark the way they conceived,
buried stillborns in deep graves of grief.
Bury your face in your hands for them.

And for the parents whose children fell
to open schoolground fire, who, uprooted,
wither upon the blood soaked earth.
Lay down wreathes of marigolds for them.

Ring bells for them.

Ring bells for a woman, pack at her heels
with knife, brick, and pipe, who dropped
in the dark, rapt with sleep, then forgot.
Cover the mirrors for them.

Ring bells for the men who balk
at the buck of the rifle butt, drop guns
and run, rogues cast out from the pack.
Raise flags for them. Free doves for them.

And for those with bodies bound by rope,
throats gagged with rags, backs strapped
and lashed, their cries silenced:
Open a window for them.

Deliver oblations for them.

For all the apocalyptic visionaries who leapt
to their ends from bridge rails, or slept drunken
on fumes in the room in a blanket of death:
Burn incense for them.

Sing chants at altars you create for them.
Carve their names deep into stone
you erect to them. Let their ashes
take wings on the wind for them.

dia de los muertos, Fruitvale

BY HALEH HATAMI

some boys in Fruitvale en Oakland

offrendas en phantom burn some boys

ancestors in Spanish some Fruitvale

no rancho no lovelorn some specters

some flutes burn floats ghostly offrenda

touch music push Spanish some come boys

en Latin ancestors some lovelorn

en otoño no touching float some

ghostly some girls burns flutes Fruitvale

touch lovelorn offrenda some candles

rancho some yes boys come otoño

some latin mestizo the candy

Post-war Fruitvale memories

BY JOHN BRENNAN

Growing up on Galindo Street in East Oakland during the 1950s was a rich experience. Indelible memories laced with a bit of nostalgia yet personally more valuable than any interest-bearing bank account. The sheer range of social variety laid at our feet in this Fruitvale district was staggering. A venerable smorgasbord of neighborhood offerings was within easy walking distance or a short bus ride away. Among other things, it is known as the place the Bing cherry made its first appearance, and to my thinking the best example there is for defining the outer-urban benefits found in location, location, location.

If you think of an extended family, that is what surrounded us kids growing up in the Foothill-Fruitvale area. Firstly, for me there was my Irish-Catholic family with a stay-at-home Mom. Bust you in the chops but tough love all the way. Also, this being the post-war Baby Boom period, most of the homes in my neighborhood were occupied during the day with babies and mothers who networked with all the other babies and mothers down the street. Then consider the business district along Foothill which us kids walked on the way to school. All these mostly independent shop owners knew and greeted their customers by name, and many even maintained a weekly grocery bill for clientele who sought this option. The last yet most influential entity in our area was St. Elizabeth Parish. A Parthenon of spiritual, social, athletic, cultural, academic, and outreach programs, it represented an anchor, foundation, and pillar of the community. Family, neighborhood, businesses, and parish. These four concentric rings of influence maintained order, forged identity, and fostered integrity.

Let's talk about Galindo Street itself. My family moved here from Berkeley in 1944. Lived in the 3006 house until 1989. Our neighbors were German, Irish, Portuguese, Chinese, Japanese, Armenian, Greek, and Italian. Many were first or second generation emigrants from the mother country. Greeting me on my daily rounds delivering the Oakland Tribune were aromatic smells commonly associated with thick speaking accents commending me for my bull's-eye paper toss onto their porch.

Luckily, the end of the month subscription collection gained me access to the exotic dens where even Lowell Thomas would feel at home.

Down at the end of Galindo Street behind residential houses was Sausal Creek. My friend Mitzu's backyard bordered the creek. He and I spent countless hours playing here. It was our own secret garden. We especially enjoyed playing war which was fueled by the many battle films locally viewed at the Foothill, Fruitvale and Fairfax theaters. Did I mention that Mitzu was born in a Relocation Camp during World War II? Also, this backyard access to Sausal Creek got utilized when running errands, and became known as the shortcut to the "fat lady's store" on E-23 Street two blocks over (aka Neighborhood Grocery). The fat lady sat on a stool and was able to reach whatever you needed in the way of candy selection. You were not allowed to pick your own.

The dominant-looking structure at the corner of Galindo was the Fruitvale Residence Club. Everyone who didn't live there called it either "the hotel" or "the castle." In its day it verged on being grand and held a lot of fascination for us kids. It was a very adult place where children did not reside. Delivering newspapers there was an eerie experience especially on Sunday morning, dashing through the hallways and up the wooden stairs to all three floors. Sometimes on a dare we'd scale the outside fire escape and climb to the hotel roof. The view was worth the risk, let me tell you. But don't ever tell my mother a word of this. Both the hotel and the tall palm trees out front were prominent enough features that they were utilized as landmarks whenever driving directions to our house were given out over the telephone. Also, after a big windstorm us kids would collect the fallen palm branches, drag them home and construct grass shacks in our backyards.

Here's a rundown of Galindo Street neighbors famous and not so famous: 3025: John Denis, owner of the Food Mill (established 1933, one of the first health food stores in Bay Area) on MacArthur; 2927: Konishi family, 50 years here; 2900: Siegel, never returned balls that inadvertently entered his property; 3002: John Nicolasi, waiter in Hollywood during the 1930s & 40s with a screen appearance in a couple of Marx Brothers films; 3006: Brennan, precinct polling site, favorite stairs for kids to sit; 3016: Robinson Brothers, mortuary owners; 3108: O'Mara, gardener for Kaiser Center & Mr. Kaiser in Oakland—also site of brutal double murder in 1915 of San Francisco banker & wife; 2401 Fruitvale: Fahey, occupied by same family since the 1920s.

Up until 1963 the Foothill-Fruitvale business district was nearly self-sufficient in its capacity to provide basic goods and services for the local consumer. That's because in '63 a big box Safeway replaced an entire block (and a tinier Safeway that faced Fruitvale) of independent shops that lined the east side of Foothill Boulevard from Fruitvale to Coolidge Avenue. My memories as a local yokel walking up and down Foothill would encompass the delights found in fine dining, cinema, hobbies, bakery, banking, hardware, shoes, cocktails, dentistry, prescriptions, postal needs, auto supplies, groceries, meats, hair cutting & salon, etc. For needs beyond the basic type, one would only walk or travel the short distance to the East 14th Street shops, the huge Montgomery Wards department store near East 27th Avenue, or the downtown stores near Lake Merritt. There was something for everybody within a few miles radius.

The venerable Foothill Theater holds a multitude of memories that I share with my brothers and sisters. Going to "the show" meant plunking down twenty-five cents and never being disappointed. Never in life afterwards would I ever get my money's worth like I did when I was a kid sitting in the Foothill for a Saturday matinee of entertainment. Prizes raffled off during intermission included a wooden rocking horse and box of assorted concession goodies, plus complimentary movie tickets. Irish luck would have it that these enviable items would be won by my two sisters whose matching ticket stubs were plucked from a tumbling mixing bin on stage, and forever become part of our family story. In 1958, the Foothill stopped featuring first run movies and through 1963 operated as an independent movie theater.

The Idle Hour restaurant at 3340 Foothill was a special place for us Brennan kids in two regards. We could buy firecrackers from the Chinese cooks out the side door. And we could "bicycle" out front against the green mirrored, vitrolite glass façade. Let me explain in the words of my brother Jim. "I would stand at one corner of the front of the building. With my chest touching the glass, I'd move my outside arm and outside leg in a circular motion, a la choo choo train motion, and MAGIC. To someone watching it would appear that both my legs would be off the ground moving in that circular motion along with both my arms! We never tired of this simple joy. It always made us laugh."

The businesses that dotted the Foothill-Fruitvale district in the 1950s & early '60s are a myriad lot that conjure up special memories. Lu's Hobby Shop was forced to relocate from the razed side of the street (3308) to new digs near the corner of 34th & Foothill (3355). Here my penchant for collecting coins was formally addressed, while just a few doors down at the Bank of America (3301), the raw materials for my collecting bug were there for the pickings. Bell Market (3327), aka Ernie Russells, had sawdust floors and superior meat (my mother claimed). Boulevard Ladies & Children's Shop (3337), aka Mrs. Bliss, was a dress shop & fabric store frequented by my mom especially because of the owner's sweet demeanor.

The east side of Foothill that was razed contained the following businesses: St. Vincent de Paul, Lake County Properties, Demi John Liquors, Merrill's Camera, Dr. Defeo Dentist, and Foothill Pharmacy. Other businesses on the east side that escaped demolition were Russ Liquor, Marion Mitar Barber, Masters Bar, and Hackman's Hardware. Of all the shops that were torn down in 1963, it was the second hand store that I missed the most, because, let's face it, a kid with limited income had few places to go that offered things that actually fitted his budget.

Continuing down Foothill on the west side toward Fruitvale: Lorraine's Bakery (3321) had a great smell and a particular curiosity known as a bread slicing machine that always fascinated me. On the way home from school, us kids would pop our heads in and ask for broken cookies. Craig's Hardware (3319), aka Ozzie's, was a place Tim the Toolman would have loved. Had an old time feeling. Ozzie was gracious, friendly & helpful, and always found time to talk to kids and ask about your parents. The Bank of America next door is where I stored my coin collection and where we all kept our Xmas Club savings accounts. The Blue Chip Stamp Redemption Store (3229) always had a crowd. Cuttings Five & Dime (3225) was a variety store that had a penny weight machine out front that gave your weight and a fortune. Also had a mirror for fixing your hat or your hair. Arizu (3221) was an Art Deco hair salon, where men never ventured.

On the corner of Fruitvale and Foothill was Guy's Drug Store. Had a side door, front door and a big neon clock above the entrance. Here passed more customers on Foothill except maybe for the old Safeway across the street or the B of A. It was a center of activity. Besides filling prescriptions, they developed photos, served up ice cream, and offered post office services. A great community landmark that sort of anchored the whole business area there. Across the street at 1933 Fruitvale resided Willie Brown's Liquor Store, owned by a football Hall of Famer and former Raider player.

Next door was Al & Jeans Market (1925), where we maintained a weekly grocery bill and which my Mom preferred over Safeway, even though my Dad was a Safeway truck driver and even though it cost more and had less variety, because she came from a family that owned a small Berkeley store like this. She had empathy and said that independents were friendlier and more accommodating.

Two service stations dominated the Fruitvale-Foothill corners which witnessed many a gas war in their day: Regular, Super or Ethyl. Standard at 2000 Fruitvale and Shell at 2001 gave out maps and pumped your gas but exhibited extraordinary displeasure if one repeatedly rang "the bell" too often when riding one's bike or walking across the small rubber hose that stretched across the ground for cars to roll over.

The biggest drawing card of the area for an afterhours gathering place, open 365 days of the year, was the fancy-looking House of Lee restaurant, 2021 Fruitvale, across from the original Safeway. Here in 1958, as the story goes, Mr. Lee had this structure built with a down payment financed from a winning Keno card that won big at a Reno casino a short nine months earlier. His establishment really gave the community a shot in the arm and lent the area a touch of class. It enjoyed a great reputation for years after, and was often written up in the social pages of the *Oakland Tribune*. Many times one would rub shoulders with Oakland Raider football players and other celebs of the era there.

Directly across the street from the House of Lee was an old Safeway store. My parents knew all the employees by name and shopped here every Wednesday, it being my Dad's payday. Imagine today on Halloween going to a big supermarket and asking trick-or-treat and getting a big size candy bar! It happened exactly like that fifty years ago at this Safeway location. Next door was the Telephone Company (2112), a monolith in the neighborhood. It had no windows on the ground floor so you couldn't see what was going on inside. I remember in 1959 or 1960 watching construction workers build several additional floors onto this building. We newspaper boys had a ringside view from the *Tribune* distribution "shack" on East 22nd Street. Also, my sister Peggy started her 30-year Ma Bell career two blocks down Foothill at the Telephone Exchange Building (3430) next door to the theater.

Traveling up Fruitvale to the corner of East 23rd Street was Scotch Cleaners (2231). A one-story wooden building, it was attached to a similar-sized structure which at the time was a hobby shop, then a bar. Both my sisters worked part-time at the cleaners, which was operated by Reba Dick. They were allowed to keep all the change they found in pockets of clothes they handled, and once a week Reba would give them a complimentary ice-cold Coke. That was most refreshing, they both remembered, in that steamy-hot cleaners.

Reaching the corner opposite "the hotel," one would see the Masonic Hall building at 3209 Galindo Street. Built in the late 1950s, this parcel was the former site of a large nursery business that provided garden supplies to the local residents. The apartments next door were also built at the same time from nursery land. I distinctly remember the overflow parking our street incurred whenever a fancy event was going on across Fruitvale at the Hall. Fancy dressed attendees in gowns, furs and suits would be curiously eyed as they exited their expensive cars and traversed the sidewalks of our humble, yet proud, blue-collared neighborhood.

Sometime in the late 1950s or early 60s, directly across from the Fahey house and "hotel" on Fruitvale, a gas station was erected where once stood an original, turn-of-the-century grand mansion. I remember delivering newspapers here in its last days when it was a multi-unit rental. Two huge, mature-sized palm trees graced the front yard as I recall. Old, weathered wrought iron fencing surrounded the raised lot where the house stood. When it was gone, the last glimpse of how old Fruitvale once looked went the way of the horses that once were common here also. Remarkably, I understand up near St. Jarlath's Church in the Dimond district sits an example of a smaller Fruitvale mansion from around the same time period. Languishing in the shadow of the MacArthur Freeway, it seems that time has passed by this former painted lady.

I tip my hat to this grand dame of the past, and all the other manmade landmarks of old Fruitvale, for they are more than just timber and plaster and nails. They are a part of our human story, and history never gets old.

GLENVIEW

WHERE: *From Trestle Glen to Dimond Canyon and from East 38th Street to Hollywood Avenue*

GLENVIEW RESIDENTS have long known that their little piece of Oakland is worth journeying to from far away. And a 1925 newspaper article corroborated it: "Homes are being built here because this relatively small area is one of the most delightful places in all the world in which to live. From these subdivisions a home can face the Golden Gate with the panorama of cities, sea and mountain like a vast painted picture spread before it. Visitors to Oakland invariably exclaim that the view from these hills is alone worth a trip across the continent."

Long before cars plied Park Boulevard, oxen used it and 13th Avenue to bring lumber down from the hills to the estuary. Over the years, Park

A 1940s look at Park Boulevard from the driver's seat.

Boulevard has gone through a number of different changes, including changing names and having curves straightened out.

Glenview was subdivided as the Fourth Avenue District in 1907 by Wickham Havens. That company crowed in an undated ad, "We have the land—the other fellows haven't: there's the situation in a nutshell."

An undated map of the tract shows wide landholdings for the "Cameron Tract" and the "Carmany Property." Cameron and Carmony were ranchers, as was Mr. Hampel whose name lives on in Hampel Street. The map also shows the huge proposed park along Trestle Glen (see Trestle Glen listing).

At one time, two "handsome and costly" entrance pillars on Park at Greenwood marked the entrance to Fourth Avenue Terrace.

"Come to Fourth Avenue Heights today . . . note the homes of millionaires just across Trestle Glen—look down into Dimond Canyon with its oaks and alders and rippling stream . . . see how beautifully the white avenues curve about the hillslopes . . . note the proximity of the Key Route Extension—and ask yourself if this is not the spot you want for your home," reasoned an April 1911 advertisement.

"There are of course more strangers in the city than ever before in the history of the city if we except the San Franciscans after the fire," said a Wickham Havens representative in an April 1911 newspaper article. "You would be absolutely astonished at the large proportion who expressed amazement at the beauty of the country within two miles of the city, and who stated with a laugh at their own expense that they had never been through either Dimond Canyon or Trestle Glen." At this time, the street-car fare to the neighborhood was five cents.

For this neighborhood, apparently it wasn't enough to simply hold picnics or build observatories to bring daytrippers out. In May 1911, a "daring aviator" from Mexico flew over the Fourth Avenue tract to bring crowds to the area to convince them to buy.

A September 1911 ad for Fourth Avenue Court pointed out that a yard of land could be had for the same cost as a yard of silk, and had a drawing of a Gibson Girl clutching her head while two gentlemen showed her lengths of fabric and a divot of land. Interestingly, although the ads repeatedly pointed out the proximity to millionaires in Trestle Glen and the Crocker Tract, this neighborhood was intended for medium-wage earners. Indeed, a Wickham Havens sales manager told the newspaper in June 1911, "It has been our custom to advance prices when the sale of property created automatically a higher value, but we have deferred in Fourth Avenue Heights because it was planned for the man of average means."

Another article marveled at the incredible population growth of Oakland and what that meant for this neighborhood. "Just picture another Oakland built almost entirely around the outside of the present city. That

The interior of the Glenview library on Park Boulevard, October 1935.

will give you some idea of the coming importance of Park Boulevard. It is going to be Oakland's great north and south artery, and it cannot be paralleled," said a developer in April 1925.

Some residents probably remember the Glenview Branch Library since it didn't close until 1981. It sat at 4231 Park Boulevard, where the organ company now operates. The library opened in October of 1935, one of those miracles of community involvement. Due to efforts of the Glenview Dad's Club, the Glenview Women's Club, the Glenview Improvement Club, the PTA and residents, the City Council was lobbied to create the branch. Proof of its necessity is the fact that within 10 days of opening, 400 people took out cards at the library.

Glenview

BY ERIKA MAILMAN

Going past my neighbor's house
Looking in all the windows seeing people
Eating their quiet dinners and
Now and then I
Visualize all of us out in the street
In full view of each other
Endlessly glad
We're home.

Lover's sonnet in Glenview

BY DARLA PRITSKY

You are ingenious because of your proud
chin and medulla that sparks unerringly.
I want your mind, want your spine
lodged in mine, want your blood to crowd
my corpuscles, your viscera in me.
Your arms are right for flying—
I've seen you fooling with the skyline.
O don't come back to pose your face
with a cocky wink and try to find
me in turn seeking you, at the base
of Wellington Avenue. I don't complain.
What matters is the pleasure of feigning
I know you, true you. I won't soar;
I am buckled to earth's very core.

GOLDEN GATE

WHERE: *Roughly bounded by San Pablo Avenue, Adeline Street, 48th Street and the Berkeley border*

THIS NEIGHBORHOOD began as a community founded by a loud, brassy man with an equally loud name. German immigrant Charles Klinkner came to town in the 1880s, bought 150 acres that had been cattle ranch land, and named the area after himself: Klinknerville.

He owned a rubber stamp business and did his damndest to advertise it, often enlisting unwitting animals. For instance, he was known for painting mules red white and blue every Fourth of July and driving them to Oakland hitched to a cart covered in signs advertising his business. On St. Patrick's Day he would paint the mules green, and so on for various color-related holidays. He would also have an elk pull a rig.

Klinkner sold several houses through a lottery of 25-cent tickets, to attract attention to the area of which he was now "mayor." Over time, he built and sold over 75 homes. His motto was said to be, "Early to bed, early to rise, never get drunk, but advertise."

This undated photo shows the Klinkner Hall at the corner of San Pablo and Klinkner avenues. Today, Klinkner Avenue is 59th Street.

OAKLAND HISTORY ROOM OF THE OAKLAND PUBLIC LIBRARY

Klinkner Hall (hosting clubs and church services on the second floor, and selling groceries and drugs on the first) was erected in 1886 at the corner of San Pablo and Klinkner avenues (today, 59th Street). This Gothic three-story structure was torn down in 1941.

Naming a village after yourself is very forward, and some didn't care for Klinkner's brassy advertising, either. Many of the old families had been there long before he arrived, perhaps lending to the effrontery of now living in or near the fabricated Klinknerville. One young woman,

This advertising was perhaps tame compared to what Mr. Klinkner was capable of. This is looking north on San Pablo Avenue.

Kate Shepard, was so repulsed that she took on the project of changing the community's name to Golden Gate because of the view of that landmark the neighborhood afforded. She started a petition, and soon the railway men were announcing the stop as Golden Gate.

The Klinknerville post office had been established in 1887, but only a year later was known as the Golden Gate post office thanks to Shepard's machinations. Klinkner got the decision reversed, but only temporarily, as citizens again intervened, changing the name back to Golden Gate. He died in 1893 at the young age of 41. Even the avenue that carried his name was changed, to 59th Street.

The Herzog Tract was one of the important subdivisions in Golden Gate, with 125 lots at San Pablo and Alcatraz avenues. In 1881, these lots were sold by auction: the advertisement for the auction read, "Save your money and buy property at your own price. The first big auction gun of the great boom to be fired by McAfee Bros, Newhall's Sons & Co., auctioneers."

In 1897, Golden Gate was annexed to Oakland.

Back in the day, Southern Pacific commuter trains used to run down Shattuck and Adeline from Berkeley, continuing into the Golden Gate neighborhood on Stanford Avenue and down to the Oakland Mole, the pier at the foot of Seventh Street in West Oakland, where they met the San Francisco ferry. Service of these red trains was discontinued in 1941.

During World War II, many African-Americans arrived in Golden Gate to work at the shipyards.

The 1918 Golden Gate library branch was designed by Charles Dickey, who also designed the Claremont Hotel. Another significant building was Golden Gate Hall on San Pablo Avenue, built in the early 1900s by Eric Lindblom. He was an Oakland tailor who went to Nome, Alaska, and struck it rich in an 1899 gold rush where gold was found by panning the sand on the beach. He returned to Oakland a millionaire.

Mean Ole City

BY JESY GOLDHAMMER

People be droppin
revolution
like it was a pick-up line.
You wouldn't use that word
if you knew what it meant—
it ain't pretty, it's bloody,
it overturns things.
- Malcolm X

1
Jerry Brown runs tours
in luxury buses
through our ghetto community—
Oak-town.
Hill folk descend to
the flatlands intrigued,
witness the African safari.
Through bullet-proof glass
write off vacation
developing gentrification.
Feast off barbecue and malt liquor,
exchange goods in a handshake.

2
Glass cognac bottle
placed behind rear tire,
caught it in time
and I put it behind someone else's.
Glass splatters like
ketchup smeared sidewalks,
our front yard idles

scenes of nomads;
pants wrapped around thighs,
booties bulgin outta Old Navy jeans,
lipstick soaked Newports,
Olde E 40s,
chips, donuts, cookies,
bags of half eaten KFC and
shady corners where
drunk men pee.

3
Sunday's an open house
next to the corner store where
the god of working thugs hides
in a brown bag.
Whadaya think of this neighborhood?
light-faced and hopeful.
Wild pitbulls abandoned
like the fashion of the month,
stale mothers spew and flare
like volcanos and aftershocks,
weary kids whacked in the heads
to the boom bap boom,
sweep up splifs, straws, syringes,
butchered trees beg for clemency.

Through town

BY KATHY NGUYEN

I'm not even there yet.
But ecstatic.
Coasting off the memories.
From last time.
He swung into town.
Crashing on his brother's sofa.
A lover's tryst.
Red light.
Stop sign.
Almost there now.
Passing Aileen,
Arlington,
Stanford,
get me there.
Get me there.
Parking meter.
No change.

GRAND LAKE

WHERE: *Between Lake Merritt and the city of Piedmont,
along the stretch of Grand Avenue*

IN THE 1870s the huge Pleasant Valley Ranch spanned much of this area, located between Greenbank Avenue and MacArthur Boulevard, along what is today Grand Avenue. Today's Pleasant Valley Road memorializes this old-time ranch.

An early resident enthused, "I stood upon Grand Avenue Heights the other day and saw the most beautiful panorama you can imagine. I could see San Francisco and on down south almost to Palo Alto. I saw the little pleasure yachts on Lake Merritt backed up by a forest of masts of mercantile vessels in Brooklyn basin. Automobiles were gliding down

OAKLAND HISTORY ROOM OF THE OAKLAND PUBLIC LIBRARY

Judging by all the skirts, this is probably the Ladies' Matinee advertised on the Grand Lake Theater's marquee. Undated.

Grand Avenue Boulevard, people were promenading past the entrance gates, and in all it was a picture I shall never forget and a picture I often expect to see as I am already living in my new house that I have erected upon one of the finest lots in the tract." This 1909 article referred to a subdivision off Grand Avenue that included streets such as Highland Avenue, Boulevard Way, Fairbanks and Weldon Avenue.

This area was "picnic grounds for the pioneers." One of the selling agents was Frank K. Mott, who was one of Oakland's more pleasant mayors. In his sales brochure, he included a form for interested parties to fill out: "I would like to go out in your automobile and see Grand Avenue Heights on (date) (hour). There will be ___ people in my party." This illustrates the fact that many potential homebuyers did not own cars at this point, underlining the importance of the streetcar line three blocks away from the tract. The cable car line ran up Oakland Avenue starting in 1890, and along Grand Avenue north of the lake in the early 1900s.

Fifty by 200 foot lots in Grand Avenue Heights were $2,500 to $4,000 in 1907, when first put on the market. By 1920, more lots had opened up, and amazingly the prices were slashed, to $1,000 to $1,500. The 1920 advertisement crowed, "$50 down for a 50-foot lot. Again the Fred T. Wood Co. has hit the bull's eye! This is the best buy ever offered by this firm. When it is remembered that the Wood Co. gave to the buying public Lakewood Park, Lakeshore Terrace, The Oaks and other exclusive lake district properties away under-priced, it will be realized that this is a bold statement to make. But it is true—all we want you to do is prove it."

Some of this neighborhood's growth can be attributed to the Panama-Pacific Exposition in San Francisco, commemorating the opening of the Panama Canal. "It is a singular thing that on the eve of the world's greatest international exposition, real estate values are on a more conservative basis here than in any other city in the United States. . . . The present low valuations, therefore, make this the psychological moment for real estate investment on this, the home building and manufacturing side of the bay," reported a 1913 newspaper article about East Piedmont Heights. This subdivision was off Lakeshore Avenue near Trestle Glen.

The Grand Lake Theater is a highly visible landmark in the neighborhood. It opened in 1926, showing vaudeville and silent films before "talkies" came out. The enormous neon sign atop the theater is a marvel of timed lighting.

The Morcom Amphitheatre of Roses, or as it is commonly known, the Rose Garden, was a project of the Business Men's Garden Club in 1931. It was designed to remind the viewer of an Italian garden. The site is naturally bowl-shaped, lending itself to the purpose. In 1953 the name was

OAKLAND HISTORY ROOM OF THE OAKLAND PUBLIC LIBRARY

This 1944 postcard shows the Rose Garden in full bloom.

changed to honor Mayor Fred Morcom who had planted the first bush. In the garden is a rose called the Pride of Oakland. A rose by any other name would not smell as sweet.

See Lakeside listing for information on Lake Merritt itself.

Voices in the Night

BY JUDITH OFFER

When Lakeshore Highlands was new,
The trains whistled and choo-choo'd in the night
Leaving the beautiful train depot downtown.
The new homeowners turned over in bed
And dreamed about places they hoped to go.

Now, above the oceanic swoosh of Highway 580,
Our very own, open-all-night, noise brewery,
A disembodied, amplified voice orders,
"Get off at the next exit,
Get off at the next exit."

Some terrified trucker is getting a ticket
To get off instead of on.
We homeowners, now off sleep instead of on,
Map the carpools and commitments
We know will control us tomorrow.

Petals in the rose garden

BY PAM SMARTT

The bee tunnels into a flower
and his wings are as soft as the petals

The rose sees its reflection in the pool
and the thorns waver in the breeze

I am entranced by the perfume
I wish I knew just one rose

a little better. I would tell her
you are a silken gift

the world has given away.
You are rising from loam

to tease the bees,
you are nodding in sleep

when the crickets whistle.
You are more than all the folds

of your petals hold.
You cannot divulge.

GRASS VALLEY

WHERE: *Land east of Highway 580,*
mostly south of Sequoyah Heights

THIS AREA encompasses the tracts of Chabot Park, Elysian Fields and Sheffield Village. It's a nice, bucolic name that illustrates the very landscape.

Chabot Park is named for Anthony Chabot, the early Oaklander who brought water and observatories to the city. His name is also attached to nearby Lake Chabot and the Lake Chabot Municipal Golf Course.

Chabot Park Estates was planned in the 1940s on a 700-acre hillside site. A February 1948 advertisement for one of its subdivisions emphasized the "ranch" nature of the area, mentioning in large print the bridle trails as well as the panoramic bay view. It read, "Buy now in romantic El Rancho Bonita estates and homesites, as low as $1750 an acre. . . .

Alexander Dunsmuir built this house in 1899 for his new bride, only to die on the honeymoon. Dunsmuir House is today a house museum.

Rambling bridle trails over picturesque wooded knolls at your very door."

The photograph in the ad showed a home with a horse corral in its side yard. This was a model home built to show buyers how the land could be used. The ad copy enthused, "This is your opportunity to see a model California ranchero. See the many things you can enjoy with just ONE ACRE! See the gracious ranch house, the picturesque ranchero stables, the paddock, the grazing pasture, the orchard or vineyard, all surrounded by beautiful landscaping and gardens. Here is living up to the hilt . . ."

Another ad, in March 1948, read, "Own a country estate right in the city of Oakland at the price of a city lot!"

Sheffield Village is at the foot of a hillside of live oaks.

Within the larger area of the neighborhood is Sheffield Village, at Foothill Boulevard and Dutton Avenue. An October 1939 newspaper article said, "Sheffield Village isn't like Topsy. It didn't 'just grow.' It began as an intangible conception of the ideal residential area of small homes. The thought came to the mind of E. B. Field, a pioneer in real estate development in Northern California." This was originally a "fertile rancho" in the Peraltas' time, and then also was a proposed site for St. Mary College, which began in what is today Broadway Auto Row and later moved to Moraga. Field bought up the land and worked with an architect to plan Sheffield Village. This neighborhood was the first place to use neon lighted house numbers developed by the Neon Electric Corporation of Oakland.

Dunsmuir House is the showplace of the area, built in 1899 as a wedding gift from Alexander Dunsmuir to his new bride. Unfortunately, he didn't make it through the honeymoon and the unexpected widow lived in the house only two years before dying herself. The 37-room mansion is today a house museum with extensive grounds.

The Oakland Zoo is also in Grass Valley, after having many homes in different areas of the city. It has been situated in Snow Park near Lake Merritt, in Joaquin Miller Park, and in Durant Park (today's Knowland Park). It began in 1943 with big game hunter Sidney Snow traveling the world and bringing back exotic animals. (For more on Snow, see Lakeside listing.)

The zoo moved to its present spot in 1960. In 1978, zoo patrons witnessed a hair-raising spectacle. Steve Wallenda of the famous Flying Wallendas walked the wire that holds up the aerial tram, blindfolded and hooded. Those familiar with the zoo's setup will be relieved to hear that the animals were removed from their enclosures directly below the tram during Wallenda's walk—otherwise a fall could mean being savaged as well as experiencing the typical detriments of meeting the ground unexpectedly. He performed only hours after hearing of the death of his uncle Karl Wallenda, who fell off a high wire in Puerto Rico.

No Snack Bar for Me Today, Thanks

BY CHARLIE MELVILLE

Once we were at the zoo and we saw something pretty extraordinary. One elephant was reaching its trunk into another elephant's . . . uh . . . anus. And from there he was pulling out clods of excrement to . . . uh . . . eat. It was so bizarre I had to watch it happen three different times before I believed it.

There was a man there with a video camera and he taped it for a while, because believe me it was ongoing and there was time to, if you wanted, bring in a star's trailer and do a light check and run some lines. I didn't think to tell him until later that he should send the tape in to one of the TV shows that plays crazy videos and maybe he'd get some money out of this particular zoo visit.

Anyway, the elephant, as it chowed through the contents of the other elephant's hindquarters, had to progressively reach in further. I would mark the place on his trunk and as he pulled out it blew my mind to see how much of the trunk that "receiver" elephant was taking. Unreal! That elephant at one point slowly moseyed over to the fake little waterhole and drank, but the other elephant just as slowly pursued, and then the buffet resumed again.

After the shock wore off, I began to feel sad. Clearly, this wasn't normal behavior. Either the elephant wasn't getting something he needed in his diet or this was a way of expressing depression from being locked up without all the hundreds of miles to roam that he would get typically.

I looked around to see if there was a plaque that talked about this behavior. Like, in an Arizona zoo, they have a sign telling you that if it looks like some weasel-type animal is stuck in the moat of his habitat, he isn't really and not to worry. There was no such explanation for this.

I meant to write a letter to the zoo to say "Hey! One of your elephants is acting weird and he must also, not coincidentally, have terrible breath!" but I didn't immediately and then enough time passed that I thought maybe whatever was bothering that elephant had already passed by.

It's really not the best memory to have of the zoo.

Study of change

BY EDNA FONG

A hillside can be green
can glow like an emerald and an opal combined
it can be as green as a grasshopper

but hot summers turn it brown
like a cow's rough hide
tufty and harsh-looking

not soft like the green
but with its own solemn beauty

like one is a color photograph
and the other a sepia tint

HADDON HILL

WHERE: *Northeast side of Lake Merritt, between Park and MacArthur boulevards*

A NEIGHBORHOOD that rises so steeply of course deserves stairs, and maybe those stairs should have, who can say, cascading water and nice landscaping and . . .

oh yeah! This neighborhood already had it—and will soon have the water running again. The Cleveland Cascade was built in 1923 by landscape architect Howard Gilkey. "Cleveland street, from Lakeshore avenue one block to the east, was too steep to be traversed by any vehicular traffic and the street was ordered closed and turned into a park. It occurred to Gilkey that the declivity offered an excellent opportunity for a cascade similar to those in Italy, which have been copied in the private grounds of a few rich Americans," reported a March 1923 newspaper article.

Two flights of stairs frame the descending basins that used to pour into each other (and will, when restoration is completed). Back in the

Land rolls untouched to the lake, circa 1910.

OAKLAND HISTORY ROOM OF THE OAKLAND PUBLIC LIBRARY

1920s, colored lights backlit the water for a lovely spectacle in the evenings. In the intervening years, however, the water ceased to flow and rosemary bushes were planted in the basins. It wasn't until 2004 that interested residents re-learned that the Cascades once had water and began work to restore it. This unique feature is located where Cleveland Street meets the lake.

In 1893, this area was subdivided as Boulevard Heights, but not built upon. After the subdivider died, his wife built several houses on the property, and the moniker Haddon Hill showed up then, around 1914, according to an Oakland Heritage Alliance house tour brochure. In 1920, Fred T. Wood began building here in earnest, using the name Lakemont to describe the tract. Houses in this neighborhood have larger front yards than in other neighborhoods, but smaller back yards. This is due to the design plan of Mark Daniels, a landscape designer who worked on the tract.

A nicety of the neighborhood is the undergrounding of the utility lines. This was one of the first neighborhoods to do so. Much attention was paid to aesthetics: a September 1920 ad refers to the fact that many of the street intersections had urns marking them and "many rare and beautiful trees and shrubs." Haddon Hill is a nice mixture of large private homes and gracious apartment buildings.

In 1910, the newspaper reported, "Peralta Heights is one of the residence districts of the city which has made such rapid advancement that it would hardly be recognized by the casual visitor who knew the open fields and undeveloped section of several years ago." Peralta Heights included streets like Newton, Brooklyn, Athol, Chicago and Hanover. The name Peralta Heights commemorated the Peralta family and Lake Merritt's original name of Lake Peralta.

Henry J. Kaiser lived in Haddon Hill. Kaiser developed modern shipbuilding to the extent that his shipyards built more than 1,500 cargo ships during World War II. Along with his ships, he launched something else: the HMO plan. He set up medical care facilities for his workers that provided the basis for programs now used nationally. As if that wasn't enough, he was also a huge steel manufacturer and a pivotal player in the construction of the Hoover Dam.

Further up Park Boulevard in the Bella Vista area was Arbor Villa, the glamorous mansion of entrepreneur Borax Smith. Francis Marion Smith earned the nickname "Borax" by discovering that mineral in the deserts of Nevada, and ingeniously figuring out hundreds of way normal households could use it. Borax was and still is advertised with the "20 Mule Team" logo representing the transportation necessary to get the borax to the railroad for shipping. Mule statues in the park at the F.M Smith Recreation Center on lower Park Boulevard commemorate those beasts. Smith also consolidated a bunch of loopy, different-gauged rail lines and horse lines into a magnificently smooth-running transportation organization called the Key System. AC Transit is the grandchild of that system.

Notice construction of the Oakland Auditorium in the background. Undated.

Finally, Smith's genius showed itself in the way that he ran streetcars into somewhat secluded areas of Oakland, showing residents new places to live and then selling the land to them. His Realty Syndicate, formed with Frank C. Havens in 1895, is responsible for much of the settling of Oakland. Havens withdrew from the syndicate in 1910, and three years later Smith was at rock bottom. Although at one point he was worth $30 million, he had taken out some loans and the lenders all called their notes at the same time. Luckily, this plucky entrepreneur reinvested in borax and had a second fortune.

Smith's mansion Arbor Villa, roughly across the street from today's Oakland High School, was demolished in 1932, the year after Smith died at the age of 85. Ninth Avenue still sports the palm trees that formed one border of his estate. Photographs show that the estate had an enormous ballroom, bowling alley, billiard room, music room, conservatory, observatory, grotto, tennis court, archery range, deer farm with rabbit hutches, lily pond—and a two-story stable that looked more like a manor house. On the other side of the coin, Smith previously lived in a tiny shack in Teels Marsh, Nevada, where he made his first big borax discovery.

Across Park Boulevard from Arbor Villa were eleven Mary R. Smith Cottages (seven of which still exist), built to house "friendless girls." Mary Smith was Borax's wife. After she died, his second wife carried on the charity work. These cottages were designed by, among others, Julia Morgan and Bernard Maybeck. The Home Club was nearby, a Grecian temple style club with a covered staircase leading to it from far below on Park Boulevard.

At one time, big game hunter Henry Snow wanted the city to dig a 40-foot cave on the Lakeshore edge of Lake Merritt, which he would supply with lions, rhinos, hippos and giraffes. The kicker was that there would be no bars to cage the animals; they would be curbed only by a water-filled moat too deep and wide for them to negotiate. Needless to say, the idea didn't get off the ground. For more on Snow—and information on Lake Merritt itself—see Lakeside listing.

Birds of the Lake

BY GENTIAN SMITH

The first time I saw pelicans
My body jolted into primal fear,
My hominid cells urging me to hide
In the dark clam of earth mud
Until that ferocious wing span
And pitiless overtaking of the sky
Ceased. But then they splashed
Down onto the lake, contained,
Their beaks the only outrageous thing
Now that the wings were tucked,
And I made peace with them,
Returned to 20th century and the
Scientific method.

I love too the hulking skulk of the
night herons, sulking where witless children
Throw bread. It's like seeing a tragic
Silent film star in her diamonds and train
Pouting in a cheerful third grade classroom.
Lighten up! I want to say. Can you
Unhunch your shoulders and participate?
The social coots have no such problem.
They swim in squadrons, bright and cute
In their black feathers capped with the beak
Of white, an almost humorous color scheme,
As if the beak were lit and leading fish
To the surface. I have seen the delicate egret
Bend like quicksilver to thrust a fish
Down its throat, like the report of a gun,

And then continue stepping with legs
Of piano wire to stir up more sediment.
Those feathers are so white they must be
Freshly laundered each day, down the estuary
Where women bend over rocks to redden
Their hands, glad with the work.
Once the metallic emerald sheen of a duck—
black and green simultaneously,
Like the shifting color of a prism—
Made me want to know the bird,
Take down its story, learn what devilish
Deal it engineered to get such plumage.
I peered long at the outfit, then saw
That the mallard had borrowed it for a helmet.

How careless they are with their beauty!
They will squat with geese and make their
Asthmatic-with-a-head-cold cry, lift their
Webbed feet and despoil that grace.
It is forgivable in the ducks who bob
Down for fish, presenting their tufty asses,
Because they make one laugh. There they are,
Stern side up, like the Titanic plunging down,
And they do it in teams, so you see three of them
With their butts foremost, shameless, mooning the world,
Saying here's what I think of you. Bottoms up!

And I can't close a poem without speaking
Of the buffleheads, those sturdy prowheads
Who swim unflappable, for they have captured
My imagination, such that I took
A block of wood and carved one,
So a piece of Lake Merritt sits on
A shelf in my house.

Park Boulevard

BY CHI PHAN

Sidewalk cracks are episiotomy puzzles
for babies overgrown and drunken unable
to sink back in or get up. Ears to the postnatal
heart that quickens with each car tricked out
without its muffler, darting through the clots
that touch each side of the vein and pass
carelessly like they may never lodge, making
the brain, some underground hell of twisted
wire we've never met, fry up. What keeps
wire lubricated? Green bike oil or the time
Larry's son brandished the gas nozzle at the Arco,
pumping at full strength until Larry wrestled
it away and the city is so full of slaps
hanging in the air dormantly, caressing
fingers to action, that this may well be
what drips down the lonely hidden armature
that is still pulsing commands to push this child
into the light

HAVENSCOURT

WHERE: *Bounded by 65th and 69th avenues,*
between International and Foothill boulevards

THIS HOUSING tract was formerly part of the larger Melrose neighborhood. See Melrose listing for more information.

The official entrance to this tract was at E. 14th Street (today, International Boulevard) and Havenscourt Boulevard, where a lovely pergola was built and a rounded gazebo on the same pattern. Nestled within that pergola was a Southern Pacific station built around 1913.

The Havenscourt Company began in 1912 as an offspring of the Realty Syndicate, building homes in an area that was at the time considered "the country." The trolley ran along East 14th, making it possible for residents to live here and commute. Most of the houses in the tract were California bungalows. Many of the residents worked at the nearby Chevrolet plant at Foothill and 69th (which was built in 1915) only a few blocks away.

Wickham Havens also offered lots for sale, and a photocopy of an

The Southern Pacific train station at Havenscourt is ensconced by the pergola in the back.

"Excursion Ticket" preserved in the Oakland History Room makes one wince. "Havenscourt is carefully restricted against cheap ugly Houses, and against Negroes, Japanese and Chinese." Many housing tracts—and not just in Oakland—were restricted in this way, sad to say. Interested San Francisco buyers who met these restrictions could gather on a particular day in front of the ferry building, where a Wickham Havens agent wearing a yellow badge would escort them via the Southern Pacific ferry and streetcar lines to the neighborhood and back.

Thanks to the lay of the land, heavy rains made this region a "small lake in the winter of 1909," according to a newspaper report.

OAKLAND HISTORY ROOM OF THE OAKLAND PUBLIC LIBRARY

The train approaches the Havenscourt subdivision.

One of the earliest housing tracts here was Putnam Terrace, which was selling in 1926. The homes were constructed off 73rd Avenue between Foothill and East 14th. Each was to be original in design with no two alike. Only two blocks away was transportation to downtown Oakland and to San Francisco.

Promises

BY OKTAYVEYA JONES

Doesn't matter what you say if you don't back it up.
If a neighbor says they'll clean up the yard,
all those strange pieces of junk that don't even
make a basement feel good, and then they don't,
then what do you do?
The world's not here for me to nag at it.

And what if they said they would stop
the dealing and then they didn't?
And if they said they were going to start fresh
and they found Jesus oh yes
but then that start got really moldy and
never even got going?

What if you found a child crying
and you promised them you'd make things right—
but that was beyond me and beyond her
and beyond all of us…
should I have made the promise?

Estate sale on 66th

BY BELINDA KLING

I am interested in her collection of nails, a true must-
smelling shed with labels on drawers that say "files,"
"bits" and "screws." I can bargain her china down
to fifty cents and lay my clothes on the thin bones
of her hangers. Afterwards, at my sink I examine
the remains of burned bread in her pan, leaning
with her posture to scrape with my own fingernail.
I will only nod now to the man who greets me
at the bakery with an armful of fat-topped loaf,
yeast almost still rising. I will slice and chew
where my kneading fingertips left whorls
and personal paisleys. The flour under my nails
says "okay" in its dry way and the oven keeps hot.
Baking bread on behalf of the dead.

HIGHLAND

<small>WHERE:</small> *The vicinity of Highland Hospital,*
14th Avenue and E. 31st Street

IN 1906, Highland Park Terrace lots were selling fast from the Laymance Real Estate Company. An ad that year rhetorically asked, "What better evidence of desirable and low-priced real estate can we give you?" It went on to say, "The location of this elegant residence property is well protected from the bay winds, and conceded by physicians as having the warmest and most desirable climate around the San Francisco bay, known as the warm thermal belt of Oakland."

In August 1906 (remember, the earthquake was in April), Mr. Laymance, the selling agent, told the newspaper that he "believed first and primarily the sale of all real estate is due to the fact that many strangers are in the city and the fact of their realization of the future importance and desirability of Oakland."

<small>OAKLAND HISTORY ROOM OF THE OAKLAND PUBLIC LIBRARY</small>

The E. C. Sessions horse railroad, circa 1890.

The area was accessible by the Highland Park horse railroad even as early as 1888, and the area was opened for subdivision around that time. Of that horsecar line it was said in 1888, "The Highland Park line is a favorite route, the beautiful region it traverses affording many inviting spots for rural pleasures, and a rare combination of rustic beauty and wild luxuriance of the wooded portions, with the artistic adornment exhibition in many lawns and gardens overflowing with fruit, flowers and tropical plants. Here is found the choicest and most bewitching departure from the uniformity of plain and hill slope, as the land is sufficiently undulating and irregular to afford a charming variety of hillside and valley, sheltered nook and crowning peak, sites for suburban homes with forestlike surroundings, almost within sound of the metropolis."

A water company reservoir was on the highest point of the property, as was a California Baptist college.

Much of this land was once owned by Mr. E.C. Sessions, who owned and operated the horsecar line. In 1890, he patented his special double-decker streetcar design. "Featuring mahogany trim, graceful spiral staircases, and well-upholstered seats, the cars provided patrons with an exhilarating and bucolically scenic journey," wrote former Oakland History Room librarian William Sturm for an issue of the Oakland Heritage Alliance *News*. Sturm wrote that "Sessions' trolley system was gobbled up by Borax Smith's Oakland Transit Co. in 1898. The double-decker trolley, like brass spittoons and ostrich plumes, vanished into the mist of an eccentrically elegant yesteryear."

Sessions was president of the Oakland Bank of Savings and founded and promoted the subdivision. Believe it or not, he initially had a hard time selling the lots, and finally broke down and sold to those who wanted to build structures contradicting his original plans. Those plans were grandiose: he wanted only two houses on a block, set back 100 feet from the street and with 200-foot frontages. Sessions, in an 1893 catalogue for the neighborhood, wrote, "It was very hard work to get the property started and convince purchasers of its value at those prices ($10 to $20 per front foot)."

Along the streets, he created a decorative border of alternating eucalyptus and cypress trees. Further, he established a picnic park in a large grove of eucalyptus trees surrounded by a high picket fence. One had to cross the creek via a bridge to enter the park. The grove was advertised as being entirely free from poison oak and planted with Sandwich Island Grass.

How did the neighborhood get named? Reputedly the first buyer was a Scot, who suggested a name that reminded him of his homeland. Poet Joaquin Miller was present at the cornerstone laying for this property and read a poem written to commemorate the occasion. This is now the site of Highland Hospital.

An early neighbor recalled, "Highland Park, being out in the country in those horse and buggy days, we had to make our own amusements.

Highland Hospital's early days, undated.

The families living there were very neighborly and the parties and dances were held at various homes… The young men got together and organized a brass band…. We also fished in Dimond Canyon and hunted quail in the hills back of Fruitvale." This account was found in the Oakland History Room files.

One of the neat features of this neighborhood is the area known as Normandie Place, a collection of Norman-style houses at 19th Avenue and East 23rd Street. A 1926 ad asked, "Have you ever longed for a charming old-world home, but equipped with all the conveniences that only America can supply?"

Highland was also the site of the early shoemaking settlement of Lynn, which joined with San Antonio and Clinton to become Brooklyn. Brooklyn was annexed to Oakland in 1872.

Highland Hospital

BY LENORE WEISS

For 20 years I've heard them race down the street
carrying the bleeding and breathless—
red flashing lights ripping off the top of telephone poles
in a chase down Beaumont Avenue to the Emergency Room
where medics give their reports to whomever will listen,
bodies exploded into sprinkler systems,
the heart of an 85-year-old abloom with electrodes—

Even as contractors built a new wing,
a three-tiered parking lot arose from steel pilings
set back several gulps from a sidewalk
where across a glass partition,
walk-ins clutch blank forms
cast in silhouette by each e-arrival,
an IV bottle weaving over a gurney.

Wherever I am in the house, I hear those sirens,
outside in the garden picking cherry tomatoes,
in the kitchen stirring a pot of minestrone soup,
at night when the ambulance layers its screech
upon our holler. It's background music
that gets played 24 / 7.

So do you think villagers living outside
Dachau and Auschwitz gradually
didn't hear each train as it pulled into the station,
wheels groaning to stop? Did they listen, like me,
then go about their business?

Here comes another, I say to myself, and another,
until it's past counting, sunk in an evening ritual
of soaking chicken in lemon juice, feeding the rabbit
wilted outer leaves of cabbage.

Good morning

BY SAM MILSTON

I think this neighborhood, this morning,
is very, very good. I like the boy
windmilling, half-heartedly catching up
to his mom, the curly-haired woman
who is getting ready to drive him to school.
Every morning I see the redhead
at her window chewing toast.
The sun that bakes my wet hair dry
will gold us all, and the jogger
who doesn't return my smile
is fatally wrong.

JINGLETOWN

BOUNDARY: *International Boulevard to the Estuary and from 23rd Avenue to Fruitvale Avenue.*

ORIGINALLY, THIS was the site of a Native American shellmound, and one of the first Westerners to settle there, Captain E. F. Rogers, named his farm Shellmound. Rogers had a fruit nursery until 1861, when the land was taken over by a man named Kennedy for use as a Civil War troop encampment, where 500 men trained. This area is also referred to as the Kennedy Tract. "Even at this great distance from the scenes of actual conflict, there was a commotion and preparation for conflict, for defense, if not for assault," reports the *Alameda County Centennial Yearbook.*

Jingletown was so called because of millworkers' habit of jingling coins in their pockets on payday to show off their earnings, says one account. Another source adds that the immigrants did not trust banks, and so kept all their money in their pockets—their children, who had not experienced poverty, laughed at the quaint custom and the term Jingletown was born.

The employer whose coins were jingled was the California Cotton

The 1,500 employees of the California Cotton Mills worked with raw cotton, like these giant bales arriving from fields in San Joaquin or Imperial valleys.

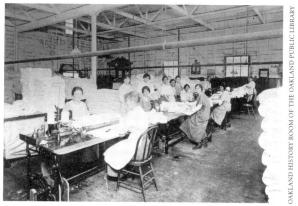

OAKLAND HISTORY ROOM OF THE OAKLAND PUBLIC LIBRARY

Women workers at the California Cotton Mills pause a moment for a photograph, circa 1917.

Mills, operating between 1883 and 1954. The cotton mills once had 20-30 buildings. Between 1915 and '28, the mills produced the greatest variety of products of any cotton mills in the country, reported Beth Bagwell in her book *Oakland, Story of a City.*

Many of the first settlers were Portuguese, some by way of Hawaii. The Portuguese founded the church Mary Help of Christians, still an important part of the community. But the area soon became a complex mixture of cultures. A longtime resident, Melvin Texeira, gave a speech at a 1974 Jingletowners reunion, typed up in a wonderful booklet at the History Room: "Integration, segregation. What was that? We had the Prushnovoskies, Poondykes, Kresoviches, Valerios, Pepitones, Roventinies, Allens, Swannigans, Hartleys, Lindsten, Martinezes, Silvas and Chong Lee living in Jingletown."

The Central Pacific Overland train ran through this area by 1869, allowing for transport of farm products. In time, two large canneries in the area, Del Monte and Prince, took advantage of that transportation. Jack London once lived in the neighborhood and began work in a cannery at the tender age of 15. Today's Fruitvale Station shopping center was built on the site of the old Del Monte Cannery.

The huge Montgomery Wards building used to form one of Jingletown's natural borders before it was torn down.

The Nimitz freeway spelled the segmentation of Jingletown, ending mill operations and in fact splitting up the mill complex, literally. That's why as you drive down Highway 880 you see the brick buildings almost touchable from the passenger seat.

A child works with cotton

BY MARIA CERVANTES

Here by the freeway
children bent over looms
in the days of the California Cotton Mills.
The foul-smelling bundles of cotton
that arrived were fogged
for boll weevils, the chemical taint
drifting out to the floors…
The machines racketed and ricketed
and they worked their childhoods away.

Payday

BY ALISON MCLEAN

It must have felt good
to jingle along
maybe adding a whistle into the mix,
making those coins sing
for all the work they entailed,
gloating in their volume.

Today, I get a statement
in the mail about an automatic
payroll deposit. I never see the money;
it's like someone whispered it
out of range of hearing
and it just shows up in my account.

Payday is not even a concept anymore;
the deposit just happens at the end
of the month and the statement arrives
a day or two later. I want to stand
in a line and get something handed to me.

I want to walk around with it
in my pocket
to get used to it.

A Job To Remember

BY MERTIS SHEKELOFF

I never felt poor growing up. Mother was a genius at disguising our true economic situation. The hopefulness of youth was on her side. Only a fourteen-year age difference separated us, and she neither thought poor nor acted poor. Escaping hard times, our family came one by one and by train to California, following the usual pattern of the Great Trek West during the WWII years. When I arrived in Oakland, Mother had two jobs: welding in the Richmond shipyards and doing janitorial work at night. (A young single mother, she managed to keep the wolves at bay.) Our lives differed little from those of other migrants in our working-class neighborhood who had left the south seeking war work.

Not even Mother could shield me from the desire for more. All around me I saw what money could buy, and as a 14-year-old , I wanted everything I saw.

Vera was my best friend and two years my senior. She had been my friend practically every since I came to California when I was 12, knowing nobody but my relatives. She always followed my lead; we did everything together. On Saturdays, sharing a pair of skates, we pushed ourselves on a single skate from West Oakland to Swan's in downtown Oakland wearing our bright-colored shorts, laughing all the way and feeling good with the wind blowing in our faces and through our curled short hair.

At the market, with our skate still on, we squeezed into the long line of housewives awaiting their turn at the chicken counter. I had Grandmother Emma's short shopping list: a nice chicken— "don't forget to get it cut it up," was always her reminder— eggs, and sugar. The two rationing stamps for the sugar had been tightly rolled up into the shopping list.

Neither of our families had money enough or had even thought of giving us a steady allowance, so Vera and I decided it was up to us to get a job that would provide us with money for movies, clothes, edible treats and all the things we craved. I don't remember consulting the school counselor or my mother, for that matter, about the idea of my working. As with many small things, I just did it. And I know Vera hadn't asked permission either. She had little to say to her small, slow-speaking Baptist preacher of a father whom she was closer to than her mother: a slow-moving silent stump of a woman. Both spent words like money, sparingly, and neither was given to conversation of any kind. So without asking permission, Vera and I made up our minds to get jobs.

There were many job opportunities, we thought, in our rather large city, and we settled on a kind of job in which workers were in demand where we could easily disguise our ages. Del Monte Cannery in East Oakland seemed a likely prospect: cannery work took no particular skill, we figured; why not apply? One day we dressed to look as old as possible and took the long streetcar ride to the cannery. We entered the imposing brick building, walking tall in our mid heels with lips splashed with wine-colored lipstick and shining like mirrors, talking loudly to disguise our fear and uncertainty. In a quaking voice, I asked a lady in rubber boots for directions to the employment office.

"Jes' keep on walkin' the way you're going. You'll see it. Can't miss it," she said.

"Thank you, ma'am," I replied, grabbing Vera's hand and pulling her along.

"I'm scared," Vera confessed, "Are you?"

"Nah," I said, beginning the first in the stack of lies I would tell that day.

At the personnel office, I walked up to the window, cleared my throat to get the young man's attention, said "hello" and asked for two job applications. The young man at the window, blue-eyed with wavy brown hair, looked us over curiously but handed me the applications.

"Thank you," I said crisply, in my new grown-up voice. I handed one to Vera, and we sat down on the wood benches in front of the gray industrial table to fill them out.

"What year should I put down if I'm 20 years old?" Vera whispered.

"Let's see," I said counting on my fingers. "Put down 1926," I whispered back

I wrote down 1928 on mine. That would make me 18, old enough to work in a cannery and anywhere else. We completed the applications and answered "yes" under the question about experience. I took them back and pushed them into the cashier window. I made a point of looking the handsome young clerk right in the eye. If I didn't look him dead in the eye, he might think I was lying. He took my paper and looked it over.

"How old are you?" he asked.

"EIGHTEEN. Can't you see it on the paper?" I challenged.

"Do you have any experience in cannery work?"

"Yes," I answered.

"Where?"

"Monroe, Louisiana."

"Doing what?"

"Canning Louisiana Hot Sauce," I loudly declared, lying through my teeth.

"O.K." the young man said and gave me a look that indicated he knew I had lied and that I hadn't fooled him one bit. I guess they really needed workers; they hired us. We were to start work the next day and work from 4 p.m. to 12 midnight. I told Vera that since we had barely enough time to make it from school to work on time, we really had to hightail it to the streetcar stop the minute school was over. She agreed.

On the streetcar going home, we laughed so we had to hold each other up. We had pulled one over on the world. We talked about what we would do with our first paycheck, all the goodies we would buy with it. I went home and told Mother I had a job. I don't think she believed me She asked me no questions, and I told her no lies.

I could hardly contain myself in school the next day. I sat in my Math class snug in my secret. It was hard to take in the teacher's instructions. This was my last class for the day, and I felt antsy until the school bell rang, I ran across the play yard to meet Vera. We skipped to the streetcar stop a couple of blocks away and, luckily, found a streetcar waiting. We got on real grown-up like; we were no longer children but young ladies with the responsibility of jobs.

We pulled the stop cord 45 minutes later in front of the cannery; we then took a short walk to the building and to the check-in station where we proudly punched our time cards. Our supervisor was waiting for us. After a curt greeting, she led us into a kind of dressing room and gave us each plastic caps and thick rubber aprons. "You'll have to buy some rubber boots," she advised before giving us a brief rundown of what our jobs would be. We listened seriously, at the same time sneaking quick looks at each other. The supervisor said because it was peach season, the plant was canning fruit cocktail. We would do various jobs involved in this process.

She took us into a room where we would spend the next eight hours. It hummed with the production of fruit cocktail and was noisy from the roar of conveyor belts loaded with tin cans of partially filled diced fruit. The pervasive sweet smell of cooked fruit made my mouth water. The supervisor started us off first on the grape belt where a double line of silent older women in rubber aprons, plastic caps and boots leaned over a moving conveyor belt filled with a single layer of small green grapes that slowly came out of a grape washing machine. She found a place for us at the belt and explained that our job was to pinch off the tiny stems still attached to the grapes. I took my place at the belt: in no time my shoes were sopping wet from dripping water. But I stood firm and PINCH PINCH PINCH—extracted the tiny stems from the small green grapes. The pads of my fingers were getting sore, and at the same time, I was discovering that this mindless task allowed my imagination to soar. It was as if my spirit detached itself from my body and was able to go any place I pleased. But even spirit flight could not totally compensate for the mind-crushing boredom of life on the grape belt.

I soon graduated to another job which required a little more mind. Not much more but some. I was put on a small belt by myself. A large machine on my right filled the cans with diced peaches and pears after I had plopped exactly 19 pieces of pineapple and six cherry halves into them. Ever after, it was difficult to resist counting the number of pineapple pieces and cherry halves in a purchased can of fruit cocktail. I soon developed a rhythm: PLOP PLOP, PLOP PLOP PLOP went my contribution to the cans of fruit cocktail.

Midnight found us sleepy on the streetcar going home. But we were able to wake ourselves up at our stop. I stole into the house without anyone noticing and got into bed. Thank God, Mother hadn't got home from work yet. I don't know how I managed to get myself up and ready for school the next morning, but I did.

I don't remember any encounters with my mother about what I was doing. As days passed, the job became increasingly burdensome; I was tired and lethargic and often fell asleep in class. Vera and I had no energy for the fun we had expected to have. We slept away our weekends. But we were determined to last until the first pay period which luckily came before I died of exhaustion. When payday came, Vera and I were first in line to get our paychecks. I tore open the envelope to look at my first earned money; the amount of the check was more than I had ever had—my money!—before. Fifty-seven dollars and eighty-six cents! I was ecstatic.

On the streetcar home, Vera and I talked about what we would buy. I said I would buy new shoes for sure. Some new school shoes—maybe those brown and white oxfords everyone who could afford them was now wearing.

At our stop we got off the streetcar and ran all the way home. I burst into the house yelling "Mom, Mom!" My 28-year-old mother came running, in her nightgown, wondering what the excitement was and why I wasn't in bed asleep as she had thought.

"Mom, look what I made," I shrieked, shoving the check under her nose. In an instant, all was changed. "This is for you," I said, pushing the check in her hand.

She took the check and held it against the light as one would do to test a counterfeit bill. "Thanks," Mother said, incredulously.

A few days later we had a new record player and Mom and I danced to Louis Jourdan's "Ain't Nobody Here But Us Chickens," the new hit record everybody was dancing to. I still wore my old shoes. But I didn't feel poor.

THE UNASSUMING and dilapidated kingpin of this area is the 1886 home of Joaquin Miller, the "Poet of the Sierras." He, his mother and his daughter lived in separate but close-by cabins by the side of the road now named for him. Miller called his estate "The Hights" and planted 70,000 trees to revitalize the landscape denuded by the logging that built Gold Rush San Francisco. Scattered around the property are various whimsical monuments Miller erected which still stand: a tower to poet Robert Browning, a pyramid to Moses, a battlement for John C. Fremont and a funeral pyre. The latter was meant to be used by Miller after this death, but as city regulations forbade the open-air cremation, mourners settled for scattering his ashes over the monolith.

Joaquin Miller sits in front of his Abbey on The Hights, circa 1904.

Just up the road is Woodminster Amphitheater, designed as a memorial to California authors. WPA Depression-era laborers worked on the amphitheater from 1933 to 1936, but it wasn't dedicated until 1941. And then, due to WWII blackout regulations, lights weren't turned on until 1944. The amphitheater boasts a series of cascades, with sinuous stone stairs connecting seven pools. At full capacity, the Cascades move 1,000 gallons of water a minute down 100 feet of drop. The middle pool was built to run through a nine-minute light show; its fountain was created for the Golden Gate Exposition on Treasure Island and moved after the expo closed. Woodminster seats roughly 3,000 people.

OAKLAND HISTORY ROOM OF THE OAKLAND PUBLIC LIBRARY

Women marvel over the Pyramid to Moses, undated.

This area was once home to a large settlement of Huchiun people, located on the grounds of the present-day Holy Names University. Native Americans had stayed so frequently in this place that they wore footpaths. These paths and a cooking circle remained to testify to their time there. This hilltop area was where Native Americans camped (good) and were preached to by the Spanish padres (bad).

In 1943, Robin McCrea donated a park to the city in his father George McCrea's name, which was the area where the Native Americans had lived. The elder McCrea had bought the 20-acre property in 1908. There were only two other owners between him and the Peraltas, one of them being a man named Walter McGee.

At the time of the donation, much was made of the site being criss-crossed with paths harking back to the Indians' use of the creek. There was also a rock-bound circle that was used for cooking, blackened with smoke, and mortar wells where acorns had been ground. The hilltop was the perfect place to scan the entire landscape and be aware of possible attackers approaching.

Also in the park was a chapel where the padres held services for the Native Americans —McCrea had converted the chapel to a dining room for his adjoining structure, but plans included restoring it to its original purpose. When McCrea had first moved onto the property, he found relics both from the Huchiuns and the padres, and a house once used by the Peraltas. Due to access problems, the city sold the historical land to Holy Names and instead gave the name McCrea to the fly casting pond off Carson Boulevard.

Holy Names University began on the shores of Lake Merritt in 1868, funded in part by a priest's sale of his horse and watch. The school moved to its present site in the 1950s. (For more, see Lakeside listing.)

Of course, in such a hilly area, mudslides during storms were a battle homeowners had to fight. Floods were heavy in 1958 when two brand-new, unoccupied homes buckled as their foundations slid, but things got worse in 1962. A killer storm fatally buried a five-year-old girl in a mud-slide and damaged a lot of property in the neighborhood. Residents charged that a faulty drainage system was to blame. The councilman for the area urged improvement of the system and culverting of open creeks. The attorney for the Crestmont Home Owners Association told the newspaper in October 1962 that 300 families "live in fear and hysteria, on the brink of disaster . . . . The death of that little girl may have been acci-dental. If it happens again it will be murder." The Crestmont tract is roughly situated between Skyline and Route 13.

Finally, Luther Lincoln was one of the original 1800s residents in the area. Part of his estate is now the Lincoln Square Shopping Center. Oakland nearly had its own Gold Rush on Lincoln's land. In the 1880s, pyrite (fool's gold) was discovered, and for a few ecstatic, heart-stopping days, Oaklanders thought they had the equivalent of Sutter's Mill. Alas, the gold may be nonexistent, but the panoramic views are just about as valuable.

The Castle in the Woods

BY SARA MOORE

Inspired by Joaquin Miller's Tower

Picking up glass like my mother
never let me. Comforted by the shards
large enough to be easily handled,
in my own kitchen with unburnt pots
and oven mitts neat on hooks.
Linoleum glossy through California glass.

The splinter she always warned of
penetrates and like the girl in the fairy tale
after the needle pricks, the wheel
spins a moment more and another inch
of fine wool yarn is rendered

Before the blood drips on the linoleum
the castle is already asleep, the cook's fat
hand sunk into the batter, the queen's lips
pursed. The servant girl lingering
at her errand, paused before some unused
window, is for one hundred years a renegade.

When I awake and brush the flies off,
it all seems clear as glass. I am not fit
to run the water in the sink or close
my cupboards with a smug smack.
I am too far and must return with clippers
for the briar. I remember the maid
whose eyes were closed before the window.

Echoes

BY JHIAN ZHONG

Sometimes I walk by myself along the creek in Joaquin Miller Park and it is like there is someone else there. These voices, the mumbling of some language I don't understand, the crackle of the fires, the noisy splash and spray in the water when they catch a fish that doesn't want to be caught so long ago…

I'm not scared; I just let the presence enter my world. I will note it, allow it. Others bang through here with their dogs, loudly talking, a cell phone, even—but when I get silent and let them come, they come.

They are whispering about trust.

They are wishing they hadn't listened when the men came in brown robes. Wished they had continued to honor the earth and not a man they hadn't known in person, a man they had never walked the earth with or eaten with or sung with.

There is sickness and sadness here. Something that thrived was snapped like a twig and thrown in the river. They speak to me because I listen. Follow follow follow your own path, they are saying. Keep keep keep keep keep what you have, what you have, what you have, what you know.

THIS LITTLE stretch of land has so much history it's insane.

To start with, there was once a museum and zoo in tiny little Snow Park at Harrison and 20th streets. The Snow Museum opened in 1922 in a converted 1899 mansion, showcasing stuffed big game animals collected on safari by Henry Snow. Not all of the animals could be displayed: the ceilings were not tall enough, for example, for the mounted giraffes. Snow was most proud of the three white rhinos in his collection, although there was only one small band of white rhinos still roaming the planet and the largest one he stuffed was never even exhibited because it, too, was too large for the mansion. Only two tons of "material" were ever on display,

OAKLAND HISTORY ROOM OF THE OAKLAND PUBLIC LIBRARY

Looking north on Lakeside Drive from 14th Street, circa 1930. On the right, one can barely make out the Oakland Museum in its small predecessor, today's Camron-Stanford House. On the left, one sees the Scottish Rite Temple with its original façade.

while 25 tons remained in storage. Reluctantly, one has to admit that Snow had many adventures: meeting Amundsen, being charged by a Kodiak bear that he killed with a bullet in the eye, and discovering mastodon bones with 11-foot tusks. As part of the white rhinos' revenge, Snow died in 1927 of Blackwater Fever, apparently contracted during his African expedition. Snow's daughter Nydine Latham carried on the curatorship of the museum until it closed in 1967. Most of the creatures were auctioned off—perhaps your grandmother has a dik-dik in her garage. A few pieces were folded into the Natural Sciences Department of the Oakland Museum when it was completed in 1969, and the mansion was torn down.

Snow's son Sidney carried on the pith helmetry, discovering the bodies of four frozen Canadian scientists in the Arctic, harpooning whales who nearly tipped over his vessel, and bringing back with him two Eskimos, who expressed great amazement at the size of San Francisco. Before the Snow Museum closed, a small zoo opened there as well in 1943. Sidney eventually became Oakland Zoo director.

A few blocks away, the Camron-Stanford House also was a private home that later served as a museum. The only remaining Victorian of about 20 that once ringed the lake when its shores were private property, the home was built in 1876 for the Camron family. They lived there less than a year, leaving in grief after their two-year-old daughter died there of food poisoning. David Hewes rented the house from them; he is famous for creating the Golden Spike that commemorated the meeting of the two sides of the transcontinental railroad in 1869. He hosted President Rutherford B. Hayes in the home during a visit. In 1882, Josiah Stanford bought the home. He is responsible for introducing the champagne grape to California. (His brother Leland founded Stanford University and was one of the railroad's "Big Four.") In 1906, the home was sold to the city for use as a museum. This was the first Oakland Museum, and when the new building was built in 1969, its collections formed the basis of the History Department collections. Today, the home is a historic house museum.

The Convent of the Sacred Heart was on the shores of Lake Merritt in 1868, begun by six French Canadian nuns and an Oakland priest. That same year, an earthquake hit which kept the new students and nuns outside most of the day, anxious about aftershocks. The convent housed ten boarders and 40 day students when it first opened. The school came to be known as Holy Names College (now, University) and moved to the Oakland hills in the 1950s.

Check your spice cabinet. If you have spices labeled Schilling, you've got a connection to German-born August Schilling, who had a wonderful estate in the late 1800s at the head of Jackson Street where it meets the lake. Schilling was a flower lover, and his gardens were a showcase enjoyed by invited guests and strangers alike. Schilling would leave the garden gates open to let anyone walk the grounds. Schilling was also involved in the coffee trade, associating with James A. Folger of Folger's coffee. Schilling's grand home was eventually torn down. In its place is the Regillus Apartments at 200 Lakeside Drive. Next door at 244 Lakeside Drive, the popularly-nicknamed Bechtel Building still has remnants of the fabulous gardens.

The Scottish Rite Temple presents an imposing face at Lakeside Drive, but an even more charming vantage point is from across the lake. It was built in 1927, designed by architect Carl Werner. Originally, the building had eight 42-foot columns capped by a triangular cornice, giving it a more classically Greek appearance than it has today. Unfortunately, wind-blown salt spray from the lake quickly deteriorated the cement façade. The 1937 revised facade has four columns encased in a boxy, more Moderne-looking front, with enormous engraved figures where the cornice used to be.

After the 1906 earthquake wrecked San Francisco's Chinatown, many Chinese came to Oakland for help. They were given tents in a segregated refugee camp at the Willows, an area on the southwestern shore of Lake Merritt. The camp was known as Chinese Camp, and at its peak on one day 1,871 residents were counted. Many other camps were consolidated at a large camp at Adams Point across the lake, but Chinese Camp remained separate.

And now, a history of the lake itself, our gorgeous crown jewel, our blue sapphire encircled by tiny diamonds.

Lake Merritt was originally a marsh, and was much larger and a different shape than it appears today. In the early days, four creeks ran into the marsh from the hills, and Native Americans used these creeks as waterways. The lake was a hunting ground for waterfowl.

Crossing the slough required a rowboat or an extended trip around the perimeter. In the late 1850's, Horace Carpentier installed a tollbridge where the present day 12th Street dam exists.

OAKLAND HISTORY ROOM OF THE OAKLAND PUBLIC LIBRARY

This is Jackson Street, looking south from 17th Street (then, Lake Street) in 1879.

It was Mayor Samuel Merritt's decision to dam the lake. This eliminated the nasty-smelling marsh and created a recreation lake. The cost to the city was $20,000; Merritt footed the rest of the bill. The tollbridge was no longer necessary, as that side of the lake was now landfill.

We can also thank Mayor Merritt for the fact that Lake Merritt was the first wildlife refuge in the United States. He influenced the state senator to introduce a bill to create the sanctuary; it was signed into law in 1870 by Governor Henry Haight.

For the next 33 years, Oakland had the honor of being the only city in the U.S. that cared enough about its wildlife to have an established refuge. In 1903, President Theodore Roosevelt followed Oakland's example, and declared Pelican Island in Florida a federal refuge.

The next mayor, Mayor Mott, was responsible for creating a park around the lake and keeping those lands for public use.

Oaklanders were becoming very attached to their protected birds. In 1915, when an oil slick from the estuary washed in, carrying bewildered, oily ducks with it, city council voted to care for the birds and buy grain to feed them. Thus, according to Paul Covel's 1978 book *People are for the birds,* this was the first flock of birds that was ever "on the dole."

The next mayor, Mayor Davie, felt the birds needed their own island, where they would not have to deal with humans or chase happy dogs on the shore. The island used fill from the creation of the municipal auditorium (today, the Henry J. Kaiser Convention Center), and was opened "for business" in 1925. Davie even ran a water line out to the island, to provide a fresh-water drinking basin for the fowl and irrigate plants at their new digs. Davie's opponents called the island "Davie's Folly," but the ducks took to it . . . like a duck takes to water.

Davie also created a log barrier across the northeast section of the lake, so the birds would not have to contend with boats.

And now you are wondering, where did all the Canada geese come from? Believe it or not, the flock was deliberately built. According to Paul Covel, who was the naturalist at the lake's wildlife refuge from 1934 to 1975, word was sent to ranchers in the Sacramento valley that the lake was looking for Canada geese. Covel and assistants traveled to Dixon to capture nine geese that were enjoying a farmer's pasture.

And then they multiplied.

And they were fearless. One goose, having laid a precious egg, reportedly hissed at bulldozers involved in constructing a new duck island.

All of Lake Merritt's birds have their own census. The Audubon Christmas count began in 1900. Dedicated birders count what they see in a particular window of time, and the results are tallied nation-wide.

And it's a good thing they get counted, too— you can tell when some are missing.

A scandal broke in 1943 where city officials were munching on our mallards. Here's the story: A park foreman was caught caging mallards and transporting them from the lake. He claimed his orders came from City Hall, but his memory clouded when he asked specifics. The forensics team found the feathers, head and feet of a dozen ducks buried in the foreman's back yard. A full-blown dinner of the luckless mallards had hosted no less than 28 park employees and officials! Furthermore, the group had really liked the meal and planned to make it a semi-monthly event.

It's especially shameful considering that previous administrations were headed up by mayors who really advocated for the birds (Merritt, Mott and Davie). The foreman was banished from the park and relegated to another park . . . one without mallards.

Stepping back a bit timewise, in 1867 Horace Carpentier—who owned not only the waterfront but also the lake connected to it by the estuary— transferred title to the Southern Pacific Railroad. Collis Huntington, one of the Big Four, wanted to fill in the lake and build a huge railroad station there. Luckily, Leland Stanford convinced his partner to donate the lake to the city of Oakland. Perhaps Stanford remembered his brother Josiah's happy years in the Camron-Stanford house on the edge of the lake, compelling him to intervene.

One of the things that makes Lake Merritt so special is the necklace of lights. At night, the reflection of the lamps in the water is so beautiful it can make the heart swell. And knowing that those lamps are intact and beaming is due to the volunteer efforts of everyday citizens makes the sight even more magical.

The necklace of lights was originally installed in the early 1900s and was dismantled for World World II blackout requirements. An effort spearheaded by the Lake Merritt Breakfast Club in the 1980s brought the lamps back up to their stellar, beaming status.

The Lake Merritt Breakfast Club was also instrumental in establishing Children's Fairyland in 1950, a literary amusement park for children. Walt Disney visited Fairyland and lore says he was influenced by what he saw there, resulting in his concept for Disneyland, which opened in 1955. Another famous connection is Frank Oz of Muppets fame, who trained as a puppeteer there.

Protected waterfowl, shimmering lights, and now an authentic Italian gondola service . . . what more could any lake ask for?

Lake at the heart of Town

BY DAN HESS

It vanishes and reappears at will.
Ethereal, translucent waves of brine
flow in and out with every changing tide—
a dark, electric pulse.
The current licks the piers,
the bottoms of the boats and sculls,
tickles the feet of wading birds
and surges through the fishes' gills.
The shore is lined by phalanxes of palms
that bow and sway in unison.
Most nights it is so still. No wind disturbs
or ripple stirs across our world.
But when the need arises, waves sweep in
across the brows of children
hot with fever, wrapped in chills.
It comes to soothe a young man's mind
unsure if his new friend will show.   Or cancel.
A girl stands gazing at the moon—
a petal floating in a bowl.
There is a thing she cannot tell.
Most nights it takes a miracle
to make the lake appear;
Some things can't be entrusted to reality,
at least, not to a permanence that kills.
The secret ripples in her mind, she lets it go;
the friend arrives of his free will;
the sickness leaves the sweating child.
All of us are bathed in the lake at the heart of town,
the water laps against our souls
and has the power to heal.

Ode to Lake Merritt

BY LENORE WEISS

I've orbited around its shore of oak trees and waterbirds,
Canada Geese, Snowy Egret, piles of cracked mussel shell left
by the Ring-Billed Gull on rotting piers that collect algae
necklaces strung with corn chip wrappers and shiny soda cans

from the time I was a young mother pushing a stroller
with my infant, happy to sit on the lawn near
Children's Fairyland, the spot Walt surveyed before going back
to Southern California where he built his own child-sized park

with the notion it had to be scaled to size. Puppet shows,
popped corn scooped from red carts with wheels . . .
When my children got older
we visited the garden with monarch butterflies and pink worms
buried in a compost heap where they chewed strips of newspaper.

How long has it been since I had my first baby, my second
as I kept walking laps around the Lake watching both grow up
learning survival from firemen at the Festival, drop, roll, and cover,
an urban fair that outgrew its own success, square dancing

between vendors, food and music that never stopped,
even gondolas where one anniversary you and I
ate black olives and drank red wine while you sang opera to me
I closed my eyes listening to sound boom from the water.

I've been circling, parking my car by the colonnade
wearing jogging shoes and a windbreaker, clocking my time,
learning how to walk again between benches,
holding on after pneumonia made me glad to be alive

near trees whose trunks look as if someone had wrung out their
sheets to dry and left them there,
run to catch the baby crying or a
tea kettle whistling on the stove, gone to chase down news of a war
ended, sprinting past swings, jungle gym,

the sun a meniscus floating on the water's top green shelf,
a contact lens someone put in the wrong way and tried to take
out, scattering bits of shine into a puzzle reassembling
itself through a tidal prism, through the constant dip of time.

Ebb and Flow

BY PHILLINA SUN

Oakland, your mama wants you home.
Oakland, these items were recently fished out of your so-called jewel
of a lake: a cell phone, a safe, a no littering sign, a football trophy, an
assault rifle, a clay mask, dentures, a television set, unmentionable
clothing, a fire extinguisher, a magic wand, an armchair, numerous car
parts, dime bags, used condoms, empty liquor bottles, drugs, a dead
man.
Oakland, I bike through you everyday
I ride on your little cash flow
past shop signs in the languages of diaspora
Spanish, Chinese, Vietnamese, Khmer, Tagalog, more,
past your bars, your warehouses, and your barbershops
past your temp agencies and your alternative art spaces
past your dilapidated Victorians and your triple-thousand-dollar lofts
past your military academy and your run-down schools
past the shadows on crack
Oakland, I bike through your ghost town of a downtown
Oakland, your poor are leaving you; they can't afford rent
so they must migrate to Stockton and beyond
Oakland, your coroner's sign is burning for your citizens!

LAUREL

WHERE: *The area surrounding 35th Avenue and MacArthur Boulevard*

"EVEN WITH our frosty mornings the grass is making good headway on the vacant lots, and contented looking cows, horses, calves and goats may be seen daily grazing upon the new grass. That is one of the charms of East Oakland life—a fine combination of the city and the country," said the newspaper of Laurel in December 1916.

Like many Oakland hills neighborhoods, Laurel arose through the machinations of the Realty Syndicate, which ran a streetcar line to the

Cows from Miss Power's Dairy on Patterson Street wander the hillside above Laurel School. An early resident remembers that Miss Power drove her cows with a stick, dressed all in black, and that boys called her a witch.

OAKLAND HISTORY ROOM OF THE OAKLAND PUBLIC LIBRARY

area and sold lots to interested day-trippers. In fact, Laurel's original 1909 name was the Key Route Heights, named for Borax Smith's streetcar company.

Although some sources say Laurel ended up being named for the old elementary school that opened in 1910, there was a contest to name the area, sponsored by the Realty Syndicate.

Business was quickly stimulated by the opening of a 38th Avenue street-car line. By the 1920s there were hardware stores, drugstores, restaurants, a planing mill, and shops for coal, hay and feed, wrote retired History Room librarian William Sturm in a short document called "Laurel: Story of an Oakland Neighborhood."

And people came to the Laurel District for prices so bargain-basement low, you will shake your head in chagrin. An August 1920 ad shows that one could buy a marine-view lot, only three blocks from the streetcar line, for—get this—as low as $250. For a view of the water! Not only that, but you only had to put $1 down and $1 a week, and you had no interest and no taxes for a year. If you could manage to pay the rest off in 12 months, you'd get a loan to build your house. Homes here were certainly afford-able for factory workers and medium-wage earners.

The ad trumpeted the terms of the sale: "We are going to hold the Greatest Sale of Real Estate Tomorrow Afternoon and Sunday that Oak-land ever knew, and you ought to get in on it." Three weeks later, the Realty Syndicate had sold 1,500 lots in the neighborhood.

By 1939, the region was sufficiently settled to warrant its own movie houses. The Laurel Theatre opened that year at 3814 Hopkins (today's MacArthur Boulevard—more on that later), and the Hopkins Theatre opened at 3531 Hopkins, where Hollywood Video is today. Tremendous fanfare accompanied the opening of the Hopkins: a blimp delivered the film shown that day, and an on-stage wedding preceded the show. On hand were celebrities Alan Hale and Sally Rand; Rand was famous for having a "nude ranch" at the Treasure Island fair, and was probably more of a draw than Hale, a film actor whose son, also Alan, later became the skipper on Gilligan's Island.

During wartime, housing needs increased, and the Laurel expanded.

Hopkins Street was renamed MacArthur Boulevard in honor of World War II hero Douglas MacArthur. Initially, it was hoped MacArthur Boulevard would run the entire length of the west coast, from Canada to Mexico, but alas we make do with a powerful freeway in his name (given

COURTESY, JENNIE JOHNSON HENDER

The Johnson family enjoys their chickens, circa 1914. Behind them is the original Laurel School. The family lived on MacArthur between Brown and Patterson avenues.

the moniker in 1966). There's only 200 feet left of Hopkins Street today, running between Coolidge and MacArthur.

The Laurel has certainly come a long way from the days when dairies and gardens were the main business ventures.

Meditation in the Laurel District

BY JACK FOLEY

Oh, Laurel, how I love your shops
They're all a hit, there are no flops
My wife and I make many stops
While walking down the street

Be careful, there's an Oakland bus
We do not want it to hit us
For we would never make a fuss
While walking down the street

We think of Oakland all the time
We think of it as free of grime
And also free of sex and crime
(Be careful on the street)

Although a man was murdered there
Where High Street crosses MacArthur
We do not feel a drop of fear
While walking on the street.

We feel the joy of Oakland's weather
We feel the neighborhoods together
While Jerry Brown sells to—whoever
We walk upon the street.

Ode to World Ground

BY JACK MILLER

A tremendous space
where all find a place

maybe they are working
on their laptops

or playing a few notes
on the piano

or talking excitedly
with a friend

or talking sadly
if someone has bad news

(the coffee will
help with this)

or they come
for live music

or for live poetry
with passion in it

or they are attending
a community meeting

or catching up
on the *Metro*

whatever it is
this place is ours

LEONA HEIGHTS is named for the mountain lion—which was once a common sight in the hills—but it is another animal that was offered up to lure potential landbuyers: the chicken.

Leona Heights began its development spurt in the early 1920s, when the Realty Syndicate offered residential tracts where previously had been one-man farms and chicken ranches.

The Realty Syndicate played up the chicken angle, advising in an April 1921 advertisement that "Chickens will thrive in this garden spot like flowers .... As for the children, just turn them loose and forget the doctor .... No healthier place in the world!" Raising chickens was said to be capable of bringing $500 a year into the family coffers.

In 1921, a down payment of $10 would buy any lot in the Leona Heights development. Potential buyers wishing to view available lots

A bench provides respite after climbing through the hills, in this stereoscopic view of rustic Leona Heights.

could take the streetcar's K line for 6 cents, disembark and transfer to a "Dinky" car (I did not make up the name) for a short ride to the Realty Syndicate tract.

A brand new street at the time, Mountain Boulevard, ran through the property, and residents could walk to the Chevrolet Auto Factory in Eastmont or take a short ride on the streetcar to see the site of the future Durant Motor Company in Stonehurst.

In fact, the rapid growth of the Leona Heights District necessitated the first streetcar extension in Oakland in 11 years.

Leona Heights also has a very interesting mining history, with sulphur mines and with four pyrite mines blasting away for 30–40 years. One iron pyrite mine was the Alma Mine. In the early 1900s, trace amounts of gold in the ore veins led to a small gold rush in the area. The industry was at one time bustling and noisy. Hikers in Leona were disconcerted but excited "by muffled thunder from underground blasts in the ore tunnels . . . and picturesque miners with lighted candles in their caps," wrote local naturalist Paul Covel, who led tours of the mine which was abandoned in 1915.

Naturalist Paul Covel leans on a Leona Heights bridge.

Nearby was a quarry dramatically nicknamed the Devil's Punchbowl. The quarry had miners' quarters, a rock-crushing machine, and a tramway that carried ore down the hill. Rocks were taken out of here to be crushed

OAKLAND HISTORY ROOM OF THE OAKLAND PUBLIC LIBRARY

to build area roads. And the roads returned the favor: the quarry was later packed in with fill from Highway 580's construction.

Leona Heights' creek is called Horseshoe Creek, and about half of it is now undergrounded. Long ago, the indigenous Huchiun people scraped clay pigments from the creek bed and used them to decorate their bodies.

The creek also provided clean spring water for one of the neighborhood's most interesting industries: a laundry. In the 1850s, a boat would come all the way from San Francisco, docking at the foot of 51st Avenue on San Leandro Bay, full of dirty clothing. From there, the laundry was carted up to Leona, to the Laundry Farm, afterwards being laid out to dry in the sun. It must have been a fabulous sight to see all the hundreds of garments sprawled on the grass. Unfortunately, the hillside laundry was on shaky ground, and a rainy day in 1857 sent it sliding down to the bottom of the canyon.

The laundry regrouped and moved business to West Oakland, but the name Laundry Farm stuck. Decades later, picnickers would come to the area in droves—one account has 1,200 visitors on a single weekend day. In 1887, a railroad was built in the area, with the carbarn across the creek from where the little laundry shack sat before its unplanned descent.

Leona was popular enough to support a large hotel, the three-story Laundry Farm Hotel built in 1892. It burned to the ground twice, the second time for good.

Laundry Farm Hotel

BY SAMANTHA TIGSDALE

You sit with the worst vacancy
because you have no shell
no walls

How is it possible
not to leave a vestige?

Men tramp these hills
with maps and try to find you

Couldn't the chambermaid
have hung a pillow slip
on a branch

carved your name into a tree

wedged part of the iron bedstead
into the ground like a gateway

something to show for all the years
of bedding miners and launderers
and picnickers?

Leona episode

BY BETTINA ALFRED

After my mother goes to sleep, she becomes a snake.
Dad finds her discarded skins in the bed.
We dance until the windows melt. I never get tired.
I never sleep. I eat boulders. I'm proud
of my hair, so long it dangles to the downstairs apartment.
I have to pay the people down there to comb it.
They coil it into a ball and put it in the tub to wash it.
There is a rooster that is an alarm clock.
He won't let any of us sleep in. But who sleeps?
Dreams seep into waking life anyway, with corn silk
fibers and algae and broom straw.
I have countless sisters. They all wear different colors,
colors that they invented. I never invented a color
so I have to wear animal furs. But I love animals
so they are all alive, writhing around my belly button,
walking up and down my legs. When I put them
in the closet, they sleep in a huddle. Good animals.
Counting sheep. Being sheep. Everything good.

MAXWELL PARK

BOUNDARY: *55th Avenue, Trask Street,*
Courtland Avenue and Camden Street

MAXWELL PARK has the very cool distinction of being a housing tract that even a child could buy into, according to the amusingly hyperbolic language of early real estate ads. Those skateboarders and basketball players you see out in the street? They may be paying off a mortgage.

Maxwell Park was originally a residence park owned by merchant John P. Maxwell. With great foresight, he purchased the property with the very aim of later selling it for housing. He arranged for the 55th Avenue streetcar line to be extended into his park to encourage sales, running to the intersection of Fleming and Madera avenues. Additionally, Southern Pacific electric lines ran only two blocks from the park entrance, allowing for fast transportation to San Francisco.

There's a reason why there's a hodgepodge of styles in Maxwell Park.

OAKLAND HISTORY ROOM OF THE OAKLAND PUBLIC LIBRARY

Laborers gather in front of the Burritt & Shealey real estate office, with Mr. Shealey on the right wearing a straw boater. Undated.

Under the headline "Maxwell Park Homes Must Be Different," a May 1923 article explains: "Every home that goes into the new series of fifty homes now under construction by Burritt & Shealey in Maxwell Park must bear the stamp of artistic individuality . . . . The result is that the architects have been able to draw freely and with good effect on the Colonial, Italian Renaissance, Spanish, French and English types of home architecture for their designs."

Maxwell Park sold out fast. In April 1921, a month before it opened for sales, the newspaper wrote, "Every day there are hundreds of people out watching the development going on and anxiously waiting for the opening of the tract to the home buyers."

An undated article says, "Four years ago, Maxwell Park, continuing 477 fine new residential lots, was soon sold out and buildings seemed to 'grow up' there overnight until now almost every lot has its home. With the beginning of Maxwell Park homes, there was a rush of buyers for all other adjacent vacant lots, on and around the (Foothill) boulevard, where homes were also speedily built." By May 1922, a year after the opening, it was reported that on average a home had been built in Maxwell Park every two days.

Burritt & Shealey clearly marked all the lotlines and posted the prices, so buyers could instantly see what they were in for: "The price and terms are plain and in full view, literally each lot being tagged and priced," said the newspaper in May 1921.

The terms started at $1 down. That figure, startling even back then, allowed the tract to "advertise" for children to buy: "Come out today— buy a lot—let the boy or girl buy one—teach them to save!"

Another attraction was the park's newness. In May 1921, a full page ad read, "Remember, this is not an old, worn-out addition covered with mortgages and trying to survive, but an all-new residence park."

A June 1921 ad said, "Picture yourself living in the clever, cosy home represented in the accompanying floor plan and you see life as it is enjoyed by the owners of homes in Maxwell Park . . . then you will understand why Maxwell Park has become the most popular home section in all the Eastbay; why many buyers came in the rain last week-end to purchase. . ."

A September 1923 ad pointed out the advisability of buying a home sooner rather than later: "Due to the present drain upon the market for building materials being shipped to Japan—visualize the importance of buying a home now . . . . Let us show you how you can own a Bard-Better-Built home." The Bard company offered 50 different types of homes to choose from in the Bard's Tract of Maxwell Park on Monticello Avenue.

J. H. A. Shealey of the construction company wrote for the 1923 *Oakland Tribune Year Book*, "These homes all radiate an unmistakable appeal in the friendly way they nestle together on the property."

OAKLAND HISTORY ROOM OF THE OAKLAND PUBLIC LIBRARY

Men and horses grade the road in Maxwell Park, undated.

Bruce Lee is undoubtedly Maxwell Park's best-known resident. He and his wife lived here with his friend James Yimm Lee in a house on Monticello Avenue. In 1964, James' wife had just died, leaving him to raise his children alone. Since Bruce was penniless at the time, the housing arrangement made sense. Bruce and James taught gung fu out of the garage.

As Maxwell Park was formerly part of Melrose, you may want to look at that listing as well.

Talking Maps to DeJuan

BY TOBEY KAPLAN

we're on route 80 north to Richmond
a windy sun through the windshield
breezes floating around the car and our eyes squinting
in the light we're fighting boredom and tiredness and exhilaration all
at once
he's thirteen ready for middle school
and I'm trying to help him make sense of out the summer free-time
get a leg up on studying and reading and poetry
he's my neighbor but we're not exactly friends
most often in the car mornings afternoons there's lots of silence
until I switch on the radio flipping through talkshows hiphop soul music
sometimes my rock'n'roll oldies mix
sometimes all news reports of crime and cuts and moneyspending
violence
there's little he'll say or ask never friendly
or chatty and I'm tired of asking questions like how was your weekend?
or what did you do after school yesterday?
and get hardly a grunt or murmur
he seats himself in with his leather baseball cap cocked over one eye
his big Dallas Cowboys down jacket in the heat of summer
protecting him from whatever

then today he says "where are we?"
like he's actually curious to know directions and
geography the function of reading a map of knowing
how to find one's way and place for now and I tell him
we're heading north from our neighborhood in Oakland
and from here the bay looks good enough to jump in take a swim he says
the turquoise water bouncing glimmering
and I tell him that when we get to our class
at Contra Costa College I can show him on the map
the distance we've covered
about twenty miles each way through Oakland Berkeley Albany

by the racetrack through Richmond for our summer program
and many summers ago I tell him
I learned map-reading as a survival skill because when I was
on vacation with my family
my dad driving he always liked to get lost
have an adventure a way of sight-seeing we didn't have to be any place
particular at a certain time
but as a kid it made me nervous so I learned to locate where we were
on a map
so I never felt lost

anywhere
"have you ever read a roadmap before?" I asked spreading out the Bay
Area in front of him
the tops of the map flopping over his knees
he says no and I trace our route with my finger so he can see where we
start in the vicinity of our homes
and where we end up   back and forth   each day

The Pizza Guy

BY TOBEY KAPLAN

my dogs aren't barking
and I've turned on the ballgame
and a young man climbs the house stairs
comes to the door the minute after I've just arrived
my porch bulb always on day or night
on the stairway in the afternoon
he's young casual but professionally-dressed
at first I assume a religious cult a business scam
but he's trying to sell me pizza
buy a coupon for twenty dollars get five bucks off
(I seriously try to follow his story)
really I'm listening I look like I'm listening
I really want to watch the ballgame
then he stops
looks around the front sloped yard of plants and little statues
and the pizza guy keeps talking they trained him
for the sales pitch
make a personal connection
asks me if I'm a painter or an artist
because then he would say he was too
I say poetry it's a kind of performance
waiting on the stairs keeping the doors open
not getting famous I teach writing and reading and thinking
at the community colleges nearby
and I almost want to ask if he's in school—
the dogs behind the door are quiet
they just want me to feed them

then he tells me he has a poem to offer
I assume something rhymed a rap he wants to lay down
friendly and personable and pushy
but I tell him I'm out of time
I don't have any money I will never be hungry
I shake his hand and wish him good luck

A Taste of East Oakland

BY ROSE MARK

International Boulevard
between 5th and 12th avenues:
Fish balls, tripe, brisket, tendons,
ribbons of rice noodles float
in steamy pho,
broth piqued with basil, cilantro, lime, bean sprouts,
and jalapeno peppers,
bahn mi sandwiches,
French rolls stuffed with meats nestled in beds of
pickled radish, carrots, cilantro and chilies.
At the market
wide eyed fish lounge next to
squirting clams in buckets,
shrimp, heads on or off defrosting,
while the perfume or some say stink of durian
permeates the air, Little Saigon.

International Boulevard,
between Fruitvale and High Street:
red, green and white carts roll along
plying
thick homemade potato chips,
sweet/tart orange mangoes, crunchy/cool jicama
splashed with lime, dash of chili,
ceviche tacos,
steaming cups of champurrado,
coils of churros bubbling in a kettle,
rolled hot in cinnamon sugar
taco trucks sit handing out
carnitas, carne asada, lengua burritos.

Overhead, BART slicing the air with speed,
Amtrak train holding up traffic,
moaning the blues of day laborers,
the struggle, sacrifice, aloneness
of the newcomer
hanging out on haunches,
standing,
waiting for the stopped car,
the job, price, agreement.

Fruitvale Avenue:
Everett and Jones BBQ,
sticky sweet smoky ribs n'chicken
bitter greens, mac and cheese, baked beans
spongy bread to wipe up that sauce
Looziana fried fish, hush puppies next door,
Salvadorean pupusas down the street,
Fried chicken and waffles up the street,
side trip to
Allendale Park,
Ventiane, a third world oasis,
serving Cambodian, Lao, Thai,
cuisines,
Red Sea catfish,
fried rice cakes
sticky rice with mangoes,
steamy pho.

MacArthur Boulevard:
The Food Mill,
bins of flour, wheat, corn, spelt, buckwheat.
Rices, jasmine, basmati, weihei, black, Imperial red,
beans, pinto, adzuki, black, great Northern peas.
Spices, cinnamon, nutmeg, mace, allspice, ginger, cardamom
mustard seed, fennel, cumin, coriander, cayenne.
Herbs, oregano, basil, thyme, marjoram, sage, tarragon and chervil.

Down the street further,
Farmer Joe's greengrocer,
collard greens next to
bok choy, five types of mixed olives,
Niman Ranch pork, purple yams,
yucca, meyer lemons, tofu,
pistachio next to mochi rice ice cream,
organic chickens, gourmet sausages,
baguettes, bagels, triple cream cheeses.

World Ground cafe,
Mills students, teachers,
old Chinese men ,
Open mic poetry night,
breakfast paninis, cappucinos, lattes, mochas.

Full House Cafe,
cornmeal waffles
portobello hash,
red flannel hash,
smoked chicken hash,
corned beef hash.

Taoist center
Tai Chi, yoga,
acupuncture,
calligraphy,
lion dances,
worship,
peace.

Laurel Books,
tiny, sweet
thoughtful selections for everyone.

Seminary Boulevard
boxes of strawberries on the corner
watermelon and oranges from
backs of trucks,
weed on some corners,

BART glides its silvery song,
Amtrak toots its horn,
makes us wait, slow down
to hear

the tinkle of bells from the paleta wagon,
the thumping bass of a teenager's car,
young children playing, laughing across the street,
ringing doorbells, running away,
dogs walking masters/mistresses,
joggers, walkers, baby buggies,
commuting bikers returning home,
peaceful breezes,
hawks fly overhead,
crows caw, squawk and cackle
songbirds woo each other with echoing melodies.

I walk the streets of my neighborhood,
Melrose Heights, lower Maxwell Park to some,
smelling red beans and rice,
greens with ham,
backyard barbecues
hamburgers, hot dogs, chicken on the grill,
jasmine rice, lemon grass, coconut milk,
paella, polenta, carnitas,
brownies, chocolate chip cookies,
apple pie,

the sweet smells of my neighborhood.

WHERE: *Roughly speaking, the area surrounding
International Boulevard between about High Street
and Seminary Avenue*

THE FIRST settlers in the area were ranchers who needed access to the railroad to ship their cattle. The area was once filled with orchards and flowers. The Peralta family sold the land around Melrose to Henry S. Fitch (one Oakland History Room account has his name as C.L. Fitch) for $14,000. He created Fitchburg, a little town that was important to the cattlemen in the area, especially since a cattle-loading stop to the railway was built near 47th Avenue.

The area was once home to a silver and gold smelting plant. After that business faded, Borax Smith used the plant to smelt "ores from mines up in the hills back of Melrose in 1896," according to a newspaper account. Smelting is the process of using a very, very hot fire to separate minerals from metals.

OAKLAND HISTORY ROOM OF THE OAKLAND PUBLIC LIBRARY

*Mr. and Mrs. Chauncey St. John stand outside their home at 1812 46th Avenue
(subsequently renumbered to 2126).*

This neighborhood was once connected by mudflats to Alameda, before the channel was dredged that transformed Alameda into an island. Like many neighborhoods, Melrose benefited population-wise by the 1906 earthquake that brought homeless San Franciscans across the bay. It was annexed to Oakland in 1909. In December 1912 when the East 16th Street streetcar line was built out to its terminal at 55th Avenue in Melrose, the whole neighborhood came out to celebrate. Hundreds joined Mayor Frank Mott in the festivities. On that occasion, Mott said, "Nature has greatly favored this section of the city in the way of climate and natural beauties, but it is not easily reached from the business part of Oakland. The completion of this carline is one of great importance to the general welfare of the community east of Lake Merritt." The mayor urged the neighborhood to band together to plant trees along the Melrose thoroughfares: now that's a good mayor!

The story of the purchase of the land for the Melrose Library branch is an interesting one. Residents who wanted a library asked one man to act as their agent to buy the land from a downtown merchant who knew the land was increasing in value and therefore was loath to sell. The agent went to visit the merchant and one by one took gold coins out of his pocket, stacking them on a table. After a pile had accrued, he took out the property deed he had written up and put it on the table near the gold. The merchant—whose name was Shylock, believe it or not—reportedly kept staring at the gold until he couldn't resist, grabbed a pen, signed the deed and hugged the gold.

Melrose Acres sold for $550 for a quarter-acre in June 1920, with the rough terms of $5 down and $5.50 a month. But the Realty Syndicate Company which offered this deal had an ingenious suggestion for how to pay it off: "You can pay for your quarter-acre home by raising chickens and rabbits and growing berries and vegetables."

In March 1923, Melrose businessmen met to consider how to draw more business to the district. According to those men, "Melrose is destined to be one of the leading industrial districts in the United States," the newspaper reported. Their plan included joint advertising and "a system of window-lighting effects and arc-lights that will make East Fourteenth Street a second 'Great White Way,'" referring to the theater district on Broadway in New York. Said one of the speakers, "Seventy-five percent of the windows in this district are now dark at night, and as a result we are losing a valuable business asset." It's true, Melrose was rife with possibility at the time with successful manufacturing plants—including auto assembling plants that, if growth continued apace, would assemble one of every 20 U.S. cars. "The way industries have been coming to this district," said another speaker, "gives Melrose a wonderful insurance of stability of its property and business values, and of their steady increase."

Those auto plants were Chevrolet in Eastmont, Durant in Stonehurst —and the Star auto assembling plant right in Melrose. And here's an interesting tidbit from November 1916: "It is said that auto factories are to start up in Oakland for the especial purpose of manufacturing a special class of low priced machines for the South American trade."

The corner of Foothill Boulevard and Courtland Avenue.

"The industrial activity which is now sweeping over Oakland is being sensibly felt in Melrose, where every house and tenement has been taken over in order to house the factory and shipyard workers. New houses are also being built to meet this demand. One party has built not less than ten three-room cottages on a single block for workers and their families," said the newspaper in June 1918.

Along with automobiles, Melrose had a more erudite industry, ostrich farming. In the days when ladies' hats featured enormous plumes, ostriches were called upon to provide them. Before domestication of the ostrich, it was necessary to kill the entire beast to earn its feathers. Additionally, at times those in pursuit of fashion were not fazed at the idea of using entire (hopefully smaller) birds as accoutrements. An 1892 article in the *California Illustrated Magazine,* charmingly titled "Ranching for Feathers," stated "Happily, the bloody reign of stuffed birds for hat trimming is over, and it is hoped that anything so unladylike, inartistic and altogether revolting will never again come into vogue."

In 1908, the three-acre Bentley Ostrich Farm first opened at the corner of International and High streets, including a repair area where old feathers were cleaned, curled and dyed. By 1913, the name changed to the Golden State Ostrich Farm, and there were 75 birds on exhibit. When an ostrich was plucked, a stocking was placed over its head to calm it. Another ostrich farm was in Idora Park in North Oakland.

The Bancroft Library holds a file of monthly newspapers created between 1912 and 1923 by Melrose grocers, titled *The Souza Brothers Store News* These papers apparently chronicle the development of Melrose from rural to urban density.

Barbecue Healing

BY STEVEN LAVOIE

The web of health takes prey with hunger.
Useless connections fade, work-related information,
as pallid teenagers leaving San Leandro
march in columns wherever
the streets widen.
The grammar of housing
left to locals
& corps of civil engineers
who have been assigned public transportation projects.
A geography forms, of cul-de-sacs.
Thoroughfares reduced to ballfields
with asphalt-turf infields.
Vice versa.
No outlet as a social condition.
The hours drag along with the crowd-laden trains.
You feel like an abstraction.
The common tongue reads in rebus,
the constitutions & rules of order
are displayed under pictures of products
visible only to motorists who pass on the skyway above.
Billboards of Hollywood violence.
With great admiration for moral certitude,
law-abiders, you convict outsiders of
incorrect brand identification,
from neighborhoods whose rules were Kools,
they violate the Marlboro statute.
Change brands while passing 35th & Foothill,
just in case.
You notice other peculiarities of locale.
A trip six blocks fills you
with a sense of adventure.
A net shirt, some extruded polystyrene material,
day-glo, with Ben Davis pants give way
to a natty baby blue ensemble
in front of Wm. Johnson's BBQ,
49th (Ave.) & E. 14th. (St.)

(degraded to "International Boulevard").
You cannot tell from the contrast
the extent of the ferment.
A situation of interiors,
disguised by decay,
probed for familiar signals.
The economic impositions
diminish choices but
increase disorientation.
The squalor is wilderness.
When you see the collapsing row
of storefronts, you can't tell
which American city this is
or that in one among them
the chi-chi of the chi-chi
of the barbecue
is in preparation.
Self-adhesive fluorescents
for illumination.
Street lights dimly intermittent,
more than adequate to secure
the values here.
Windshield fog immerses us,
exposing our lack
of exposure:
the heat of the sauce,
the thudding beat,
now brought to you in Spanish
when the signal is clear,
temporary relief to the isolation,
atmospheric conditions
permitting.
Braving the vacated architecture,
as we are,
where the sauce brings us
back among the proud profusion,
from aging uncles to
fresh-faced refugees.
Make ours medium,
to go.

Funk and Triple Funk

BY MARGARITA SOARES

You made it funky
but we made it funkier

you doubled it
we tripled it

it's like that
when you need it

it just flows through you
on the avenue

on the most international
of all 14th streets

on the wrong side
of a name

so we made it funky
and funkied it up further

that's just a game
(not a name)
we have to play

MILLSMONT

BOUNDARY: *Millsmont reaches from*
Seminary Avenue to 72nd Avenue

OH JOY! *No more rent!* That's how a May 1924 ad for Millsmont started. It went on to state that the neighborhood "just fits the need of the family with a small income. Here you can buy a big, level lot for a few dollars down. Fine garden soil, room to raise a few chickens . . . and San Francisco transportation right to your door."

One of the subdivisions was called Mills College Park, which promised in an April 1923 ad, "You're not pioneering here—but moving into a thoroughly developed section. Paved streets, curbs, sidewalks all completed. Schools on tract. Stores on tract. Sewer, water, gas, electricity already installed. Street car company bus to center of tract every 20 minutes."

Two students stand in front of Mills Hall, which once housed the entirety of Mills College. Although the college was originally a seminary for women, men are now allowed into the graduate programs.

Another was Chimes Terrace. A dramatic June 1926 ad pictured a drawing of a gigantic man arising out of Oakland's soil with a sledge-hammer to drive a stake labeled "Close in, values rising" into the Chimes Terrace land. The legend read, "Oakland Progress is driving this fact home!" The tract was named because it was within sound of the chimes from El Campanil, the bell tower on the Mills campus designed by Julia Morgan.

Yet another subdivision was Chevrolet Park, four blocks north of Foothill, along Seminary Avenue, "across the street" from Mills College.

This shows where Laird Avenue met Seminary Avenue, in an age-speckled 1925 photo.

War interrupted its settlement. "The war came just as the property was to be offered to the public, and little was done with it during that period of anxiety and excitement," read an August 1921 newspaper article. Many bought here after the war on the $1 down/$1 a week plan, and even though the tract subsequently sold out, many purchasers did not keep up with payments and the lots were then reopened for sale. The article mentioned that several Mills faculty were buying lots in Chevrolet Park.

Another subdivision was Melrose Highlands (Millsmont was origi-nally part of the larger Melrose neighborhood), of which a grocer said in a November 1926 ad, "Glad I moved to Melrose Highlands . . . . It is warmer here in this little valley than it is any place else along these hills, and the kids are healthier out here because they can be out of doors all day." This area was part of the old Houston ranch, which was previously used as a rifle range by the National Guard.

One tract was on a section of land previously belonging to Mills College and known as the "old meadow." "Because of sentimental reasons, the Wood Company developers offered a prize of $50 to the students of Mills College for a name for the new tract. Out of the large number of names submitted, the choice was Mills Gardens," reported a February 1924 newspaper. The tract was bounded by 55th and Seminary avenues, the campus and the Nelson estate. Nelson was a captain whose large estate was near the campus.

Mills College began as the Young Ladies Seminary in Benicia in 1852. At the time, there was no University of California (nor even the College of California, the Oakland school that morphed into UC before it ever set foot in Berkeley) and no Stanford. Pioneers who had just completed the danger-fraught journey to the west coast were loath to send their daughters back east to be educated. The seminary fit a need.

Cyrus and Susan Mills bought the school and relocated it to the Oakland hills in 1870. The main structure on campus, Mills Hall, was originally the college in its entirety, with classrooms and dormitories for students and teachers. The campus was self-sufficient with vegetable gardens, an orchard and a dairy to feed students.

The Mills land was once the site of a Native American village; bones were found which attested to the original inhabitants' presence.

The 1776 Juan Bautista de Anza expedition, which brought a teenaged Luis Maria Peralta to the Bay Area, stopped on a hill on what would become the Mills campus, off Underwood Road. There is a plaque in a field there to commemorate it. Nearby on Underwood is a palm tree near what was once the "Home for Aged and Infirm Colored People."

One enclave that gets a lot of attention each December is Picardy Drive at Seminary Avenue. Here, a charming 10-acre plot contains French and Old English-style homes built in 1926, originally called Normandy Gardens. Each year residents decorate their homes with holiday lights in grand style. Most importantly, the lights are strung between the homes, connecting them as true neighbors.

Picardy Drive

BY ZACH HOFSTEDER

It is a sight.
Lights connecting neighbors.
Everyone going all out
to be part of this.
It doesn't matter if it's
your religion or his holiday
or her Chanukah or what—
it's just about the neighbors.
And when I walk there
under all those twinkling
crazy lights, the strand
that doesn't stop, I wish
it was more than metaphoric:
I wish the understanding
really ran that deep.

Mills College

BY SUSAN BRYANT

Julia Morgan is far more alive here than she ever is at San Simeon. There, she was put upon and beset by a man's dream, a man's vision— a skewed vision that she tried to dignify with her skill.

But at Mills, she is active and moving and her buildings house girls— bright, smart girls the likes of her. She approves of the campus set aside to make women more powerful, more sure of themselves. Here in this grassy environment, the women forget that they are softer-voiced. They speak up for themselves. They do as they wish.

Just as Julia did, going to Paris to become an architect when the school wouldn't let her in. She stayed in Paris and just kept being there and trying to convince them. And then she became the first female graduate from the Ecole des Beaux Arts. She came back to the U.S. and used poured concrete. She was an innovator in so many ways—because of that concrete, some of her buildings best survived the 1906 earthquake.

So she is present here, in the tower of El Campanil, in the buildings she designed, in the stout hearts of women who are fearless about being themselves.

MONTCLAIR

WHERE: *The large hills area on either side of Route 13, between Upper Rockridge and Joaquin Miller area.*

MONTCLAIR WAS once the land holdings of Colonel John C. Hays, the famous Texas Ranger who served as San Francisco's first sheriff during the rough years of vigilantism. This fascinating man succeeded on two fronts: the bloody battlefield and the halls of government. He was an accomplished and some say dirty fighter in the Mexican-American War and against Native Americans, then later shifted gears and was an 1876 delegate to the National Democratic Convention.

Hays arrived in California as part of a wagon train he led after hearing the reports of gold. He was San Francisco's sheriff 1850-53. In 1853, President Franklin Pierce appointed him California's surveyor general. The placid little town of Oakland suited Hays after all his fighting: he settled here to take things more slowly. Although Texas made him famous, we got him last: he's buried in Mountain View Cemetery.

This Montclair observatory provided a tangible reason for people to make the trek out to the hills. Once there, they might consider buying real estate—exactly the reason that developers erected it.

Three years after his 1883 death, residents erected the Hays School (where today's Moraga Avenue firehouse stands) in his honor. Many of the students were the children of Portuguese-American laborers who worked in the orchards, farms and dairies which then dotted the area. The schoolmistress lived downtown and rode her horse to school each day, which was a three hour round-trip—luckily her commute didn't involve traffic. The school closed in 1913.

The Medau family (for which Medau Place in Montclair Village is named) had a house in what is today Montclair Park (and owned 487 acres encompassing today's entire village of Montclair). The Medau parents were German immigrants. They grew fruit and raised stock, later switching to grain and hay. At one point, the Medau dairy had 100 cows. In 1901, John Medau sold the ranch to the Realty Syndicate for a mere $130,000.

In 1913, the Sacramento Northern Pacific railroad track was laid along the edge of what soon became Montclair's commercial center, and the remote area began bustling with real estate dealings.

Developers launched into action to bring potential homebuyers to the secluded area. Like the old schoolmistress, some came on horseback to check out the sales hut. The canny salesmen built an observatory in the hills as a destination for daytrippers. Once visitors saw the beauty of the land, it was far easier to convince them that this could be home. That lookout tower no longer stands.

Two great examples of Storybook civic architecture stand in Montclair, the 1927 firehouse and the 1930 library. The firehouse's white painted roof today suggests "snow," but originally copper roofing blazed in the sun, intending to look like fire, and indeed the roof finials curl up like flames. Today the building is abandoned. The library, on the other hand, still flourishes, with its pitched roofs and gables that conjure up a medieval fairy tale cottage.

That railroad that helped launch development in Montclair once ran through Montclair and Shepherd Canyon on its way to Sacramento. The canyon (and a now-culverted creek) is named for farmer William Joseph Shepherd. Originally from England, Shepherd came to the area in 1869 and owned land for the next 20 years. The trains carried passengers and freight through the densely-wooded hills, stopping at two stations in the Montclair hills, Havens and Sequoia. Havens was right in Shepherd Canyon,

The 1927 Montclair firehouse made firefighters into storybook characters who lived in a heart-embellished cottage. The men of Engine Company 24 appreciated their charming station and built terraced gardens, plant houses, a fish pond and an aviary.

while Sequoia was further east, closer to Moraga. The train that crossed Lake Temescal was known as the Comet.

The railroad began in 1909 as the Oakland & Antioch Railway. Two years later, the Sacramento Northern Railroad leased the O&A right-of-way through the canyon. For a while, business boomed, but then the Great Depression hit. Even the 1937 construction of the Bay Bridge (which then carried trains on its lower deck) couldn't help increase passenger traffic, so the railroad mostly focused on freight. It had another heyday during World War II, transporting materials, but the final train ran in 1957 and the tracks were dismantled.

Lake Temescal was created by damming Temescal Creek in 1868. Tons of dirt were washed from a 160-foot-deep canyon to create the dam, and herds of wild mustangs were run at the site so their hooves would compact the earth. The process of using horses to trample earth until it is rock hard is called "puddling." Believe it or not, this makes the ground as water-resistant as cement. The resulting reservoir was a source of water piped to homes by the Contra Costa Water Company—but that "right to pipe" involved a long battle. The Contra Costa Water Company was owned by Anthony Chabot, who went head-to-head with William Dingee, who owned the Oakland Water Company. Dingee's personal cesspool drained into Chabot's water supply, and Dingee alerted the papers that his competitor's water was bacteria-laden. In turn, Chabot accused Dingee's water of being full of alkali. An 1876 newspaper reported, "The water furnished the inhabitants of this city has carried more people to the grave... than all the rotgut that has been sold and consumed in this state . . . . The water has been so filthy that a respectable cow would turn from it in disgust." Dingee tunneled into the Montclair hills to obtain water: for a while, millions of gallons daily poured through the now-closed-off tunnels. Eventually, the feuding water companies merged.

In 1938, Lake Temescal was opened as a swimming/recreation area. The boathouse was built by the WPA that year and is an example of the National Park Service rustic style.

One of the subdivisions adjoining Montclair was Piedmont Pines, tucked in where Mountain and Park boulevards used to meet before the construction of Route 13. This Mitchell & Austin subdivision was open for sale in 1934. That year, the newspaper reported, "Display homes in Piedmont Pines are the Mecca for thousands of prospective home builders interested in observing new details of home construction."

"With an elevation ranging from 1,300 to 1,400 feet, LeMon Park in Piedmont Pines commands a view of which its residents can never be deprived," said a July 1937 newspaper article. LeMon Park was named for retired New York capitalist R.F. D. LeMon who walked the property one day and was astonished by the views. Telling the subdivision rep "I'll take it" on the spur of the moment, he bought a house and 60 acres, where he then launched his building program. Piedmont Pines was advertised as being "for those particular people who put a premium on seclusion . . . not isolation" in an August 1937 ad.

Another area in the Montclair hills was the Wickham Havens subdivision Forest Park. A 1924 advertisement enthused, "Trees! Sunshine! The invigorating air of the hills! Ferns! Flowers! It even has a forest pool for property owners and their friends to swim in." The titular forest was planted by Frank C. Havens in 1904. The pool was originally a watering hole for cattle, then a muddy swimming hole, and then was cemented into a $10,000 pool (nearby homesites were $475.) Its close proximity to Thornhill Road prompted concerns in the mid-1940s about traffic during swim season. Today the fountain in the middle no longer exists, but the pool does, as the Montclair Swim Club on Woodhaven Way.

The neighborhood of Hiller Highlands was built on an abandoned rock quarry site. The Fred T. Wood Company began building there in 1926. "Within a few months, or a year at most, this beautiful section of Oakland will have a new skyline—a skyline of homes," said the tract manager in a May 1926 article. This, like many of the Oakland hills tracts, was a daily picnic spot, and while building occurred Wood put up benches to continue use of the property. "While lots are selling rapidly in the Highlands of Oakland, picnickers are still welcome to enjoy the panorama of hills and bay," reported a May 1926 article. In that same article, the subdivision manager said, "Freedom from fogs and protection from the wind which the pines and eucalyptus afford make this an unusually healthy homesite."

Hiller Highlands was named for Stanley Hiller, an inventor born in 1888. Among many other things, Hiller helped invent the seaplane and installed underground utilities long before they were considered feasible. In 1912, he flew an amphibious monoplane off Lake Merritt. Many of his accomplishments were aviation-based, as was his production of his son Stanley, Jr.

Stanley, Jr. had a staff of 300 working for him building mini race cars to the tune of annual gross of $1 million—when he was fifteen years old. He went on to develop and build the helicopter beginning in 1942 and established Hiller Aviation Institute and Museum in San Carlos in 1998, among many other achievements.

Must have been something "flighty" in the genes.

The Hills Fire of 1991

BY PARADISE FREEJAH LOVE

I had a bird's eye view of the whole thing from start to finish from my second-floor window and sixth floor roof at the Harriet Tubman Apartment Complex on Adeline in Berkeley. About an hour or so before noon on that fateful October Sunday morning, I noticed a huge but somewhat innocent looking cloud of white smoke rising up from behind the Claremont Hotel a little over a mile away. By and by the smoke grew darker until it made the reddish-orange midday sun disappear.

The weather was weird-hot that day.
And even more intense than it was during the '89 quake.

It seems like God has a propensity for speaking to the world through the Bay Area! In '89 he shook the A's-Giants World Series game off the air with a quake. And now the smoke from the Oakland hills had reached across the bay and blanketed Candlestick Park where the '49ers were playing, and John Madden was doing a play by play of the game—and the fire!

The wind, which usually blows cool air inland from the Pacific Ocean and San Francisco Bay, was now blowing dry-hot air from east to west and southwest, as it would all day—but hard! As if there was a dragon behind them there hills trying to stir up the raging flames of fire on purpose. "Where was this wind coming from?" I asked myself.

Supernatural forces were at work behind this fire, and the helplessness of man against Nature's fury was quite evident here as the firefighters dropped little 500-gallon thimbles of water on the fire from their helicopters and airplanes, but would have been just as effective trying to put the fire out by spitting on it. Stupid Man . . . . Nothing could've stopped that fire from spreading to the ends of the earth, I imagined, if God had wanted it to.

It was beginning to dawn on me that this fire was serious. Apocalyptic, even! And here I was in the middle of Judgment Day, with all hell breaking loose, watching a '49ers game. And I was supposed to be a spiritual person!? No wonder we were doomed.

I started to think about my family—our escape—our rendezvous. Who did I know in San Francisco? I pictured the fire coming down from the hills, the Bay Bridge jammed with cars, pandemonium. People trying to swim across the bay . . . boiling like the crabs and lobsters they had eaten. Was this the day the Lord would come like a thief in the night and destroy the world by fire?

Nooooo. I wasn't ready yet. How come you didn't tell me? What about my career? My mission? I got down on my knees and prayed as if I might be the only one who could stop this thing. I prayed for my family. For an ex-girlfriend of mine who lived up there (and would later tell me the fire was put out about a hundred yards from her house).

Near sundown I got on my bike and rode toward this historical event to get a close-up view. Soot rained from the sky as I rode down Telegraph Avenue's evacuated streets. I turned up 43rd Street to go to Tech High School, one of the designated relief centers.

But instead of scenes of horror, I saw a bunch of friendly-looking people helping each other out. Huge Safeway and Lucky trucks offering free food. Hmmmm. Five thousand homeless before the fire. Five thousand more after the fire, from the hill. And just three days later, the folks from the hills would all be sheltered again. Boy, does money talk!

I wasn't needed there. So I grabbed one of those nose and mouth breathing masks the authorities were making available and headed into the night towards the hills and Rockridge Terrace, where all the television stations were keying in. Man, what horrific beauty. The two symbolic pillars at the entrance and foot of the hill. Behind which all those beautiful homes were going up in flames . . . along with so many memories. I hoped there were no people up there.

I looked down at the freeway. That was the first time I had seen it completely empty. The whole scene looked surreal. Like something out of the Twilight Zone . . . until this long red caravan of fire trucks streamed up it to battle the fire. I stayed up all night until I heard the fire was under control.

The weather the next day was completely different—Dante's Inferno was followed by the breath of an Ice Age, as a cool, eerie mist passed over the hills as if to say, "It is finished; time for healing now."

Oakland survived the '89 quake, and it will rise again—phoenix from its own ashes, even as it will overcome the Crack Holocaust plaguing it over the last 15 years. Because the story of Oakland has not yet been completely told: We will thrive again!

American Dream in Action

BY YVONNE BYRON

My swim club in the Oakland hills is the perfect
example of the American Dream in action.
I have traded recipes or solved the problems of the
world with either first or second generation
Italian-Americans, Chinese-Americans (Malaysia),
Chinese-Americans (Singapore),
Chinese-Americans (Hong Kong),
a Lebanese-American, African-Americans,
East Indian-Americans, French-Americans,
a Chilean-American, a Peruvian-American,
Mexican-Americans, a German-American,
a Swiss-American, a Nicaraguan-American,
an Israeli-American, New Zealander-Americans,
a Finnish-American, a Norwegian-American,
an Egyptian-American, a Russian-American,
an Irish-American, a Dutch-American,
Belgian-Americans, Armenian-Americans,
and a Vietnamese-American.
Most are members, some are staff
who have become friends over the years.

Redwood

BY WENDY DUTTON

In my yard there is a redwood. At about 120 feet tall, it is well over 150 years old. There are some other redwoods in the neighborhood, but the tree in my yard is lone. It still remembers the time when this whole neighborhood was redwoods, back before Montclair got pricey, before the 7-Eleven came in, before the school was built, even before the Thornhill corridor was a major logging operation—back when Thornhill Drive was just a creek full of trout. The hills were lined with redwoods.

Here is what I know about redwoods. The redwoods (Sequoia sempervirens and Sequoia gigantia) only grow in one place in the world, a region stretching from Big Sur to just above the California/Oregon coast and only within 20 miles of the ocean They can easily reach 300 feet—taller than a skyscraper. They can live for 2,000 years or more. They have not only been in California since the Indians, but since the dinosaurs.

Because redwood is superior for outdoor building, logging—such as what took place in the Montclair region of Oakland at the turn of the century—has wiped out all but 5% of old-growth redwoods. They used to cut the big trees along Skyline Boulevard and send them down the waterfalls into Temescal Creek. The trees came splashing and crashing by, guided with giant scythes from the shore.

Imagine the waterfalls. You can still see water seeping out of the hillsides of Montclair. This is where construction occurred without regard to the numerous natural streams that are constantly struggling to join up with the larger creeks that head for the Bay. One such creek goes directly under St. John's Church, which is in my back yard. You can hear the creek gushing in a culvert in the garden there. The church must have been quite a watering hole, terrific for swimming, before the creeks were captured and contained in giant pipes.

The creeks of Oakland run through the city like streets on a map. Indians used the creeks like maps as well. They followed Temescal Creek from its base at the Bay up into the Thornhill corridor where they summered among the cool redwoods. Now that the creek has been dammed at Lake Temescal, it runs through most of Oakland in huge underground pipes until it reaches the gigantic shopping mall in Emeryville next to the gigantic furniture store where once there was a gigantic shellmound and Indian village.

This neighborhood was first a hunting ground for the Indians, and then a hunting ground for adventurous San Franciscans. Lots of the old houses in Montclair were first hunting lodges or vacation cottages. They are tiny, plain homes. My house was built in 1915. It looks like it was built in 1915. One of the rooms still had a dirt floor, and three of the rooms don't have heat.

The house is owned by St. John's Church. They own four houses in this neighborhood. They plan to tear down one in order to build a bridge over Thornhill Road and a new "park-like" parking lot in what is now an orchard. The process of gathering permits is taking a lot of time, and there is neighborhood opposition to these plans. Two of the oldest redwoods on the church's property are right in the middle of their plans. Meanwhile, the land is in limbo.

Often I think, "Why oh why did I move here?" Usually I think that when I am contemplating skunks under the house or working on the laundry room floor again. The answer lies with the redwoods.

One night I was standing in the yard at dusk. I was praying. Actually I was complaining about my fixer-upper life. Suddenly I forgot about this because all around me I could hear the trees talking. It was sort of a loud shwooshing sound. I realized I was standing in the bowl of a meadow with hills all around me lined with monster trees, mostly Monterey Pine, also redwood. At first I thought the trees were talking to each other, but then I realized they were talking to me. They were welcoming me to the neighborhood. They were hoping I was a tree-planting type rather than a tree-removing type. And could I plant some redwoods? Could I help them get the forest back?

So far I have planted 15 trees, eight redwoods. I am curious to see how many redwoods I can fit into one yard. I wonder if the church will object to this or if they will even notice. When they come to reclaim a good chunk of this yard for their parking lot, they will find the baby redwoods already there, taking root along the edges of construction.

Now you know my plan.

MOSSWOOD

WHERE: *The area around*
Broadway and MacArthur Boulevard

WE HAVE Mosswood Park to enjoy today because a turn of the century city attorney had the guts to bid $100 over what he was allowed, at a probate auction for the property.

Mosswood was first owned in 1862 by J. Mora Moss, a San Francisco businessman. He longed for a country estate far from city activity and found it in the East Bay. At that time, Oakland's city limit was 22nd Street (then Charter Street), so he was 10 blocks away from "civilization." His lands were a lot larger than today's city park: they stretched from Broadway all the way down to Telegraph, and between 35th and 38th streets, comprising around 30 acres.

Moss created a charming estate with plenty of good rambles through orchards, live oaks, ferns, grain fields and gardens. There was a running brook on the property (Glen Echo Creek, which was undergrounded in

One of the rustic trails twisting through Mosswood Park, 1932.

1945). His wife, Julia Wood, whose name conjoins with his to form the estate's name (how lucky their names were so woodsy!) was a skilled gardener who did much of the landscaping.

Moss was a pillar of the community, serving on the board of directors of the Deaf, Dumb and Blind Institute in Oakland and being one of the first regents of the University of California (which was sited in Oakland before it moved to Berkeley).

Moss died in 1880 and his widow in 1904. They had had no children, and some of the land was subdivided for homes. The rest wound up in a probate court auction in 1908, and that's when the mayor got involved.

There's a document in the Oakland History Room called "The Story of the Acquisition of Mosswood Park," written by Mayor Frank K. Mott. This progressive mayor took office in 1905, and he states in his paper that his most important policy was the acquisition of park lands.

When he saw the Mosswood estate going to auction with the city treasury empty of funding for its purchase, he rounded up a group of banks to provide the city a loan. The banks agreed they would bid no more than $65,000.

Their representative in court that day was City Attorney John McElroy (the large fountain in Lakeside Park is named for him). A syndicate that wished to further subdivide the property was McElroy's opponent, and it opened the bidding with sweeping $1,000 bids, which he matched. After a bit, the syndicate dropped its raises to $500, and McElroy kept up. Finally the syndicate was only raising by $100—and it bid $65,000, the amount McElroy was supposed to stop at.

But McElroy took a chance and raised to $65,100. The syndicate dropped out.

The banks put up a fence to protect the land from vandals while the park was being formed. It was a grand iron affair but was scrapped for metal in 1942 to help the war effort. The chairman of the Salvage for Victory Committee told the newspaper: "If we lose the war the fence won't mean a thing, and when we win it, we can build a new one—probably out of relics taken from the German and Japanese armies." Luckily, the fence was never rebuilt with such gory materials.

By 1911, the city was able to take title to the park.

The Moss mansion is still in the park, a Gothic Revival cottage built in 1864. Many of its fittings were brought over from England. Stained

OAKLAND HISTORY ROOM OF THE OAKLAND PUBLIC LIBRARY

From left, Summer, Autumn and Spring act in a pageant at Mosswood Park put on by the Oakland Recreation Department in 1921. The pageant was a benefit for the American Physical Education Association.

glass windows featured the couple's respective coats of arms: his showed the head and shoulders of a buck arising from a crown, and hers showed two human arms rising from a crown and holding a globe. More recently, the home had been used for the Oakland Africa Sister Cities International group, which supported Oakland's sister city relationship with Sekondi-Takoradi, Ghana, but it is now closed.

Mosswood Park used to house the Junior Center for the Arts, opened in 1954, before it was moved to Lakeside Park.

MacArthur Boulevard used to be called Moss Avenue after Moss, but the City Council changed the street's name to honor General MacArthur. That name change set a precedent: Soon an 8-year-old boy named Franklin Delano Winston (himself named after a great man) suggested that Mosswood Park become MacArthur Park. The 1942 city park board quickly OK'd the suggestion, unwitting that Oakland would roar in response. Mere months after the park's name was changed, the decision was reversed.

(See Piedmont Avenue listing for information on Glen Echo Creek.)

Doing Laundry

BY PHILLIP RICHARDS

Maria told me she'd meet me at the Laundromat there by the 7-11. We were going to do our laundry together. I hardly knew her but I guessed this was her idea of a date; she suggested it. So even though I didn't even have enough for a full load (I'd already done my laundry earlier at my own apartment building where there were washers and dryers in the basement), I rumpled up a few clean T-shirts and threw them in my laundry basket on top of the few legitimate dirty clothes and drove to the Laundromat.

And then she wasn't there. I didn't know if I should start my load or not—was this like picking up your fork and eating before the hostess does? I decided to wait, but then it was strange how everyone else there was staring at me like I was lazy or crazy. So, I went next door to the 7-11 to get a drink and keep an eye out the window to see if Maria would show up.

I moved really slowly, tried to do some small talk with the clerk just to kill time, but eventually I had to go back and look at my laundry basket. Except now my jeans were gone.

What the fuck!

"Hey," I said to the family there reading books: a mom and young son. "Did you see anyone take my jeans out of this basket?"

The mom shook her head with a pained smile. She knows it hurts to lose your jeans. I walked around, just wondering if the jeans were still on the premises and not even sure I'd be able to positively ID them. Like a police lineup with the Levis and the poseurs. All I knew was that there had been jeans lying on top of the T-shirts and now there weren't. I knew it was my fault. Everyone knows jeans are ultimately stealable and sellable, but I was used to doing laundry in my little apartment basement where the front door is locked and you have to be buzzed in and I know all the neighbors and no one would do this.

I mentally pictured who was there before I left to get my stupid, stupid slushy drink, and tried to replay watching the parking lot out the front window. Who was the culprit? It really didn't matter.

What mattered was that I was a dupe. A double dupe. I was here trying to do laundry I didn't even need to do, for a woman who hadn't bothered to show up or call me on my cell. I grabbed my basket and threw it in my car and locked it. I left it there in the parking lot, just in case Maria showed up super late (it was 20 minutes now, at this point) so maybe she'd recognize my car from when we met before and she'd hang at the Laundromat and wait for me for a goddamn change. Meanwhile, I walked over to the Mosswood Park and sat on a swing smoking.

I could tell all the parents around weren't too psyched about a grown man sitting there lightly swinging with his cigarette going, but I had just lost my jeans and been stood up and I couldn't give a shit. One of the dads just gave me this long, bold stare like as if to say, "Move along, pedophile," but I didn't let it penetrate. No pun intended.

After two cigarettes, my mood was different. On the way back to my car, I told everyone, "Those are nice looking jeans. You look great. I'm glad you do. Everyone should wear jeans and look great."

I only said that in my head. I took my laundry home, not the girl.

Calling all Arthurs

BY STEVE CHOW

The M/B Center: I always thought
it stood for Milton Bradley
and I thought there would be
fun and games.

Actually, there was
Kick'N It for a while,
which sounds like a kind
of a game. Why did I leap

to this association? A childhood
of too many board games
and too many sisters.
But I digress.

M/B stands for MacArthur
and for Broadway.
I think a better way of referring
to it would have been "BroadArthur Center."

Or the "MacWay." McDonald's
could then subsidize the sad thing
and we'd all be better off.
But also more broad

in the waist, so really "BroadArthur"
would be the better description.
Especially if a fair percentage
of Oaklanders were named Arthur.

How many
of us
are named
Arthur?

IN NORTH OAKLAND's heyday, Idora Park brought throngs to enjoy the entertainments there starting in 1903. The amusement park was on the west side of Telegraph between 56th and 58th streets and had a figure-eight rollercoaster which traveled at 90 mph, advertised as a "race through the clouds." Idora Park offered a mock volcano eruption and also had an ostrich farm, rollerskating rink (where Charlie Chaplin won a competition one year), baseball park, opera house and dance pavilion. Celebrities who performed at Idora included Lon Chaney, Buster Keaton and Fatty Arbuckle.

Like many Oakland neighborhoods, transit was key to its growth. The streetcar line extended along Telegraph Avenue starting in 1869, making this area a suburb. Idora Park was actually built as a lure to bring real estate buyers further out from downtown. After the 1906

OAKLAND HISTORY ROOM OF THE OAKLAND PUBLIC LIBRARY

This circa 1915 poultry plant was at 6015 Shattuck Avenue.

earthquake, several thousand San Franciscans camped out at Idora Park for weeks, sleeping on cots and under blankets donated by the Realty Syndicate. Being housed in an amusement park hopefully made the disaster easier to surmount, and certainly many of those San Franciscans decided to stay permanently, causing a growth spurt for North Oakland. Idora Park closed sometime before 1929.

Nearby, the Santa Fe Tract boasted that its residents were only 28 minutes away from San Francisco, with Key Route trips every 20 minutes. The tract was located at Fifty-Fifth Street between Shattuck and Adeline. Not only did it offer Key Route service, but also access to the Santa Fe railroad and the Southern Pacific local and various electric streetcar lines passing through.

This April 1910 photograph shows the walkway to the Idora Park Theater festooned with lanterns.

This neighborhood has a connection with the Black Panther Party. In 1962, Bobby Seale and Huey Newton met at Merritt College, which was then sited at Martin Luther King, Jr. Way and 58th Street. They had been taking classes through the Afro-American Cultural Program and after getting to know each other organized a small group of Merritt students. They began as the Black Panther Party for Self Defense, the "self defense" part being a conscious move away from the nonviolent stance Martin Luther King, Jr. had advocated as well as an tribute to a Louisiana civil rights group called the Deacons for Defense. The group's Ten Point Platform and Program included a call for "decent housing, fit for the shelter of human beings," "free health care for all black and oppressed people," and for the federal government to give everyone employment, among other things. While the Party's platform was rooted in understandable anger at the state of racial affairs in America, the controversial later actions of Party members make this a deeply complex group that is difficult to label.

The Merritt College that the Black Panthers attended was formerly the University High School. Built in 1923, it now houses a senior center and the Children's Hospital Oakland Research Institute, which is working on vaccine development and other research. Merritt College moved to Leona Heights.

Nearby, the Children's Hospital began as a facility to treat those even smaller: the Baby Hospital. A nurse named Bertha Wright and a group of women wanted to create a place where all babies and children could be treated, no matter what their family's financial circumstance was. Since it was 1912 and women didn't have the vote yet, they gathered up a male Board of Directors and started fundraising. They bought land at 51st and Dover streets with an old stable on it. The women cleaned the stable of its horsiness and opened as Baby Hospital in 1914. The facility has grown enormously since then, and still offers free treatment for those who can't afford it.

The Brownie McGhee house is in this neighborhood, at 688 43rd Street. McGhee was born in Tennessee in 1915. At the age of four, he contracted polio and due to the time he spent at home recovering, he began practicing guitar. He became renowned as a guitarist in the "Piedmont-style blues" tradition, sometimes referred to as the East Coast blues, a form that originated in the American south in the 1920s. McGhee was the longtime partner of Sonny Terry, a harmonica player. In the 1950s and '60s they were important to the folk music scene. McGhee died in Oakland in 1996 at the age of 81.

Alley Cat

BY DAN HESS

Just close your eyes and you may dream
    the darkness isn't what it seems
but something lithe and loose that glides
    from tin-pan shadows to your side.
Just close your eyes and you may feel
    the midnight brush against your heel.
It's only me, I promise you
    to prowl the alleys, avenues,
where we have felt the darkness fall
    the hardest, we will walk them all.

untitled

BY ADELLE FOLEY

Early plum blossoms
On the streets of North Oakland
Announce the new year

WHERE: *Bordered by Sausal Creek, Route 13
and the Fruitvale and Dimond neighborhoods*

OAKMORE WAS simply a meadow with a great view of downtown Oakland in the distance . . . until the Leimert Bridge was built in 1926, that is. The Palo Seco Creek bed to the east (where Route 13 now runs) and the 325-foot Dimond Canyon on the northwest had effectively "stranded" the land. Building the Leimert Bridge over the Sausal Creek allowed building and development to happen.

The cement and steel bridge was designed by George Posey, who built the Posey Tube between Oakland and Alameda. It spans 357 feet and is 117 feet high, a dramatic-looking structure straddling the gorge.

OAKMORE HOMES ASSOCIATION/JOHN BOSKO

The Leimert bridge made the development of Oakmore possible. Here it is in the process of being built, 1926.

It carried the #18 streetcar across the creek, which still flows. In September 2002, city landmark plaques were placed on the bridge by the Oakland Heritage Alliance and the Oakmore Homes Association. The bridge's importance to this neighborhood cannot be underestimated. In an early real estate advertisement, it was referred to as "the Bridge that Wrought a Miracle for Oakmore Highlands."

Realtor Walter Leimert set up the subdivision of Oakmore Highlands in 1926, and the homeowners association he created is still very active today. This quaint neighborhood was once Antonio Peralta's land, from the immensely larger land grant to his father, divided between the four sons.

There were four tracts in the subdivision, and Leimert and his brother Harry took pains to match the area's natural beauty with architectural beauty. They created model homes designed by local architects Miller & Warnecke, so people could use them as a jumping point to talk with the contractors and viscerally "see" themselves living in Oakmore Highlands. One such model home, built in 1934, brought in 8,000 visitors in only three weeks, due to a partnership with the *Oakland Tribune* and Oakland's own Breuner Furniture Company to help furnish and advertise the home.

Sales were handled by tract agents Mitchell & Austin. A representative of that company told the newspaper in September 1936, "The inauguration of motor coach service in Oakmore several weeks ago by the Eastbay Transit Company has been of material aid in the advancement of this close-in subdivision. The coaches operate daily through the property and provide transfers to the Park Boulevard streetcar line." Another Mitchell & Austin ad from that year emphasized the area's wooded atmosphere yet easy access to downtown, stating that Oakmore was "for those who want quiet with convenience."

According to a Leimert Company brochure, "Homesites in Oakmore Highlands are of splendid proportions, based upon the natural contour and beauty of the property. Beauty, and not the arbitrary rule of so many front feet, forms the basis upon which the lots are plotted. Every homesite is a little bit different." The company's tract office was nestled next to the bridge on the Oakmore side, on Oakmore Drive.

The Oakmore Homes Association 1926 Declaration of Restrictions had a section devoted to the oaks that are part of the neighborhood's

OAKMORE HOMES ASSOCIATION/JOHN BOSKO

Here is the bridge with some of its first foot passengers and automobiles, undated.

name: "Before cutting down trees of any property within the jurisdiction of the Oakmore Homes Association, you should secure the approval of the Tract Committee. Before applying the axe, obtain written approval from the Association Manager."

To a Lost Friend

BY MAGDA WHITE

What are you doing now?
You are rolling an herbal cigarette
You are changing moods
You are sitting on a back stoop
regretting your life
You are thinking I am fey
to wish to bring the dead back

You yearn for your stolen toolbox
You move your beautiful fingers
You look perplexed
Sending odd postcards to me
a city away, in Oakmore, in Oakland,
you are plunging into darkness
with a brush torch in both hands.

I miss you and love you
The stars become ashes
but you know the darkness

Under the bridge

BY BRIAN TSO

Climbing down the steep patch
under the Leimert Bridge
and walking down the creekside

almost able to pretend you don't hear
the Park Boulevard traffic whizzing by
there is solace here

sit on a rock and watch for as long as you can
there's a miniature round of traffic here
bees and flies constantly on the move

water skimmers, ants with big ideas,
drifting pollen without any at all
and always water that is restless and can't

stop to talk –but I listen anyway
and still think I heard what it said

PIEDMONT AVENUE

WHERE: *This neighborhood generally stretches along
Piedmont Avenue, from the cemetery to Broadway*

A WONDERFUL brochure for the Oak Park Tract waxes rhapsodic, "It's no fancy name. There ARE oaks—big, spreading, deep-green, gnarly, old fellows—and the men, who have just divided into beautiful residence lots these wonderful grassy acres in the heart of Oakland, have left them all! Not to the venerable trunk of a single tree has the ax been laid! Wouldn't you like to live there? And listen: Right through the middle of the Tract is a little wooded stream, spanned by rustic bridges, and on each side of it run broad white boulevards. Fairyland? Oh, no—not quite!"

This 33-acre Wickham Havens tract lay to the east of Piedmont Avenue. The stream they were speaking of was Glen Echo Creek. One of the branches of this creek was called Cemetery Creek since it began as runoff from the hills behind Mountain View Cemetery. The reservoirs

Preparing the land for tracks at Howe and 40th streets, 1904.

OAKLAND HISTORY ROOM OF THE OAKLAND PUBLIC LIBRARY

in the cemetery were created by damming in the late 1800s, and the resulting creek is today alternately undergrounded and opened.

Richmond Boulevard, at the more southwesterly end of the creek, developed in the early 1900s. It benefited from Mayor Frank K. Mott's support of the City Beautiful movement. Therefore, this tiny urban street was blessed with a park, pergola, mosaic tiles and lion's head fountain. Stairways and cast-iron light standards completed the picture. In 1908, Charles Mulford Robinson, a consultant who also endorsed the City Beautiful ideal, suggested that a park be formed from Mountain View Cemetery to Lakeside Park, with Glen Echo Creek as its center. This unfortunately did not come to pass.

OAKLAND HISTORY ROOM OF THE OAKLAND PUBLIC LIBRARY

Taking care of the landscaping at Mountain View Cemetery, 1913.

The subdivision at 40th and Broadway was called Alton Park. A March 1910 advertisement for the neighborhood illustrated the morals of the day. It stated that the property could be visited on Sunday, "altho [sic] our down-town office will be closed. As a general thing we do not approve of devoting Sunday to business but realize that most business men cannot get away during the working hours and for their sake have concluded to make an exception and have the Tract Office open next Sunday."

An interesting ad for the Linda Vista Terrace subdivision plays on renters' desires. "A man rents a flat of six rooms for which he pays $35 a month. For this privilege, he has the pleasure of listening to the strenuous efforts on the piano of the budding second generation in the flat on the right; the quieting influence of the noisy thoughts of an idle fellow—the baby—in the flat on the left; and the hundred and one other sounds which to the maker are delightful but to the enforced listener , to say the least, 'lack that certain indescribable charm,' particularly when he is trying to woo Morpheus after a strenuous modern business day. At last, realizing that he is getting tired of this sort of life, he looks for a quiet home in the Hills, away from all noise and confusion. He purchases a lot for which he pays $,1500, builds a beautiful and comfortable home of seven rooms for $2,700 . . . ." Linda Vista Terrace was developed in the 1890s and was located east of Piedmont Avenue below Monte Vista Avenue.

And now we will end with those who have also ended. At the terminus of Piedmont Avenue is Mountain View Cemetery, formed in 1863 with Samuel Merritt acting as president of its association. The association hired Frederick Law Olmsted to design the grounds. Olmsted, who also designed New York's Central Park, had been dismayed by the growing trend of using graveyards as parks, and disliked the sight of picnickers spreading their baskets' contents over the bodies of those unable to protest. He planned the 200-acre cemetery to be a dignified resting zone, far enough from day-to-day traffic of the city that visiting the dead would entail a trip.

By 1867, most of the bodies from the city's former cemetery on 17th Street had been moved to Mountain View or the adjoining St. Mary's cemetery. But as an 1874 newspaper noted, the procedure had been somewhat haphazard because some people had built homes over sections of the old graveyard, complicating the relocation, and because the man in charge of the old cemetery was illiterate and there were no records of how many people were buried there.

Many well-known people are buried in Mountain View Cemetery: beloved architects Julia Morgan and Bernard Maybeck; Anthony Chabot, responsible for creating a municipal water supply for Oakland; Governor George Pardee; Mayor Samuel Merritt; Charles Crocker, one of the Big Four railroad tycoons; Frances Marion "Borax" Smith, Key Route street-car founder; Henry J. Kaiser of HMO and shipbuilding fame; and two people you'll recognize from the products which bear their names: Domingo Ghirardelli and James Folger.

Friday

BY MARGARITA SOARES

It has to be fish tacos
and then we walk down to the cemetery

where every statue is hungry
and wants our tacos

we climb the hill
until we earn the rich sauce inside

climbing away the calories
taunting the statues

and then at the summit
we open the bag

and we eat our tacos
from the Baja Taqueria

and we toast the view
(it is immense)

and we praise God
we are alive

(unlike everyone else here)
to eat these tacos

Mountain View

BY TRACY ADAMSKI

I like to wander around the dead
letting my dog sniff out
their pneumonia, their tuberculosis,
their 1918 flu, their consumption,
their syphilis, their cancers,
their death in childbed,
in childhood.

We climb to the top
where we see the huge vista
of those still living,
boats in the bay, cars flashing
on the bridge, skyscrapers
with people in them
on every floor

Breathing heavily,
we calm down and look.
Breathing slows and we are like
the statues on the hillside below,
a dog beloved enough to be sculpted,
a woman with her hand cupped
over her eyes so she can look west
without squinting, a good pose,
really, like a pioneer except for
the shorts and tank top,
short hair and sneakers.

PILL HILL

WHERE: *Roughly bounded by 34th Street,
Broadway, 27th Street and Telegraph Avenue*

THIS NEIGHBORHOOD carries a slightly humorous and certainly descriptive name. Since a cluster of various hospitals at various times sat on this hill, the pill dispensary lent its influence to the entire area.

But the name of this neighborhood was formerly Academy Hill, since so many different schools had used it. Merritt Hospital was built on the site of the Pacific Theological Seminary, and at different times the Female College of the Pacific and Hopkins Academy were there, along with the nearby St. Mary's College.

And it also once had the moniker of Blackstone Hill, because many attorneys lived there. (Blackstone was the 1700s English lawyer whose *Commentaries* were referred to when Americans drafted the Constitution and Declaration of Independence.)

The main big boy on the hill was Merritt Hospital, founded by Catherine Garcelon in accordance with the wishes of her brother, Dr. Samuel Merritt (of lake fame). When he died in 1890, he left her his

Merritt Hospital, undated.

This photo looks westerly from Pill Hill down 34th Street to Telegraph Avenue, circa 1890. On the right is the Plymouth Congregational Church.

fortune ($2 million) with the understanding that she would use it to establish the hospital. Garcelon died only 18 months after her brother, but in that short span of time she made arrangements for the hospital. Interestingly, heirs fought to have her trust declared invalid—apparently generosity didn't make it through all the branches of the family tree. The fight lasted more than a decade.

So, the delayed construction began in 1905 and was nearly finished when the 1906 earthquake destroyed major sections of the brick structure. Not only that, the blueprints were in San Francisco and burned in the fire. The next iteration was of steel frame construction, built 1907-08 and opened in 1909. That same year, the Samuel Merritt Hospital School of Nursing was opened, today's Samuel Merritt College.

The hospital was opened with space for only 36 patients, and additions and new wings were added over the years. Garcelon was a forward-thinker who provided in the original deed of trust that medical care be given free of charge to those who needed it (this was abandoned in 1955).

Originally, Garcelon wanted the hospital sited on property bounded by 13th and Oak streets and the lake, but instead property near St. Mary's College was purchased. (St. Mary's was then on Broadway in today's Auto Row, before its move to Moraga.) Thus was Pill Hill started.

Soon other hospitals followed suit by settling close by. Today's Alta Bates Summit Medical Center merges Merritt Hospital, the 1928 Peralta Hospital and the 1904 Providence Hospital, all located on Pill Hill.

Gift

BY ALAN HOWARD

When I first dragged my new scalpel across his sternum, I thought that I was pushing too hard. I had made the cut with trepidation, worried that I was going to interrupt the hard plate of a sternum underneath. He may still need it, I thought. Sarah came by, looked at my jagged handiwork and said, "You need to push a lot harder. The guys next to us just scored the bone really hard and cracked it with their knuckles." I took her advice and pushed harder than I thought I could, so hard I thought the blade would snap off and fly into my eye, blinding me. The blade didn't break and did, in fact, score the underlying bone. I cocked my fist, paused slightly in the backswing, and delivered a neat hard blow right between where the ribcage is joined. I hadn't paid attention to the fact that the guy had had open-heart surgery in the 1950s, back when they joined the two halves of a sternum with the surgical equivalent to baling wire. My fist connected with the weakened breastbone of a 94-year-old investment banker and plunged neatly into his corrected heart, resulting in a punishing spray of formaldehyde, phenol and slimy intestinal oil that squarely met my open-mouth face and panic-closed eyes. My right hand had been neatly sliced open from the bone shards of our assignment, a man we would come to call Burke.

It was our first day in cadaver lab, a moment we had all been dreaming of forever.

What Pill Hill means to me

BY HANH TRAN

A sadly haunting place for me. I have spent too much time there. You call it Pill Hill; to me it has been home. In my frail body, I have learned not to take anything for granted. I have had other people's blood in my veins; I have been so sick someone had to wash me. I have had nurses know everything about me and get upset when they switch my room while they are off work, believing when they come back the next day that I died.

I am grateful to modern medicine for keeping me alive. Only a century before this and I would be dead. What will it be like in the future? Every time I drive past, I look over and think of what I endured, what I went through. I don't sweat the small stuff anymore. I'm even glad when I'm irritated—because I lived to be able to experience all the emotions. Against all the odds.

Thank you doctors, thank you nurses, and even thank you to the people in the billing department who liked to give lots of calls to my family when I was in there. It doesn't matter. Thank you, all of you.

PRODUCE MARKET

WHERE: *Lower Franklin Street,*
between 1st and 4th streets

THERE IS something timeless about the marketing of vegetables and fruit. After all, this commerce has been around for thousands of years. Oakland's historic Produce Market District preserves this ancient art of putting the fruits of the earth into our hands.

The Wholesale Produce Market was originally started at 11th and Washington streets, but as Oakland grew it was pushed to lower Franklin Street in 1916, where it is today. Most of the buildings for the latter produce area were designed by Oakland architect Charles McCall.

One of the first produce businesses was started by Warren Rouse of Michigan in 1877, according to an issue of the Oakland Heritage

OAKLAND HISTORY ROOM OF THE OAKLAND PUBLIC LIBRARY

Produce men congregate around the Produce Exchange which Borax Smith's wife built. This 1915 photograph shows 11th and Harrison streets, looking west on 11th.

Alliance *News*. A decade later, several others had located near Rouse at 11th and Washington. Around 1903, a fire destroyed the Bacon Building at 11th and Washington, necessitating the market men's move to 11th between Webster and Harrison. Borax Smith had somewhat of a sideways hand in this, as he had his fingers in many of Oakland's other pies. His wife owned the entire block and consented to build a new Produce Exchange, tearing down an old Mills Tabernacle on the site to do so. Forty-six stores were in the building.

For a while, relations were "fruitful." An April 1903 newspaper crowed, "Oakland will possess the biggest and best equipped market edifice in this State," while another paper spun it even further the next month, "Best equipped wholesale, retail and commission house west of Chicago." The building was lit with 1,500 outdoor lights, and the May 1903 paper reported, "Illuminated as it will be tonight, the Produce Exchange will present a rare attraction. Quite different is the every morning scene when hundreds of wagons from the farms and gardens of Alameda county throng the streets adjacent to the market, bringing the day's supplies of produce."

But as development sprang up nearby, the men with their fruits and vegetables were deemed unwelcome. In 1916, City Council created an ordinance whereby the only place sidewalks could be used to display merchandise was the area bounded by Broadway, Fallon, 7th Street and the waterfront.

This area actually made much more sense to the produce men, because they would be nearer the waterfront and the rail station, allowing for convenient shipping. They incorporated the Fruit and Produce Realty Company and gathered 38 lots along Franklin between 1st and 4th streets where they built market buildings in 1916—17.

Italians were the main players in this enterprise, but a Chinese man owned Western Produce, which the OHA *News* says reflected "the importance of the Chinese in Oakland's retail produce trade, from the 19th century 'basket brigade' of San Francisco peddlers on."

The designer of the market buildings was named McCall. His father ran a grocery business on San Pablo Avenue, perhaps giving his son an insight into how produce should be displayed and stored. Those McCall buildings may be some of the best surviving examples of produce markets in the U.S. since many have been demolished over the years (like Mrs.

OAKLAND HISTORY ROOM OF THE OAKLAND PUBLIC LIBRARY

Behind the bags of potatoes, men carry on the work of the day. This is the market district, 1930.

Borax Smith's Produce Exchange). While they are not fancy, they are simple and functional. "The success of the pattern is seen in the buildings remaining virtually unchanged since the day they were built," says OHA *News*.

Tomato Journey

BY ROBERT STEELE

Imagine the simple tomato.
It is wet beneath its dry skin.
It traveled in a truck to get here.
It looked up at the sky from
the open truckbed.
And then it went to market,
where a store took it,
or a restaurant, and it went on
a new adventure.

Produce Market

BY CLARISSA METTICA

Square, solid buildings
Dirty and loud, starting their noise
early in the orange morning

Ending too early in the afternoon
All things are heavy and square
and metal and dirt and wood.

All of these things come together to clean, pack
and sell to me, to us.
Round, soft, sweet, clean fruit.
Earthy, heavy, leafy vegetables.

REDWOOD HEIGHTS

WHERE: *While the neighborhood association's official boundaries are quite specific and detailed, we can say that Redwood Heights sits below Route 13 centered around 35th Avenue/Redwood Road.*

THE HISTORY of this neighborhood is inextricably linked to the enormous trees that give the region its name. Beginning in 1840 and continuing for the next 20 years, these towering, fragrant redwoods were harvested. One tree had a 33.5-foot diameter, yet it too succumbed to the saw. A drawing in the Oakland History Room shows a perhaps apocryphal scene: a redwood stump serving as a dance floor, large enough to hold several waltzing couples and the band. And not only were they thick, they were also tall: one was used as a landmark by sailors in the bay to navigate around dangerous rocks near Alcatraz.

This sawmill on the Palo Seco Creek operated between 1849 and 1854 and was one of the first steam-powered mills in the area.

One sawmill on the Palo Seco Creek is credited with being one of the first steam-powered mills in the region. It operated between 1849 and 1854. The Palo Seco Creek still runs through Joaquin Miller Park, above Woodminster Amphitheater, a tributary of Sausal Creek.

There were, believe it or not, nine other sawmills in the area, all working furiously to render tree into lumber. One was run by waterpower. It is said that timbers from a steam-powered mill composed the home of Moses Chase, the first squatter on Peralta land (see listing for Clinton Park). The now-endangered California condor was a frequent sight for the lumbermen: reportedly in one hour, they counted 50.

Despite the birdwatching, the loggers were a rough sort (often ship deserters) who performed their own vigilante justice, lynching horse thieves and cattle rustlers (see listing for San Antonio). In 1854, a search party composed of 110 men searched the area for 25 felons who had escaped from San Quentin.

According to one account, the redwood men accused the flatlanders of stealing their oxen and threatened to burn down Oakland. At this time, circa 1852, there were many more people logging in the hills than there were living downtown. Reportedly, Horace Carpentier ended the threatening situation by settling with the men for cash.

Redwood was especially popular for building since it is resistant to rot and insect penetration. And of course, the newly burgeoning Bay Area cities needed lots of wood to build. The redwoods were rendered not only into boards but also into shingles for roofing. In place of hewn redwoods, oily, quick-growing eucalypti were planted: a decision with severe repercussions in 1991 when the hills firestorm ate the trees like they were candy.

So how did the behemoths come down, without chainsaws? Men would carve out a notch near the base of the tree and wedge a board into the notch, upon which they stood to hack away with axe and saw. It would take two men all day to cut down one tree. After stripping off the bark and branches, the tree would be cut into 16-foot lengths by drilling holes and stuffing them with dynamite. These smaller lengths were dragged by oxen to the mill and to the estuary on skid roads, which were created by greasing smaller logs.

Park Boulevard and 13th Avenue were once logging roads used to transport the logs down through Dimond Canyon to reach Brooklyn Basin.

If you're dying to see the sole remaining original redwood, you'll have to do some bushwhacking over in Leona Heights. The tree is visible from

Although not necessarily taken in Redwood Heights, this photograph from the Oakland History Room shows how an oxen team would drag the lumber. Note the huge logs and stump in the background.

the parking lot of Carl Munck Elementary School, where there is a plaque in "Old Survivor's" honor, but not too accessible. As you stare into the hillside, you'll see the stalwart nature of this tall and sturdy tree, but not necessarily a good way to get over there and commune with it.

One of the first areas to be built up in Redwood Heights was Avenue Terrace, which a subdivider's 1925 advertisement nicknamed "The Piedmont of East Oakland." Avenue Terrace stretched across the hills, giving a panoramic vista of land across the bay from San Rafael to Palo Alto. "World travellers are lavish in their praise of this magnificent marine view," continued the ad.

Sales were big that year for Avenue Terrace, such that the following year another newspaper ad made the astonishing claim that "Oakland is destined to be the New York of the Pacific Coast. During 1925, Oakland grew faster than any previous year in its history. The coming year is expected to run far, far ahead of 1925." Several of the 1925 homeowners had already sold their holdings at a profit.

Several other subdivisions emerged in the 1930s. One was Sunset Manor on upper 35th Avenue and Victor Avenue. Another was Redwood Gardens at Redwood Road and Detroit Avenue. Redwood Gardens can consider itself a literary, moneyed tract, for the first Western inhabitants were a playwright named Oliver Morosco and then, building on the site of Morosco's mansion, a banker named Carlston.

Dunn Trail

BY CONSTANCE CALLAHAN

The slam of the car door echoes weirdly in the parking lot. I'm not the first one here; there's a green pickup over by the corral. The dog whines anxiously until I open the back door and he bounds out onto the pavement. I snap the leash to his collar; he submits with poor grace.

Cars pass by on Skyline Drive, whip-whip-whipping to the light at Redwood Road and from there down the hill to the unenviable drive across the Bay Bridge. From here I could just see San Francisco if it were clear, but instead the fog drapes low over the tree tops, creeping down the canyon walls on both sides of the ridge.

The first half-mile of my run is a grind, uphill in the cold, stiff muscles protesting and the dog trying to mark every stump and post along the way. This gravel path is heavily used, the surface uncertain and eroded from the winter rains. It hasn't rained recently, and I'm thankful: mud makes this trail hard on the uphills and dangerous on the downhills.

I hit the top of the first rise and settle into an easier jog, taking my time. The point isn't speed, and the dog is too old for a race anyway. From here the trail loops along the edge of the canyon, snaking ever inward into the park. The ground falls away sharply to my right, the thistle edging the trail giving way to manzanita and other scrub. On my left the canyon wall climbs up, spotted with laurel and pines, but some of the brush nearest the trail is poison oak, so I keep the dog close to my side.

At the junction I go left, and start climbing again, a little more easily now that I've warmed up. After a few hundred yards the dog perks up, ears cocking, and I pull him closer to me, still on the leash. It's a wise move: three horseback riders pass me on their way downhill, hips rolling with the horses' long strides. I've heard horror stories about off-leash dogs attacking horses; although I'm pretty sure my dog never would, it's good not to test him. I keep him on a short leash as we continue, and eventually he settles down.

The trail narrows, and the trees close over it, keeping the air moist. Redwoods and Douglas firs fill my view, the surface of the trail is soft with fallen needles, and I get to go downhill a bit as the trail dips and loops sharply to the right.

Then it's another climb, and man, I'd really like to stop and rest, but I know that this is the worst of it, the hardest part; I slow down almost to a walk, and keep moving, panting hard, the sweat sticking my shirt to my back. My hands feel funny, I'm squeezing them into fists: I try to shake my arms and shoulders out while still moving too slowly uphill.

The trail tops out by a picnic area: if I go straight, I'll find myself at another parking lot. Instead I follow the switchback around, almost 180 degrees, and take a break to breathe. Here, I walk in slow circles, inhaling and exhaling, rolling my head from shoulder to shoulder. There's a muddy patch on the trail marked by the prints of running shoes and another dog's tracks. I wonder if I'll see them, whoever they are, or if they're already home, drinking coffee in a sunny kitchen window.

My pulse slows, and it's time to start running again. This is the part I like best of the entire run: here, the trail runs straight and wide, an avenue dropping slowly off the ridgeline, bordered by stately eucalyptus. In the summer, it's shaded from the sun; in the winter it's dangerously slick from the fallen leaves, but I love the view of the hills through the trees, and the smell of the eucalyptus and the laurels.

What was this countryside like before Europeans arrived, I wonder, as I start down at an easy lope. No eucalyptus, no thistle; tall pines and red-woods covered these hills, and instead of fire roads there were game trails and tribal trading routes. A jet growls overhead, but from here, deep in the park, I can see no cars, no highway, no houses—just trees, trail, and the occasional deer track.

I'm only halfway through my run. The sun glints through the trees, laying tiger-stripes on the path before me. I let myself move a little faster, arms and legs swinging easily. It's still early, I'm breathing well, and the dog leans against the leash. I unclip him, open up my stride, and let gravity take over, until I'm galloping downhill.

The dog dashes ahead, kicking up dust as he runs. All I hear is my own breathing, the jingle of his tags, the thump of my feet slapping against the ground. I feel like I could run like this forever. The sweat cools between my shoulders, the sun blinds my eyes at every second step, and it's so easy, I could be flying.

I could be flying.

The Giving Trees

BY RUSSELL YEE

Five miles and fifteen minutes from downtown Oakland, I'm standing alone in a redwood forest, about halfway up a steep hillside. The only sounds I hear are the chatter of birds, the wind in the trees, and a creek splashing far below. The canopy of branches high above bathes everything around me in dappled shade. It rained yesterday, so the forest floor is glistening and fresh. At first glance, other than the trail I'm on, nothing I see—the trees, the huckleberry bushes, the wild ginger and sword ferns—tells me humans have been here. But then I notice that all the redwoods are unnaturally uniform in age, all fairly young for the species, maybe a century old or less, and crowded in clumps. Someone has been here. Something happened.

And the Lord God made all kinds of trees grow out of the ground . . . . In the middle of the garden were the tree of life and the tree of the knowledge of good and evil.—Genesis

Before the 19th century, about two million acres of virgin coast redwoods stood in California, about four times the area of Alameda County. These trees stood in six major "islands," all within reach of the coastal fogs. The most southerly island was a thin archipelago along the Santa Lucia range from above San Simeon almost up to Monterey. The next island north was the much wider belt starting from above Watsonville, overspreading the Santa Cruz mountains (including Big Basin, which in 1902 became the very first California State Park) and up the Peninsula.

Across the Golden Gate was the third island, from the slopes of Mt. Tamalpais almost to the top of Marin County and scattered eastward into Napa County. This third island includes the most heavily-visited stand of virgin redwoods by far: Muir Woods National Monument, personally saved in 1907 by Congressman William Kent from flooding as a reservoir.

Continuing north, the fourth and fifth islands make up the Redwood Empire, each larger than all the others combined. The fourth was the great belt from the Russian River to the Lost Coast, where Highway 1 heads inland. Much of it is no longer even forested, having been logged and cleared for pastures, farmland, and vineyards. Some beautiful but small virgin stands remain in a handful of State Parks and Reserves, mostly along Highway 128.

The fifth and greatest belt is from the bottom of Humboldt County up to just over the border with Oregon, which now includes Humboldt Redwoods State Park (with the largest intact stand of virgin trees), Redwood National Park (with several of the world's tallest known trees), and the now-famous Headwaters Forest (with the last large stand of virgin trees to have been in private hands). There the abundant rainfall but still moderate temperatures combine to produce redwoods in their greatest glory, with many large, pure stands, and many trees in the finest groves exceeding 300 feet tall.

The sixth island virgin redwoods was tiny compared to the other five. Covering about five square miles, this stand began in the westward-facing valleys of Palo Seco Creek and Leona Creek in the Oakland hills, covered a mile or so of the skyline, and filled the valley that is now the heart of Redwood Regional Park plus a few small groves in upper Chabot Regional Park. It also filled the northeast-facing slopes of the valley of upper San Leandro Creek from just above what is now the town of Canyon to just below the intersection of Pinehurst and Canyon Roads. Some early Spanish maps called this stand "Palos Colorados" ("Ruddy Timber"). Along with fully 96% of the original two million acres of virgin redwoods in California, 99.999% of the Palos Colorados are now gone, first cut in the 1830s by European nationals, then logged off in earnest by Americans from about 1846 to 1860.

The 0.001% is a solitary virgin tree in Leona Heights Park in Oakland. To see it, drive up Redwood Road and turn right on Campus Drive towards Merritt College. Turn left into the parking lot of Carl Munck Elementary School. There, a plaque points the way, across the valley, to "Old Survivor." It's grizzly, shaggy, misshapen, not a tree that ever thrived. It survives precisely because it's perched precariously on a steep, rocky slope, because it has had a hard life and so is not very big for its age (currently about 440 years, based on a 1969 core ring count).

As with the Chinese under Mao, sometimes it pays to be poor. Along with the Jack London Oak in front of City Hall, and the 64 palms on Ninth Avenue, Old Survivor has the honor of being a City of Oakland Landmark Tree. It's certainly the oldest tree in Oakland and probably for quite some distance around, dating back to the time of Elizabeth I and the middle of the Ming Dynasty. It stood when Sir Francis Drake became the first European to land somewhere around here, and it stood two centuries later when the early Spanish expeditions first mapped the Palos Colorados. It stood while Junípero Serra's missions were planted and when they declined, while the Californios enjoyed their brief season of glory, and on through the Bear Flag Republic, the Gold Rush, statehood, the arrival of the Transcontinental Railroad, the coming of cars, two World Wars, and the building out of the eastshore cities. And it still stands, our one witness to the time before our time, our one and only truly ancient local denizen.

The remaining trees of the forests will be so few that a child could write them down.—Isaiah

I love big, old trees. They humble and inspire me, having survived and thrived for so much longer than my life, so very much longer than any of my problems. Like gothic cathedrals and old-world cities, old trees humble the individual because they exist on a time-scale far greater than any individual. For America, ancient forests and other natural wonders were also the splendid consolations of a continent that had no Coliseum, no Versailles, no Vatican, no castles, no pyramids, no Great Wall. Big, old trees are our living connection to the distant past and a towering presence in the here and now. John Steinbeck called redwoods "ambassadors from another age." The rest of us are merely passing through. Such trees inhabit a splendid world quite beyond the realm of human accomplishment or ability. No amount of money can create a great tree in place. It takes sunlight, rain, air, the divine spark of life, and far more time than any one of us has been given in this life.

And California is arborally blessed. Garcí Ordóñez de Montalvo's chivalric fantasy *Las sergas de Esplandián* (1498) imagined our eponymous Queen Califia and her she-race of Amazonian giants joining in a siege of Constantinople. As it turned out, there were giants in the land: trees. California is graced with the world's tallest, most massive, and oldest trees— making them the tallest, most massive, and oldest living things on earth.

And the largest coast redwoods ever measured may have actually stood in our hills. In an 1893 article in *Erythea* (then the organ of the UC Berkeley Botany Department), Dr. William P. Gibbons reported the results of his post-mortem on the Palos Colorados. What is astonishing were his measurements of the larger stumps he found: many from 12 to 22 feet in diameter, one averaging 30 feet without bark (nearly the cross-section of the Campanile), and a prodigious triple-trunk that had merged to yield 57 feet of solid wood. Since no currently living coast redwood exceeds 26 feet in diameter it's hard to know what to make of such dimensions. While it is much warmer here than up north and there's more sunlight, our hills are much drier than places where the largest redwoods grow today. This is one of the mysteries—and one of the heartaches—left for us to ponder.

The cedars in the garden of God could not rival it, nor could the pine trees equal its boughs, nor could the plane trees compare with its branches— no tree in the garden of God could match its beauty.—Ezekiel

As lumber, coast redwood is immensely useful and workable: straight-grained, lustrous, famously durable, readily accessible, and long available in gigantic quantities. "As timber the Redwood is too good to live," complained John Muir, bitterly. By the final decades of the 20th century, only four percent of the virgin stands remained, with well under half a percent still in private hands. That smallest fraction of original old growth is what all the fighting was about: Earth First!, 1990's Redwood Summer, Charles Hurwitz, Maxxam, Pacific Lumber, Judi Bari, Woody Harrelson, Butterfly's Tree Luna, Forests Forever, and all the rest.

But the fight came far too late for the Palos Colorados. They were gone before the Sierra Club or Save-the-Redwoods League, before photography, before state or national parks, before anyone knew just how thinly our beneficence of forest stretched, how quickly it could disappear, or how much its loss would be lamented.

It's hard to now imagine several hundred loggers speaking a handful of European languages roaming the Oakland hills, felling the giant trees, burning, blasting and sawing them to pieces, hauling them with oxen down to the waterfront, haggling over their price—all only a century and a half ago. I get dismayed just thinking about the sheer physical effort it took. But for these loggers, many of them ship-jumpers and disappointed gold-seekers, taking a profit by squatting on others' land was irresistible.

Those others were Antonio Peralta, Joaquín Moraga and the public, who held the San Antonio, Moraga, and middle sections of the redwoods respectively. In our moral accounting, we Americans didn't think it right that a few Californios should enjoy the good life on immense, mostly undeveloped pieces of land. Land is to be used: logged, cleared, ranched, farmed, subdivided, sold, paved—whatever. It couldn't just be. It was immoral for profit not to be taken in whatever way possible and as quickly as possible.

They will chop down her forest, dense though it be. They are more numerous than locusts, they cannot be counted.—Jeremiah

The trees were not the only things stolen. From the Ain't Nothing New file comes this diary entry from one Joseph Lamson of Maine, who stayed in the Oakland hills in 1854.

> My neighbor, Mr. R., has lost an ox. It was stolen; and a horse stolen also. Another neighbor, Mr. A., has lost three valuable oxen in the same way . . . . [there are] too many inducements to the numerous idlers and vagabonds that prowl about the land to be visited; and consequently theft, robbery, and I may almost add, murder are but every day occurrences.

(Of course, most of the livestock had originally been stolen from the Californios.) It was the wild, wild west, set in a redwood forest. Only, in the end, it was the forest itself that was driven out of town.

When Alameda County was formed in 1853, its boundary with Contra Costa County included a very careful jog dividing the redwoods in half. By then there were upwards of 450 lumbermen who needed to be divided into equitable voting precincts. But the need didn't last long. The Contra Costa County redwood precinct was abolished in 1857 and the Alameda County one in 1860. By then, only a sea of stumps remained in the San Antonio, middle, and Moraga redwoods that had made up the Palos Colorados. It was long thought that not a single virgin tree had been spared until Old Survivor was discovered in 1969 by Oakland Park Naturalist Paul Covel.

Arborgenocide. Dendroholocaust. The first clearcut of an entire virgin forest in California. The destruction of a whole population, not for reasons of hatred, only reasons of gain and greed. When a forest suffers so, whose loss is it? Wherein is the offence? Who is there to forgive? Who can do the forgiving?

By your messengers you have heaped insults on the Lord. And you have said, "With my many chariots I have ascended the heights of the mountains,

the utmost heights of Lebanon. I have cut down its tallest cedars, the choicest of its pines. I have reached its remotest heights, the finest of its forests."
—Isaiah

There is no turning back the clock. Of course I would bring the trees back if I could . . . but to do so might preclude my own life. So many of the advantages I've enjoyed—a first-world standard of living, access to world-class education, and work that is greatly removed from any worry of day-to-day survival—are possible only because of the wealth that has been created on this land. (My ancestors didn't come here for the natural wonders.) In just a few generations after the Gold Rush, European and American settlers and an assortment of immigrants of color had prospered here and built the growing new towns and cities that became a destination of hope for my grandparents, an eagerly embraced alternative to the chaos, crowding, and abject poverty of southern China early last century. Here, met by exploitation, indifference, curiosity, hatred, opportunity, and kindness, they lived out their wholly transplanted lives. Here they set into motion the events that led to my own life, a life that is surely blessed even far beyond the hopes they brought to these shores. Without the wealth that was created on this land, I would not be here, and not be near these trees both living and gone that so inspire me.

So I can't fully begrudge the settlers who took and changed this land. Yes, they could have been more respectful of the Ohlones and the Californios, less bent on their Get Rich Quick efforts, and earlier to recognize the enduring value of unspoiled natural wonders for coming generations. But many of them had to worry about survival—about having food to eat and a place to live—in ways I've never had to. Contemplating big trees is pretty high on Maslow's pyramid. Perhaps I'm the one who needs to be forgiven, for taking for granted the debt I owe them for their choices and efforts, from which I benefit so greatly. And for standing in some untraceable line of benefit, however long and indirect, to the cash and construction value of the trees that once were here.

In the end the very species that first brought depredations to these redwoods will, it would seem, ensure the forest's survival. In 1928, the Save-the-Redwoods League intervened to preserve the "Hights" around Joaquin Miller's estate. The City of Oakland eventually acquired it to help assemble today's 512-acre Joaquin Miller Park. That park, upper

Dimond Park, and Leona Heights Park include most of the former San Antonio stand. In 1939, the 1,494 acres that would become the bulk of Redwood Regional Park were acquired from the East Bay Municipal Water District by the still-new (and still breathtakingly foresightful) East Bay Regional Park District. That preserved the former middle stand. The former Moraga stand is now mostly EBMUD watershed lands extending south and west from the town of Canyon, between Pinehurst Road and Redwood Regional Park. Thus, the former Palos Colorados in substantially all its original range is free to continue regenerating a forgiveness forest. Somehow, we found it in ourselves to not turn it into housing, highways, farms, or rangeland.

In my native boosterism I revel in the daydream that the world-famous Oakland Redwoods are still standing, far greater than Muir Woods, perhaps even including the World Champion Redwood. I daydream that as a cable car mounts the crest of one of those overbuilt hills across the Bay, the knowing tourist could look eastward and see the mightiest sylvan skyline of any city in the world. What a treasure that could have been! For now we have our forest of memory, of contention, of preservation. We agonize over who benefits and who loses over the fate of trees we did not create and did not grow. And if so inclined, we lament what was once in the hills overlooking what became our home.

Wail, O pine tree, for the cedar has fallen; the stately trees are ruined! Wail, oaks of Bashan; the dense forest has been cut down!—Zechariah

I'm thankful I wasn't born a century earlier, when the slopes above my city Oakland were still denuded and the ugly scars of clearcutting were still open and bleeding. I envy those who will come of age here two and three centuries from now, who will once again have an ancient forest by which to contemplate their lives.

That is, barring some cataclysmic environmental disaster or societal collapse that leaves the trees vulnerable again. It's only been one and a half centuries since the forest began falling. What will life be like a hundred years from now? Two? Five? Another millennium? Some of these same trees could still be standing then. But by then, who knows if our civilization will have fallen and another taken its place. Perhaps some distant descendant of mine will write this very same essay in another century, after a new era of war, pestilence, and migration takes its toll on these trees. Another season of offence; another occasion for forgiveness.

Meanwhile, the trees reach for the sky, drink up each year's rain, endure each year's summer drought, crowd and push against each other, teeter and fall when they lose their balance, and sprout and send up new growth. The forest forgives. God, who made the forest, forgives. And I am learning to forgive.

On each side of the river stood the tree of life . . . . And the leaves of the tree are for the healing of the peoples.—Revelation

ROCKRIDGE

WHERE: *Along College Avenue and Broadway from Alcatraz Avenue to 51st Street. Upper Rockridge curls up along the north side of the Claremont Country Club along Broadway Terrace.*

THIS WAS once the property of Horatio Livermore, who was the first to build a house there. Livermore's wife named the region after a very big boulder in the area that was once worthy of summiting. Many picnickers and horse riders used the rock as a destination point. It is located near the corner of Glenbrook and Bowling Drive in Claremont Pines, but due to grading is no longer impressive and is nearly hidden by vegetation. "Most of this landmark has been blasted away," said Livermore's daughter to the newspaper, reminiscing in 1954, "but a portion of it still remains."

The "rock" of Rockridge provided a destination for picnickers and horse riders.

When the Livermores settled, there were no other buildings for miles. Horatio's brother Charles owned surrounding property but lived with Horatio's family. "My father, who was always doing the unusual thing, decided to move our home to the present site of the Claremont Country Club," said Livermore's daughter. And "moving the home" didn't refer to moving the items and furnishings: it referred to repositioning the house itself. That home burned sometime during World War I.

The Livermores planted eucalypti, pine and cedar on the property, and pastured stock on the current grounds of the Claremont Country Club. Around 1900, they began selling off the land. The first portion of the estate went to the Claremont Country Club, which opened in 1904; another (including the land where their home sat before its move) to banker Philip E. Bowles, who bought 58 acres between Acacia and the Claremont Country Club; and the third part to Rock Ridge Properties to develop.

In 1906, Laymance Real Estate company opened up the tract, taking three years to lay out the streets and prepare the area. There were three subdivisions: Rockridge Place, bordering Broadway; Rockridge Park, in the hills to the east; and Rockridge Terrace, the highest point, part of which is now Claremont Pines. As the land increased in elevation, so did it too in minimum house prices. In order to preserve the flavor of the neighborhood, the developers made lot buyers promise to spend a particular amount in building their homes.

A June 1910 ad for Rock Ridge Place emphasizes the exclusivity of the neighborhood: "Not for every Tom, Dick and Harry. Not for every man who has the price to purchase a lot. There is a line drawn very distinctly. Rock Ridge Place is a home for people who have the same ideals. Apartments, flats, double houses, houses in the rear and so forth will not be allowed. Orientals and colored people will not be allowed in Rock Ridge Place except as servants. Your home is protected. And your family is protected." In this ad, land could be bought for $20-$30 a front foot—if you met the criteria.

The white gates topped with spheres are a well-known entrance to the property at Broadway and Rockridge Boulevard. Walter Reed created them. His brother Fred E. Reed, whose tract office was located just inside those gates, was subdivision manager for Laymance Real Estate Company.

Gentlemen talk outside the Fred E. Reed tract office, circa 1910.

"We determined to build Rockridge to an ideal. Not a near-ideal— but absolutely as near as we could conceive it," said Fred Reed. Laymance provided transportation to potential buyers from as far away as Sacramento. Reed's efforts paid off: On the first day of sales, he sold $186,000 worth of lots.

All those people moving into the neighborhood needed a place to read. Rockridge's original library was located at the corner of Miles and College avenues– where BART parking is today. Further up College, a mining family named the Treadwells lived where California College of Arts and Crafts now is; the Treadwell mansion is a city landmark still on the campus.

The Big Build

BY GARY TURCHIN

From Gary's Montclarion *column "There There"*
in October 2001, describing the building of a new
community playground

If you didn't make it to FROG's Big Build at Hardy Park this past week you surely missed something special. I showed up Saturday expecting to find a few dozen hearty souls banging nails but found instead hundreds of busy-bee workers and the play structure rising like a great wooden ship. It was, and still is, a remarkable event. Community being a community in the old fashioned sense, a barn raising where the barn is a playhouse of quirky delight. Words are inadequate to evoke.

Across the field toddlers rubbed long screws in soap bars to make them easier to drill. Slightly older kids sanded wooden animal cutouts. Workers of all ages wheel barreled in gravel to level the ground. Extension cords crossed and criss-crossed from one end of the park to another. We shared drills and jigsaws, rasps and hammers, shovels and rakes. We waited patiently when someone doing their job was in our way. Then they waited patiently for us. Need a tool? Sign one out from the tool shed. Hungry? We were fed like kings and queens. Lunch, dinner, snacks, treats; there was no end.

And the structure grew.

College kids came down from Cal. High schoolers from College Prep and Oakland High and Tech and elsewhere. Crews of fireman pitched in. Oaklanders from neighborhoods across the city joined the fray. Camaraderie was the order of the week. No one seemed in a big hurry, but everyone worked. When it got dark, they turned the bright lights on and the work continued.

And the structure grew.

There was time to pose, smile for the cameras. Document the history. In a patch of dirt, under a freeway, in a lost corridor of Oakland a park bloomed.

And not just a park—an imaginative, complex, creative, amorphous, delectable, delicious play structure worthy of a second, third, or even fourth childhood. Hey, neighbor—grow down! And get down and help this weekend for phase two at Redondo Park. Don't do it to help anyone else. Do it to help yourself. It's that kind of experience. Trust me.

"It's better than anything we dreamed," Theresa Nelson, one of the forces behind the project, told me, beaming. "It's worth all the hard work, all the frustrations, all the time away from my family."

Steve Costa, FROG's chairman, wore a smile like a proud papa the whole day. Over 800 people had signed up, but maybe more than that actually showed up over the days. The experience was bigger than the build. Bigger than the park. An affirmation of life itself.

"Amazing, isn't it?" Councilwomen Jane Brunner glowed. A few weeks ago, Jane presented a check for $125,000 from her discretionary account to the project, a sum equal to her whole year's allotment. Her reward: last week she was redistricted out of the assembly district she is running for. With friends like that in the Capital, who needs enemies? "Just goes to show, politics is a nasty business," she said, before grabbing a shovel and getting into the work at hand.

Jane has, by the way, rented a house a few blocks from her home of 25 years and is still making the run. On Monday she dragged the likes of Harry Edwards and George Musgrove down to the build to see what true city managers can get done without the crock and bull of bureaucracy and turf wars. Here's wishing the likes of those two, along with the rest of the administration, would get their hands a little dirty and pitch in. This is how a great city really gets built.

On Sunday, busy with my life but following the news of war, I found myself drawn back to Hardy Park. Not to work, but just to gaze, measure the progress. The spiral-tube slide was in, the climbing bars, the super-web, the cement frog in the sand box was taking shape, the fences were mostly picketed. With the bone-chilling reality of war darkening my spirit, Hardy Park was aglow like a warm campfire. Rubbing my hands in the heat of good people doing good work for no reason other than it's the right thing to do.

And still the despair of bombing and terror hung over me. How can people be both so good and so bad? How can the same world that builds and drops techno-bombs build silly train cabooses and crooked climbing structures? How can the same species that designs and carries out terror-izing mass-murder also design and build such glorious, inspired frivolity? The head reels with incomprehension. Focus on the good, I tell myself. Warm my hands in the deeds of the righteous. Pitch in. Be all I can be. Choose life. Build, build, build.

The Initiation

BY THOMAS NASH

Little did our friends know, what was in store for them, as we began
to descend down the slippery path, that lead to the underworld of
darkness
and haunting echoes.

My brother was always first into the pitch black, and I was glad
as always that he was taking the lead. It is an eerie feeling to lose
your primary navigational sense.

We were going to travel for miles under the city, in a vast network
of storm drains, without any light, relying totally on our lead scout.

Everyone walked silently, with extreme concentration, as to avoid
falling into the rushing water.

I always went second in line, in anticipation of what came next.

After a half hour or so of tense, slow walking, our fearless leader
would break into a horrifying dead run, with myself following awk-
wardly behind.

This left those too scared to run blind into the void
more alone than they had ever been.

Later, walking home, the tapping of my brother's white cane
reminded me of the disabling unknown that I had just been led out of.

On other non-initiation jaunts into that underworld, we would take
our journey befittingly during the night, without candles or flashlight.

I would set my alarm for two in the morning, to make sure my parents
didn't hear my brother and I leap out of my bedroom window
into the thick ivy ten feet below.

We would scamper, giggling, up one of the many stairway paths
that ran between the winding streets of the Oakland hills, all alone,
free in our own nocturnal playground.

Often, on the way to our below-the-city entrance, we would stop
at a neighbor's open garage and raid their freezer for something
to cook-up in the underworld.

I distinctly remember scalding the roof of my mouth, on a bite
of berry pie that we tried to cook on a fire. Half of the pie
was still cold and the other half burnt.

Then there was frozen chicken-on-a-stick, blackened on the outside,
icy-raw in the middle, with charcoal baked potatoes.

Although definitely not gourmet, these primitive meals in the dancing
shadows were a delight.

Sometimes traveling down one of the various tunnels that ran
towards the bay, we would up-periscope to determine our location.

At the top of a small tunnel leading straight up, with a built-in ladder
on the side, there would be a manhole cover.

Climbing to the top, hoping to avoid any large hairy black spiders,
I would listen intently for cars. When it seemed that the coast
was clear, I would cautiously push up the cover and peek around.

If the sky seemed like it was close to daybreak, we would crawl out,
replacing the cover and then walk home.

Hopefully we would get a short nap before the start of our daylight
world, which seemed somewhat bland compared to the dark
unknown of our dual reality.

Upper Rockridge: A Personal History

BY ANNA EDMONDSON

I live in a part of the Oakland hills that is below Montclair and above Rockridge, a California hybrid of the city and the 'burbs. Here I can get my jazz fix at Yoshi's downtown but return to the coziness of birdsong, tall trees and meandering hilly streets— without having to enter a tunnel, take a long commute, or make a wrong turn into a bland cul-de-sac of three-car garages and symmetrical gardens. I can see downtown Oakland, San Francisco, and Berkeley from almost every major intersection. I can feel the easterly winds and smell the salty air from the San Francisco Bay. I can hike in the woods ten minutes uphill, and shop at the Berkeley Bowl ten minutes downhill.

It is a curious juxtaposition of elements: beautiful wildlife and dangerously fast car traffic, elderly singles and families with newborns, the "old" neighborhood rubbing shoulders with the newer Fire Zone. The latter part of our neighborhood boasts multi-million dollar homes, haphazard architecture, buried infrastructure, and tiny gardens with young trees. I live in the older part, the "pre-fire" zone. Its homes are smaller, older, the trees taller and greener, the sky still crisscrossed with overhead wires. At times it feels like someone's sci-fi fantasy of two neighborhoods spliced together from different places in time and space.

* * *

It was 1996. My visiting mother saw the sketch on the real estate sheet lying on the kitchen table of the dark-shingled house we were renting in Berkeley. "Go see this one; it looks interesting," she ordered, sure as a Polish priest. First I looked down at the rendering of the Cape-Cod style house built in 1937 and its Oakland hills address. Then I looked at her, my right eyebrow raised, skeptical. "This house has great potential," she said. "And besides, we artists have good instincts."

"What does 'Upper Rockridge' mean anyway?" I wondered, reading the sheet more closely. I knew of Montclair and Rockridge. But Upper Rockridge? Who names a neighborhood "upper" anything? Where was this mysterious, other part of Rockridge that suggested a higher realm?

The phrases describing the house caught my attention: "needs a little love" and "good public elementary school." A fixer-upper would be okay. The school thing—well—my child was so young still, I did not really understand the importance of a good neighborhood school. But our agent did. I kept hearing her voice in the back of my head repeating the phrase "location, location, location." After our umpteenth house, she was ready to close a deal and move on. She chimed in with my mother and said "Go!"

I drove up Broadway Terrace above the dense flat stretch of little Craftsman-style bungalows, sidewalks, and shops of Rockridge, past a wide expanse of undulating, manicured golf turf which I had never seen before, thinking "How odd! How suburban!" Perturbed, I moved on, past the fenced golf green, past a tall stand of towering Eucalyptus, up Clarewood Drive. The rising landscape turned into swaths of Live Oak, Cedar, Monterey Pine and Yellow Broom brush marking the northern boundary of the Oakland cemetery. Amazed, I spotted a doe grazing delicately on the cemetery's hillside, sweet and watchful.

I finally approached the wide intersection of Harbord Drive and Florence Avenue, the view telescoping onto an image of sorry neglect: motorcycle parts in the cracked driveway, an empty oil can, peeling paint, crab grass and untrimmed junipers. This was the correct address, I noted, checking the real estate sheet on my lap.

Inside the 1937 house I took in the old carpets covering wide-plank oak wood floors, valances covering big windows, linoleum, an architectural spiral of split-level floors and many rooms recalling a by-gone era of dinner parties and Friday afternoon martinis. I could feel the previous owner's life still in the house. There had had been some really good times —the faded heavy silk curtains in the living room, the old bar in the converted basement apartment—before the downhill slide into divorce and near-foreclosure. I was told three generations had lived here. The house had been worked hard, had survived an earthquake or two, and still its foundation held firm. A scavenger at heart, I liked the idea of giving something well worn a new life.

Back outside, I imagined my cottage garden instead of the crabgrass and junipers that prevailed, envisioning natives, lavender and ornamental grasses instead of the ivy that clung to the hillside. In the late morning sunlight I walked the neighborhood and took mental notes: bird song, clear sky, eerily quiet streets interrupted by the periodic rush of cars zooming around corners, lawn mowers and leaf blowers, dog walkers, a few children, and old people. I saw the clearly-delineated Fire Zone one block above, along Proctor Avenue, and the smaller '30s and '60s-era homes below. There was St. Theresa's Catholic church, school and playground, First Church of Religious Science (both parking lots overflowing on Sundays), St. Mary's High School, Hillcrest Elementary School, Aurora School, the Oakland cemetery, and Village Market.

As I walked further upward along the winding roads, I turned to look westward and was reassured to see as far north as Richmond and the Campanile at UC Berkeley, the hills dotted with terra cotta tops of houses, as far west as Marin and the Golden Gate Bridge, and south toward downtown Oakland and San Francisco across the bay. Not only were the views beautiful, they were important to me.

I grew up with the notion that the city symbolized cultural and economic progress, that it was where people from all over came to start new lives or improve on old ones. The city was where differences of ethnicity, culture and lifestyle were at the very least tolerated and sometimes embraced, where class differences were less apparent than in the suburbs. I had lived in cities all my life: Santiago, Quito, D.C., New York, Port-au-Prince, Berkeley and Oakland. If I was going to live in a suburban enclave of the city, I needed to be able to see that city every day. Not having lived in the true suburbs, they made me anxious. This neighborhood had its suburban elements: the country feel, the open space, the larger houses, a mostly white population, but this too seemed to be changing. We decided to take it: the house, the neighborhood and all.

During our first year, our son still small enough to sit in a stroller, I walked the streets for exercise. I barely knew anyone still. Most couples worked during the day and had babysitters. I was in the minority of stay-at-home mothers. The silence of those morning walks, punctuated by the random assault of a lone leaf blower blasting into the air, drew me into dark chasms of ambivalence and isolation. I looked at my watch way too many times during the day wondering if we'd made the right decision.

Yet my mood would be buoyed by natural discoveries such as a secret trail of Redwoods along a wet ravine below Amy Street's western end, extending down to Moraga Avenue. The first signs of plum blossoms in mid-February conjured images of geisha promenading in Kyoto. Bored, but with a vivid imagination, I took as inspiration a series of stunning neighborhood gardens and started my own garden design business. My mother, also an excellent gardener, would brainstorm garden ideas over the phone, long distance from D.C., her voice hinting at envy of our mild weather and vastly long bloom periods.

We had a second child. Years went by. We befriended our nearest neighbors, shopped at Village Market and Broadway Terrace Nursery, renovated our house, enrolled our children in Hillcrest, and hopped on Moraga Avenue and Highway 13 to go downtown or out-of-town. Having spent the years before homeownership living and working overseas, we had begun to sink in roots. We finally unpacked our stored boxes from the three-year stay in Thailand, sorted through old college textbooks and papers, tossing and sorting each spring. My husband launched a business in our makeshift home-office. Five people worked in one room for three years straight until he found an office in an old Oakland warehouse.

I continued to take walks and soak up the details. I noticed houses of every imaginable style, some appealing and fanciful, others not to my liking, as if someone had the grand design to create a neighborhood evoking architectural tolerance as a civic virtue. Other young families moved into the neighborhood, a few with teenagers, most with very young children buying their first homes from the older generation who were moving on. Upper Rockridge was an extension of the old but hallmarking the new, of shifting demographics, lifestyles and building trends. In eight short years, our neighborhood had become one of newcomers and frequent for-sale signs.

In 2002, when our two sons were enrolled in elementary school, something interesting happened: My neighborhood had become part of the digital world. Most of the school's parent community had been fully online for at least a year or two. I had acquired a portable laptop computer with wireless Internet access, which allowed me to cook dinner and check emails at the same time. My own schoolyard acquaintances with parents were evolving into friendships online. An initial email discussion about after-school art programs would become a deeper exchange of ideas and walks in the woods.

Our pace of life quickened and my old feelings of neighborhood isolation gave way to a new connectedness. Emails zipped back and forth among the parent-teacher community about the kids, school policy, friendships, and interests that extended beyond our identities as parents and homeowners. What could have become a gossiping small-town culture somehow failed to materialize. I would like to think that it had something to do with our community's connection to the greater world "out there," to the city and beyond.

In more recent times, neighborhood safety issues—something taken for granted—began to emerge after a spate of robberies. Neighborhood e-boards cropped up, keeping us in the loop about robberies and police response. Political e-boards communicated various viewpoints on election events, and so on. A sense of community beyond the physical had emerged. That earlier feeling of physical and social isolation no longer predominated. I had finally become part of the neighborhood.

* * *

These days, my sons are now old enough to play on the edge of the street. Cars and the occasional bus, upon which we depend for access to just about everything, rush down our local streets like scary metal death boxes causing near-misses and frequent accidents. I am forced to be vigilant. I struggle with the push and pull of keeping my children safe and teaching them freedom. Sometimes my rules seem restrictive; other times they seem too dangerously free. I encourage my children to play outside but find myself driving them to play dates only blocks away.

I succumb to the deceptive comforts of this semi-suburban city enclave: I shop at Village Market for barbecue and drive mere minutes to get anywhere thanks to Highway 13. My conscience keeps track. Months go by when I realize I have not had a good chat with Carol, my next-door neighbor. Awakened out of complacency, I am outraged when I learn the police have accidentally profiled an African-American acquaintance after a spate of neighborhood burglaries. She says I am naïve. We email energetically back and forth for a few days then drift back to our busy schedules and routines. Some of us talk of organizing to make our intersection safer, calling in our city representatives, building speed bumps.

Our neighborhood's natural resources remind me to think long-term. The young native Live Oak trees, symbols of environmental conservation with an eye to the long view, continue to grow and spread. The Monterey Pines are approaching seventy, eighty years, coming down one by one from age or illness to mark the end of an era. Turkey Hawks with their distinctive calls continue to fly high and proud but now seek fragile haven in the last of the tallest old pines and cypresses. Hummingbirds thrive like little jets in their own universe zipping in and out of gardens, scooping up nectar with their tiny sword-shaped beaks. In the wetter months, my children hunt and discover salamander families under the flat rocks right in the back of our garden.

The young trees in the Fire Zone are taller and fuller, approaching adolescence. Our children thrive. My digital community grows and connects me to those I rarely see. Halloween has become a joyous neighborhood gathering of familiar faces. The start-and-stop, connected-yet-disjointed sense of neighborhood continues. With each passing year, my experience of Upper Rockridge becomes richer and more interesting. I remind myself to stay vigilant of old habits and impulses and to actively nurture and rediscover this unique, peculiar place called home.

NEXT TIME you're at San Antonio Park, look over the grassy expanse
and picture a bear pulled from the Oakland hills fighting a bull to the
death. Right here in the 1850s such a thing happened, with a special
ferry bringing crowds over from San Francisco. But the rough mayhem
didn't stop there: there was also a bull ring, gambling, fandangos and
horse races. On Good Fridays, Judas was hanged in effigy. There were
even lynchings, with lumbermen called Redwood Boys, Redwoodites or
Redwood Rangers coming down from the hills to stop thieves and cattle
rustlers for once and for all.

Antonio Peralta was the son of Don Luis Maria Peralta who wound
up receiving this portion of his father's 45,000 acres. This area had a big
connection to the cattle industry. Here, hides and other products were

This photograph was taken from Independence Square (now San Antonio Park)
in 1868, looking towards the estuary.

OAKLAND HISTORY ROOM OF THE OAKLAND PUBLIC LIBRARY

shipped out through Brooklyn Basin . . . not to mention the lumber that was being cut in the hills. The wood was brought down via the street that in the hills is now called Park Boulevard and in the San Antonio stretch is 13th Avenue. In 1851, a settler named James LaRue arrived in town and bought the tract from Antonio Peralta. Three years later, it was subdivided under the name San Antonio.

OAKLAND HISTORY ROOM OF THE OAKLAND PUBLIC LIBRARY

Traffic jams used to look way cooler. This is East 12th Street near 22nd Avenue.

In 1856, the settlements of San Antonio, Clinton and Lynn (a shoe-making settlement named for Lynn, Massachusetts) merged to form one entity called Brooklyn. In 1870, the town of Brooklyn was incorporated, and two years later it annexed to Oakland. The Brooklynites agreed to the annexation, because they had been promised that the county seat, then in Alvarado, would be moved to San Antonio Park, then called Independence Square. For two years, the county seat *was* in San Antonio, although not in the park. Today you can still see the courthouse and the jail next to it (some sources refer to it as the "Hall of Records"—I'm sure those behind bars would have liked to know for sure) at International Boulevard and 20th Avenue. The yellow building with the red fence was the courthouse, now apparently apartments, and the one next to it, also yellow, was the county's first jail. Gray material now covers the first floor's double-brick security construction.

Another vestige of the old days you can visit is "Big Hollow." If you drive along International Boulevard and notice the big dip at 14th Avenue, you've found it. A wooden bridge on stilts used to span this expanse, and had a lively history. A 1927 *Tribune* article reports that someone in the 1800s dumped a body off the bridge, only to be stabbed moments later by a woman with a stiletto.

San Antonio is a very diverse neighborhood today, with Asians, Latinos, Ethiopians, Cambodians, African-Americans, Thai, Native Americans and whites all living together. In 1976, the *Oakland Tribune* characterized San Antonio as "primarily black"; by 1992, it was calling it the "new China-town," as many Chinese were finding cheaper rent and available space in San Antonio. At one point, it was reported that 34 languages were spoken in San Antonio.

Soccer weekend

BY MANUEL LOPEZ

There is nothing like kicking
that soccer ball around
San Antonio Park.

We have a team
from work; we just play
each other

Swift feet,
fast bobs,
and then we all get in our cars

for pizza and beer
afterwards at the Leaning
Tower of Pizza

Sweating and happy
Tired and alert
we always rib Danny

about his two
left
feet.

No good reason

BY DONOVAN HOCH

She lived on Gleason Street
and that's where I kissed her
the first time, while her parents
tried not to watch out the window

I lived on Commerce
and that's how I knew her
and my parents were waiting up
at the window for me to come home

And now she and I
watch out the window
when our daughter says goodnight
to someone we don't trust

ADVERTISEMENTS FOR this hills neighborhood were obviously geared towards the wealthy. "Is your fortune growing as rapidly as Oakland?" asked an undated ad for Country Club Park, continuing on in a grandiose vein, "Through the centuries, the tide of commerce has ebbed and flowed—following always the natural channels of travel—seeking

This circa 1928 brochure is for the company that insured all the lots in Country Club Park.

always the centers of population—in each century men and women of keen vision have taken advantage of this flow of commerce—have studied the natural laws governing the growth of commercial centers. And as a result, they have built the large fortunes of their time. Now you can buy insured lots in Country Club Park with the certainty that its value has nowhere to go but up!"

The tract took its name from two nearby country clubs: the Oak Knoll Country Club and the Sequoyah Country Club.

Sequoyah was not far from three different motor plants (Fageol, Durant and Chrysler were nearby, with Chevrolet a little further), and it was the rise of the car that made access to this hills neighborhood possible. "It was not an earthquake, but . . . with the advent of the automobile, our beautiful foothills just naturally got up and moved closer to the bright lights of Broadway," joked an April 1923 ad. "Since then, those who could afford a 'gasoline Pullman' or a 'tin Lizzie' have taken advantage of Nature's generous gift—the oak-adorned foothills of Oakland, with the marvelous panorama of the city below."

Lots here were generally bigger than in some other areas of the city. Sequoyah Hills, for instance, offered half, three-quarter and acre estates. That tract was planned before World War I and resumed sale in 1923, when many folks were flush with wartime industry dollars. Said the builder, "No homesite has less than 100 feet frontage, with an average of 125 feet. Not more than one home per lot. No flats or apartments or stores. No home can be built for less than $7,500 independent of the cost of the lot."

A March 1924 ad for Sequoyah Hills praised the "large, scenic lots, commanding a wonderful view of the verdant hills of the magnificent Country Club Estate and of the San Francisco Bay. A panorama such as only 'Oakland-Most Beautiful of World Cities' has to offer. No fog, no dust, no roar of city traffic. Protected by rigid building restrictions. Many palatial residences already built."

An April 1926 ad for Sequoyah Highlands, where each lot fronted on Golf Links Road, stated, "One has but to see this spot to be convinced of its future. Many have called it the Beverly Hills of Central California."

Durant Park Highlands, a tract located between the Sequoyah golf course and the municipal golf course (at Lake Chabot), consisted of lots where 80 percent had an "unobstructed view of the Oakland skyline with Tamalpais, San Francisco, Burlingame and Redwood City visible in the

OAKLAND HISTORY ROOM OF THE OAKLAND PUBLIC LIBRARY

Two women play the links at Sequoyah Country Club in this vintage postcard.

background. The crest of the property immediately overlooks the new St. Mary's college site, and many East Oakland subdivisions, the scene of Oakland's greatest home building activities," reported the newspaper in an undated article in the Oakland History Room.

Sequoyah also encompasses Oak Knoll, where a naval hospital stands. The hospital was built in 1942 as temporary wooden barracks on the site of the Oak Knoll Golf Course, housing injured men returning from the Pacific during World War II. It expanded during and after the war, becoming an established naval hospital. It was closed in 1996.

L. Ron Hubbard, the founder of Scientology, was a naval officer hospitalized at Oak Knoll. There, he availed himself of his ill compatriots to test out his theories of removing mental blocks to allow them to improve.

Sequoyah

BY SISSY ACTON

Dreams melt into grassland
and the wind ruffles all those dreams
and we are hearing the thoughts
of all those before

Everyone had the same thought:
live with your own house
and be happy

I am lucky my grandfather
bought in and that when he died
and grandma died, my parents
didn't want the house and I am
the only child.

My dreams are here.
Grandma and Grandpa are here.
The grasslands flutter with
everyone's footsteps

the lucky ones
who live here

Stars

BY MARK ROGERS

Stars at night
and stars reflected
in the city lights below

surrounded by light

a holy broadcast
from earth and man

natural and unnatural

earth brings sky
to the dark mirror
and we all three look

STONEHURST IS named for Lysander Stone, a pioneer who came to the area in 1847 by wagon train. Gold seeking didn't do much for him. Before settling here, he threaded mule trains through the rough terrain of the Sierra, and then finally decided agriculture was the way to go. He set up shop on 250 acres, and the newspaper reported in May 1922, "His splendid cherry orchard became one of the show places of the county and for miles around people came in the spring time to see the apricot orchard in bloom." His ranch encompassed both today's Elmhurst and Stonehurst. He had bought the land from a man named Daniel Webster, who in turn had bought it from the Peralta grant in the 1870s.

An August 1910 advertisement calls Stonehurst "the paradise of Oakland and Alameda County: a subdivision which stands like a Pompeiian pillar, conspicuous by itself." It contained a "special mention: each lot

OAKLAND HISTORY ROOM OF THE OAKLAND PUBLIC LIBRARY

An estate in Stonehurst. Undated photo.

contains either cherry, apricot, plum, peach, pear, orange or apple trees. All bearing luscious fruit."

One of Stonehurst's subdivisions was Iveywood, described in a 1911 advertisement as the "Cream of East Oakland." One of the selling points of this land was the Southern Pacific Electric Loop system which was underway, a faster way to run trains—when completed, developers boasted it would be possible to reach downtown in less than 12 minutes

Note the windmill at the end of the street in this circa 1910 postcard.

and San Francisco's ferry building in 36. The ad stated, "We know . . . that if you are interested in real estate a salesman will not even have to tell you anything about the tract. The property itself at the prices we are asking is our best advertisement." These lots, though, were only available to certain persons; restrictions prohibited "the sale of a lot to Chinese, Japanese, Hindus, Negroes or people of their type."

Another 1911 ad for Iveywood made a big promise. "To the man or woman desiring to own a lot that will increase in value very rapidly let us start out by saying this is the most important real estate announcement you have ever read or will ever read."

An August 1920 ad harked back to the tract's early days by stating the lots had "cherry, apricot, peach and other trees. The very richest of valley loam soil. Will raise vegetables of every description." Another ad that same month reinforced the idea: "One can go to Stonehurst and build their little home there and save the high rents, raise their own vegetables, chickens and fruit and really enjoy health and perfect happiness."

By August 1923, Stonehurst was pretty well settled according to this ad: "Hear Ye! Hear Ye! Hear Ye! Stonehurst at 104th Avenue and East 14th Street [today's International Boulevard] to be closed out. Fine lots will be closed out as low as $250 . . . . Buy now and stand on your own ground."

In the 1940s, Federal Housing Authority monies could help with home purchasing in Stonehurst. Hawthorne Gardens was one of the subdivisions selling at that time, located at today's International Boulevard and 102nd Avenue. Homes sold there for $4,300–$5,250 in 1941, all approved for wartime funding.

The Durant motor plant was situated in this neighborhood on International between 105th and Durant avenues. At various times connected with Buick, General Motors, Cadillac and Chevrolet, William C. Durant began transportation operations as a horse carriage company. He produced cars at the Durant plant beginning in 1921, and by 1928, the plant's 1,000 workers were spitting out 3,500 cars a month. But this feisty company could not fight the Great Depression and the declining market, and Durant Motors failed in 1933. (Eastmont's Chevrolet plant, where the mall is today, survived a little longer, into the late 1950s.) Afterwards, the man who had wheeled and dealed with the biggest men of automobile production became convinced that bowling alleys were the wave of the future. He owned several alleys in Flint, Michigan, before his death in 1947.

Short poem

BY RUDY GRAY

I don't know what to write about anything
My teacher told me to write about where I live
I live in Stonehurst and that's enough to say

Ain't it?

What was here

BY SOPHIE BENNETT

Oranges and cherries and pears and plums
Things to gather

Autos and gears and brakes and wheels
Things to drive

Neighborhoods, people, homes and lives
Things to remember

TEMESCAL

WHERE: *Centered around*
Telegraph Avenue and 51st Street

THE TEMESCAL story begins with the Huchiun Indians, who built a village on the banks of Temescal creek. One of their religious practices was to sit in a sweathouse and then rush out to plunge into the cold waters. The word "temescal" is an Aztec word for sweathouse, which was then adopted by the Spanish who later settled in the area.

Next came the Peraltas. Vicente Peralta's dirt floor adobe house stood here in 1836, behind present-day 5527 Vicente Street.

Around that time, other types of settlers began arriving. Solomon Alden was one of these. In 1832, he bought land from Vicente Peralta, and in 1868 began dividing his land into tracts, hearing word about the horsecar line being extended to the area. The Temescal library was called the Alden branch in his honor.

The interior of Caesar Orio's store at 5010 Telegraph Avenue, undated.

The interior of the Liberty Bakery at 43rd and Telegraph. Stefano Persoglio is on the right. Undated.

By 1870, sure enough, a horsecar barn was erected at 51st and Telegraph, with 52 horses. A horsecar driver at the time worked 14 hours a day, seven days a week, for the weekly pay of $16. The trip itself cost a rider 5 cents. By 1892, horsecars were phased out in favor of streetcars, which themselves were abandoned in 1948.

By the early 1870s, Italian immigrants began moving to Temescal, building its character as a strongly Italian one and giving Temescal the nickname "Little Italy." A testament to that influx is Colombo Hall, opposite the DMV on Claremont Avenue, built in 1951. The Genovese fraternal organization was established in 1920 with 36 members and originally met in a different location. Today there are 900 members.

In the 1860s there were many cigar factories in the area to employ the immigrants, as well as garbage collection services. Italians began the Oakland Scavenger Company and ran a steamship to dump trash at sea, a practice fortunately halted during World War II.

Settlers planted fruits and vegetables, which of course led to the industry of packing and canning. At one time, Oakland's fame was that it contained the largest cannery in the world, the Josiah Lusk Canning Company at Claremont and 51st. Employing close to 1,000 workers, the cannery produced 3,000 cases of canned fruit or vegetables daily. It operated for 20 years, starting in 1868. Many Chinese immigrants worked in the cannery but due to housing restrictions were not allowed to live in Temescal and instead settled in Chinatown.

In 1897, Temescal became a part of the city of Oakland.

Besides the cannery, a few cool things in Temescal that no longer exist are an observatory tower that stood at the site of Global Entertainment and burned in the 1800s and a free-flowing creek. Once, the banks of Temescal Creek were 100 feet across from each other, and the water was deep enough to swim and catch salmon in. Nearby was the Bilger Quarry, at the corner of Pleasant Valley Road and Broadway, which employed many of Temescal's Italian workers.

The Cannery

BY REBECCA STURGIS

I like to think of all the fruit they canned here,
the flies that must have gathered,
the sticky syrup on the workers' aprons.

It must have been an odor they would
never forget, coming home smelling sweet,
like bartenders up until a few years ago
used to go home smelling of smoke.

They must have brought home
dented cans. They must have gone to the boss
to recommend that he hire their sister
or their cousin or their father's half-uncle.
Sweetness. All around them.

Horses

BY REBECCA STURGIS

Whatever happened to the horses?
When they caught sight of their first
automobile, did they see that they would
sink from daily use to being something
only rich girls could afford, paddocked
far away in the hills? Did they know
the streets would no longer belong to them?
That an entire industry would also
die along with them, the blacksmiths
who made their shoes, the livery men,
the hay men, the muckers?

Maybe they were tired of pulling things
and getting whipped. Maybe it was just
as well to step aside and let another
beast try.

But I bet in their stables now,
they think about it in awe, like
can you believe that really happened?
Hundreds of us in the streets,
interacting with humans,
making daily life possible?
To have that kind of easiness
in the city—what a mind-blower.

TRESTLE GLEN

WHERE: *The area along Trestle Glen Road to Mandana Boulevard, between Park Boulevard and Lakeshore Avenue*

ONCE, A stable of forty horses was housed on the upper reaches of Trestle Glen, their task to do nothing but grade the long stretch of Trestle Glen Road. Those horses did a great job: this area is one of the coziest spots in Oakland.

Trestle Glen was a subdivision formed as Lakeshore Highlands in 1917 by Wickham Havens and Walter Leimert. This subdivision fell along both sides of Trestle Glen Creek from Lakeshore Avenue to Park Boulevard. Trestle Glen Creek was called Indian Creek by the pioneers, because Native Americans lived along its shores where Trestle Glen meets Lakeshore Avenue.

The canyon was called Indian Gulch, which later formed a partial border between the lands of Vicente and Antonio Maria Peralta, two of

OAKLAND HISTORY ROOM OF THE OAKLAND PUBLIC LIBRARY

The double-decker streetcar was an elegant way to cross the canyon, circa 1895.

Horses grade Trestle Glen Road where it meets Lakeshore Avenue, circa 1918.

the four sons of Luis Maria Peralta who scored the entire East Bay as a gift from the Spanish government in 1820.

After that point, the land belonged to the Sather family. After Peder Sather died in 1886, his wife Jane allowed the land to be used as a park (and yes, she is the woman behind UC Berkeley's Sather Gate). In 1893, Borax Smith ran a trolley line up Park Boulevard, and the trestle that crossed the canyon gave the area its name. That trestle ran from the present-day Holman-Grosvenor intersection to the Underhills Road-Grosvenor intersection. (For more on the double-decker streetcars that once crossed the trestle, see the Highland listing.) Mark Twain was reputed to have been on the maiden voyage of the first car to cross the trestle over to Sather Park. In 1904, Borax not only brought picnickers to the area, he also bought it. Two years later, the trestle was dismantled.

In 1897, Trestle Glen was the site of a Salvation Army Camp meeting that was expected to bring a thousand people. One hundred fifty tents were set up with stoves, furniture and carpeting. The camps had been held there for the last six years and perhaps went on much longer.

Neighbors hoped that Trestle Glen, instead of being built up residentially, would be the site of a huge city park greenbelt, connecting Dimond Canyon, Mountain View Cemetery and Lakeside Park. Plans were actually underway in 1914, but financing issues quelled it. Mayor Frank K. Mott, proponent of the City Beautiful ideal, worked to make it happen, but the next man to occupy office, John L. Davie, was less interested, and in two years the subdivision was forming.

At least if there had to be houses, the tract could be beautiful. The sons of Frederick Law Olmsted were hired to lay it out. Their father was famed for his hand in the landscape design at Chicago's Columbian Exposition in 1893, New York's Central Park and, closer to home, Mountain View Cemetery where the landscaping is so beautiful that people are dying to go. Clearly, he passed a good amount of his sensibility to his sons, because while Lakeshore Highlands is heavily settled, it still feels expansive. The entrance gates at Trestle Glen and Longridge roads are made of wrought iron and still stand.

In 1918, Leimert took over and continued the building through the 1920s with other homebuilding companies. Lakeshore Highlands is home to some houses designed by Julia Morgan and Bernard Maybeck. This neighborhood, like so many, was subject to racial covenants that kept out minorities.

Much of Trestle Glen was still undeveloped in 1921. A visitor that year stated that after a 10-minute walk from the trolley tracks, he was in a "wild jungle," as far as the eye could see. He was lucky enough to stumble across a 20-foot waterfall.

In 1922, Trestle Glen Road hosted the California Complete Homes Exposition, with ten homes designed by renowned architects, and then of course available for sale after the Expo closed.

Nearby Crocker Highlands is named for millionaire William H. Crocker who bought the land from Hiram Tubbs (who built a grand luxury hotel in Clinton Park). Crocker was the son of Charles Crocker, one of the Big Four of transcontinental railroad building.

Sun Puddles

BY JUDITH OFFER

Felinely perfect, perfectly still,
Our apricot cat
Hugely guards the dollhouse door
Like Shaw's Egyptian God,
In a blaze of autumn afternoon.

Beneath the dining room window
The dog sprawls snoring,
Yelping from that far land
Where rabbits in meadowgrasses
Often get caught.

On quilts and pillows
Piled at the foot of her bed,
Hair damp after a long soak,
Our soccer goalie dreams away
That awful ball she missed.

Maiden voyage on the trestle

BY SANFORD AMES

A famous person on the train
is that writer Mark Twain

he takes it once across the trestle
and after that I guess he'll

have to make it back again
for as the light begins to wane

he'll have no way to safe return,
and stranded, he'll say "Durn!"

THIS NEIGHBORHOOD grew so fast that there's a wonderful tale to illustrate it. A December 1897 newspaper reported a doubtless apocryphal story about a man who went to sleep in a vacant lot and awoke to find himself "in the basement of a four-story building which was going up."

The district certainly benefited from its proximity to Fruitvale. "While the Twenty-Third Avenue district does not come within the precincts of Fruitvale, the avenue itself is a sort of dividing line between Oakland and Fruitvale . . . . The immediate vicinity of the local station is considered a most desirable business locality, and since being connected with the electric railway system, one round of lively traffic is in progress from morn to night," said a March 1893 newspaper article.

The trolley is on East 14th Street (now International) and 23rd Avenue is the cross-street by the bank (right) and the dry goods store (left).

Indeed, Twenty-Third Avenue was having "phenomenal growth" and the newspaper could reflect back on simpler times by December 1897: "Fifteen years ago there were a dozen or less homes where now there are a thousand. Snake fences, brambles and weeds held place where now Eastlake cottages, trim gardens and concrete walks prevail."

The district had the cotton mill, pottery works, bakeries . . . but few saloons. "The prohibition element is very strong in this community, but it has been whispered that if one entered the places where 'root beer' signs were rampant and asked for that innocuous beverage with a manner resembling [writer] Bret Harte's 'Heathen Chinee'—his 'smile that was childlike and bland'—a root beer would appear the like of which was never before seen—as root beer," reported the newspaper in 1897, well before the established Prohibition of 1919–1933.

Two other developments were the Grande Vista Terrace at East 26th Street and 24th Avenue and Latham Terrace at East 22nd Street and Twenty-Third Avenue. Of the latter, an early brochure said, "The atmosphere in this part of the city is especially soft and pleasant. Notwithstanding the elevation, there is a marked absence of keen winds, and orange and other citrus plants in the vicinity thrive, and fruit comes to full maturity in the open air. This section of town has long been justly noted both for salubrious climate and for healthfulness. No miasmatic vapors gather on these heights."

In June 1911, hopes were high for the neighborhood. The paper reported, "Twenty-Third Avenue represents to the city of Oakland what Filmore streets [sic] represents to San Francisco. It is a well paved, electrolier lighted thoroughfare that is faced with stores on either side from its juncture with 14th Street to Twenty-Third street and beyond. The district has its own banks, political and improvement clubs, and its business men are always on the job and always wide-awake."

When Twenty-Third Avenue was extended to Hopkins (today, MacArthur), growth escalated, both residentially and commercially. Said a November 1916 newspaper, "Twenty-third Avenue is a happy combination of the useful and the beautiful." A branch library was once located at the corner of East 15th Street and 24th Avenue.

Here's an interesting item from December 1916 that seems to break a few laws: "The factories of the Twenty-Third Avenue district are working 12 hour shifts in place of eight hours, but of course the wages are based upon an eight-hour day. It simply means that the factories are so crowded with work that they are working a day and a half where for-

A fire draws a crowd at the Western Pacific tracks, Twenty-Third Avenue and East 12th Street. The fire was in May 1910.

merly they worked one day." To make matters worse, children worked there—and the mill workers worked a six-day week.

Although the neighborhood was fairly industrialized, it was still rustic enough for the newspaper to report this in May 1917: "Several fine patches of growing spuds may be observed these days bordering on E. 14th Street between Twenty-Third and Fruitvale Avenues. These spuds are not saying much, but they seem to make a noise like cheaper potatoes in the near future."

Twenty-Third Avenue Widow's Song

BY TISHA KENNINGS

Charcoal is the excrement of her old estate.
Examine the ruined ends of the wall
to find the widow's bones and her very last groan.

Five diamonds had she and a husband and land,
but all of her joy has the worth of sand.
Her diamond ring rests on some other hand.

Disapproval

BY MONA REICH

You thump that car around here one more time
vibrating the sidewalk and making my head hurt
I swear to God I will pull your pants up!

WATERFRONT

WHERE: At the foot of Broadway and along the waterfront, the Waterfront Warehouse District and Jack London Square.

WHY WAS Oakland not allowed access to its own waterfront for 60 years? And why was it in danger of never having access?

Because of one of our earliest residents, a plotter who machinated himself into mayor.

Horace Carpentier was a squatter in the mid-1800s, and he chose land near the Oakland waterfront on Vicente Peralta's property. When Peralta objected, Carpentier, who was an attorney, allegedly donned priests' garb (or at least described himself as a priest, depending on what source you look at), and tricked Peralta into signing a mortgage against himself.

So began Carpentier's scheming tenure in Oakland.

In 1852, he ran for California legislature. The now-defunct *San Francisco Call* newspaper reported that after the election, Carpentier himself was in charge of counting most of the votes! He claimed 519 votes in his

OAKLAND HISTORY ROOM OF THE OAKLAND PUBLIC LIBRARY

The Oakland estuary in 1894 was a quietly majestic place.

favor, even though a census 10 weeks prior to the election reflected only 130 eligible voters.

There were no chads in these days—tickets for Carpentier were yellow, while those for his opponent were white. The *Call* reported that the pile of tickets to be counted were yellow at the top, and one had to dig quite a bit to find a white ticket, even though many of the very last voters before the polls closed had voted "white." A man made an affidavit that he overheard someone saying he voted seven times, and that people were given a free ferry ride to San Francisco in exchange for voting for Carpentier.

Despite the doubt cast on that election, Carpentier still became a legislator, and one of his first acts was to introduce a bill for the incorporation of Oakland as a town. A 1928 newspaper article quotes a former county clerk reflecting: "The first the citizens knew of Oakland was through the name used in this bill. It was not such a bad name, for the community at that time was oakland: a beautiful woodland carpeted with flowers, a great many of them wild lupin."

An uncited document in the Oakland History Room states that Carpentier used the name Oakland to disguise exactly which town was being incorporated, so soon-to-be Oaklanders had no idea there was a bill pending that affected them. Whatever his motivation and no matter the despicable maneuvers Carpentier later made, he did one thing right in giving us the great name Oakland.

When Oakland was incorporated as a town, on May 4, 1852, it was to be run by a group of five trustees. The language of the act also specified that along with incorporation, wharves should be built. Carpentier already had his beady eye on the waterfront.

On May 17, a scant 13 days after incorporation, the new trustees granted Carpentier the entire waterfront (estimated at 10,000 acres) for a 37-year period.

In turn, he would pay the town $5, and build three wharves and a public schoolhouse. One of the wharves was to built at the foot of Main Street (now Broadway) and the others nearby. The prices residents would pay Carpentier for wharfing were not to exceed 5 cents for a footman, 20 cents for a horse or cow, and 40 cents for a loaded wagon. The following day, May 18, the vote was reconsidered and the ordinance was amended to remove the caps on wharfage fees. Apparently Carpentier worked hard on the trustees overnight.

Roughly a year later, on May 9, 1853, the people of Oakland called for a reform election to oust the trustees. This election was also tampered with. The townspeople rioted. Some of Carpentier's property was damaged, and he had the audacity to sue the town for relief.

By August 1853, Carpentier had constructed the schoolhouse and two wharves. Upon those tasks' completion, a new ordinance granted him the

Heinold's First and Last Chance saloon was where the literati came for their whiskeys. That's Johnny Heinold at the door—the saloon is still open today at the foot of Webster Street on the waterfront.

waterfront in fee simple forever, the 37-year cap apparently forgotten. Or was it? One guess is that Carpentier was angry about the riot, and thought, "Well, you thought 35 years was bad??! How about forever?" and convinced or paid his cronies to go along with it.

The town later filed a complaint against Carpentier for the third wharf he was supposed to build. He said he built it, which was accepted.

City Council asked for a legal opinion to be prepared to see if the waterfront grant to Carpentier was "good." The attorneys opined that it was, saying of the trustees' outright gift of the waterfront to Carpentier that "Such a course might be impolitic and unwise, but it would be a lawful exercise of power."

One guy owned all the waterfront.

In 1854, Oakland's incorporation was upgraded to city status. The trustee board was put aside in favor of a mayoral form of government—and guess who was Oakland's first mayor.

Carpentier apparently didn't consider owning a city's entire waterfront malevolent enough. He created a toll bridge across Lake Merritt and designed a 20-year monopoly on ferry service to and from San Francisco. When another ferry company, operating in San Antonio just outside Carpentier's waterfront boundaries, dared in 1858 to take a piece of that action, he launched a fare war. A year later, the competitor joined forces with him (and it doesn't take much to guess Carpentier got the better terms of that deal).

The waterfront was always lucrative property, but with the coming of the transcontinental railroad, the waterway was worth far more. He sold (for an undisclosed amount) to the Big Four, taking a seat on the board of directors of the Central Pacific Railroad.

Meanwhile, City Council had applied to the state legislature for a bill granting the waterfront back to Oakland. The bill passed, yet still the council made the bad decision to deal for the land it had already won. As part of the "Compromise of 1868," Carpentier conveyed title to all land to the newly formed Oakland Waterfront Company, which not coincidentally seated him as president with a controlling interest, so it and the railroad could sign a contract. The city was given title to a little bit of waterfront. In later years, the Southern Pacific Railroad, which ended up holding the land, agreed to give up claims of ownership to the land in exchange for a 50-year lease, which began in 1909. Finally, Oakland held control of its own waterfront. Today, the waterfront is managed by the Port of Oakland, which also controls the airport.

During Carpentier's stay in Oakland, he lived at a "sumptuous estate" at Third and Alice, according to the *Independent & Gazette*. He named Alice Street after his sister. He worked out of his law office in San Francisco. Carpentier was born in July of 1824, so in 1854 when he had manipulated the city out of its waterfront and become its first mayor he was only 30 years old!

He died in 1918 in his 90s. After he had made millions off Oakland, he returned to his native New York state, and also traveled extensively in the Far East. He gave generous bequests—but none to any Oakland institution.

As a side note, Borax Smith tried in 1916 to lease much of the waterfront for 99 years. But the beleaguered city had had enough. Mayor Davie told the Alameda County Civic Association, "I will fight to the last ditch, if necessary, to prevent the voters of this city from entering into a lease which will take out of their control property for which I have fought a lifetime and lost a fortune to secure for them." And just in case Borax didn't feel his seething anger, Davie added in no uncertain terms, "Any man who would turn over municipal lands for this damnable purpose ought to be taken out and hanged." He strode out of the meeting in silence.

One tiny structure along the Embarcadero, at the foot of Webster Street, holds enough history to make it seem larger than life. This is Heinold's First and Last Chance Saloon, built in 1880 as a bunkhouse for oystermen. Legend says it was built from the timbers of a whaling ship.

The still-operational bar memorializes the 1906 earthquake, with the sharp slant of the floor caused by the tremors and the clock stopped at 5:18 and never reset. Gas lamps and low ceilings complete the atmosphere.

According to the current owner, the back door once opened directly onto the water, and men were "shanghaied" through it. Shanghaiing was the practice of kidnapping someone to serve as a sailor. Often, drunk men would wake up to find themselves on a vessel already underway on a two or three year voyage.

The waterfront was once a very dangerous place where women never ventured, until about the 1920s or so. During Prohibition, Heinold's served mild hard cider. The name of the saloon comes about because it was, naturally, the first and last place to get a drink before stepping on or off ship.

As if that's not colorful enough, the bar had some pretty famous patrons, including its most beloved son, Jack London. Former owner Johnny Heinold paid for London to attend college to get him off the bar stool. London returned the favor by constantly returning to buy rounds and always sending his benefactor autographed copies of his new books.

Other illustrious patrons were President William Taft, Robert Louis Stevenson, Joaquin Miller, Ambrose Bierce and Alexander McLean, the model for Wolf Larsen in Jack London's *The Sea Wolf*. The saloon is reputed to be haunted.

Next to Heinold's is the Jack London cabin, reconstituted with logs from his 1987 Yukon cabin. We have half the logs; Dawson City in Canada has the other half.

Where there are sailors, there is typically prostitution and Oakland's waterfront was no exception. At the turn of the century, prostitutes generally banded together in brothels or in rows of shacks called cribs rather than working singly. The Fat Lady restaurant on Washington advertises itself as having once been "the wharf's busiest brothel." A crib prostitute in 1912 made 20 cents a trick, while brothel workers earned $1-$5 for the same act. At the time, the latter price was what most other working women could make in an entire week. Brothel prostitutes kept half and gave half to the madam. Although these women should have been filthy rich, few prostitutes ever made it past the pitfalls of alcohol and drugs—or everyday goods sold to them with outrageous markups by the madam.

Beginning in or around 1890, Oakland actually had a legalized red light district in the area bounded by Fourth, Seventh, Webster and Washington streets. Only 72 cities in the U.S. at the time tolerated prostitution as long as the women registered with the police and presented themselves to a doctor every four days for a venereal disease examination. The doctor would stamp the prostitute's booklet, which she could present to clients to show that she was clean. The booklets included her photograph and a description of her. Reports say that women initially mistrusted the system and would make faces for their photograph so they couldn't be recognized, but as they learned to appreciate the arrangement they would return to have their photos retaken. Many Oaklanders were not happy about the red light district and about the continued rise of the Red Plague (venereal disease). In 1913, the Red Light Abatement Act was passed. Anyone still practicing after that was given jailtime or charged $2,000 (an enormous amount at this time). Since whistle-blowers were given a percentage of that fine, the prostitution district was quickly dismantled.

Back to the waterfront proper, Jack London Village, a funky wooden network of shops and restaurants designed to look like a fishing village, was built in 1975 and torn down in 2002. With wood pilings, pedestrian bridges, outlooks and a view of the working waterfront, the village called to mind Jack London's youthful days as a sailor and oyster pirate, when he would raid people's nearby oyster beds under cover of night.

Jack London Square, on the other hand, is still doing its best to promote tourism. It was established for that very purpose in 1951. The U.S.S. *Potomac* is docked here, Franklin Roosevelt's yacht that is now a floating museum. Visible from the square are the enormous shipping cranes of West Oakland.

Stretching from Jack London Square the other direction is the more than 60 acres of the Oak to Ninth project. On the land sits the historic Ninth Avenue Terminal, Oakland's last remaining marine terminal. The terminal was built in 1930 and has been in continuous use since then. Proposed plans for the huge waterfront plot involve a private company tearing down the terminal and contradicting the Estuary Plan, created over five years by residents as a road map to open up the waterfront for public enjoyment. That battle reminds some of the Horace Carpentier days of private waterfront control.

A good news story is the Waterfront Warehouse District, declared a historic district in 2000. It encompasses about ten blocks roughly bounding the Produce Market, Madison Street, Third Street and Fifth Street. Its importance is due to the profusion of industrial and warehouse buildings that once busily shipped goods out of the estuary and the Third Street railroad line. The depot is still there on Third Street.

Ode to Jack

BY PETER KUNKA

Jack London is a man we admire
Because he walked the wire
and made us hold our breath
as he tried "to start a fire"

A bartender at Heinold's
paid for him to go to school
better than him sitting soused
upon a small black barstool

We named a square after him
and this is not mere gabbin'
you can go there and peer inside
his relocated cabin

And our good friend you should know
you are that meteor in magnificent glow
Any worry? You should ban it—
you are not that sleepy, permanent planet.

Boat Parade

BY DIANA IVERSEN

One of my favorite memories is sitting to watch the Boat Parade in December. There were so many people crowded around it was hard to see, so my boyfriend and I ducked under the windows of one of the seafood restaurants and walked along a little ledge until we were sitting, hidden from view from everyone, including the diners behind us and through the glass.

It was just so beautiful to watch the silent boats go by with their lights beaming, kind of surreal, really. We watched this quiet parade and reveled in our secret hiding place. When we began to kiss, it was like the boats were slow earthbound fireworks in my peripheral vision.

I love the boat parade. And I still love him.

WEST OAKLAND

WHERE: *Land west of Highway 980*
between the estuary and Highway 580

WEST OAKLAND's history is a rich one, full of many different ethnicities coming together to live in what was once a countryside landscape. West Oakland began as a few homes strewn under the oak groves and along the creek banks. There were two buildings at the Point, which would later become the railroad terminus and where the rails met the sea for further shipping. The Point, named for its jut of land, was at the foot of Seventh Street, which then became the region's commercial center. In later years Seventh Street would be the hub of cultural life with famous jazz clubs such as Slim Jenkins and the Creole Club.

One of the earliest West Oakland residents was James DeFremery, who was born in Holland in 1826 and arrived in San Francisco in 1849. His original nine-acre estate on Adeline Street was called The Grove because of the many trees he planted there. He died in 1899 at the age of 73, and

An apartment block on Seventh Street, undated.

OAKLAND HISTORY ROOM OF THE OAKLAND PUBLIC LIBRARY

his family continued to live in the house until 1910 when it was sold to the city. In the 1940s, it was used as a Hospitality House for servicemen. The home and grounds are today preserved as DeFremery Park. Some call it Bobby Hutton Park after the slain Black Panther Party member, since the park was used for Party barbecues and meetings.

In 1861, rail and ferry service began between San Antonio (today, the San Antonio neighborhood, but back then its own settlement) and San Francisco. The train connected to the ferry at the Point. After that, house prices in West Oakland rose 50 percent. Then in 1869, when the transcontinental railroad arrived, African-American families began settling near the Point, as many of the men worked as sleeping car porters.

And then things blossomed from there. The Long Wharf of the Central Pacific Railroad was opened at the Point, and the Mole, a wharf that was over a mile long, was built in 1881. By the late 1880s, there were nearly 600 African-Americans living in Oakland, more than in any California city other than Los Angeles.

"As to healthfulness, excepting in the immediate vicinity of the marshes, West Oakland will compare favorably with other parts of the city. Here the west winds blow fresh and pure from the bay before becoming impregnated with the poisonous gases of the marsh, which are then wafted over to the other sections of the city," a December 1891 article read.

It went on to praise the character of the residents: "Of several things West Oakland can justly boast. Its residents are progressive and public spirited. They are not sectional nor clannish. They do not envy the good that may come to other districts of the city by public improvements." This last bit refers to the fact that West Oaklanders were then rallying for public park to be created over the "foul, sewer-defiled marsh lying on the borders of the bay north of Sixteenth Street" and for new schools.

But another article pointed a finger at a few bad characters in July 1891, under the headline "West Oakland Morals: they are threatened by some gambling places." Objecting to a handful of saloons and gambling rooms, the article stated that West Oakland residents "look with disgust on the scenes of vice and shame that are daily enacted in the most open manner . . . Only a few days since, a railroad man employed in the West Oakland's yards carried his month's salary from the pay car to this notorious place [a room in the rear of a cigar store on Wood Street] and dropped every penny of it into the pockets of the patrons of the game, returning home to his family at an early hour in the morning, without a cent to support them for the month to come."

One of West Oakland's pioneering residents was Barbados-born William T. Shorey. In 1886, he was named commander of a sea vessel, a groundbreaking promotion. This was extraordinary, for a black man to be master of a ship only 20 years after slavery was abolished—and with largely white crews. The newspaper called him the "only colored captain on the Pacific coast." In 1907, his ship was caught between two typhoons, with winds so strong they actually took the sails off, and was later stuck in fog masking the fact the ship was only 20 feet off a reef.

OAKLAND HISTORY ROOM OF THE OAKLAND PUBLIC LIBRARY

Myrtle Street near 12th Street, 1913.

After the return to land, the crewmen told the newspaper that "nothing but Captain Shorey's coolness and clever seamanship saved the vessel." And indeed, tales of Shorey's success were often reported in the daily papers. He and his family, who often accompanied him at sea, lived at 1774 Eighth St., subsequently renumbered 1782. In fact, he once allowed his three-year-old daughter to "navigate" the whaling ship further north than any other whaler had penetrated that year. Shorey retired from commanding in 1909 and died in Oakland in 1919 at the age of 60. He and his family are buried in Mountain View Cemetery.

The 1906 earthquake brought many refugees to Oakland, and some of them settled in West Oakland, including many Italians who had formerly lived in San Francisco's North Beach neighborhood.

West Oakland began to take on an industrial feel rather than residential beginning in 1916 with the establishment of the Shredded Wheat Company factory at 14th and Union streets.

Another population boom came around wartime. "Large numbers of Portuguese, Greeks, East European Jews and blacks moved to West Oakland in the years just before and after World War I," reads a July 1982 article. Despite this mixing pot, West Oakland still was predominantly Black. "In the early 1920s, although San Francisco had more than double the population of Oakland, there were almost twice as many blacks in Oakland as in San Francisco. And Oakland, for most blacks, meant West Oakland," the article continued.

By the time of World War II, thousands of people who had been recruited to work for the Kaiser shipyards moved to Oakland. But when the wartime jobs vanished at peacetime, West Oakland began a rough patch where the vibrant community became economically depressed. Many homes were removed for construction of the large main post office, the Acorn housing project, the Nimitz freeway and BART, adding to the disjointed feel of this neighborhood trying to get its legs back under it.

Little sister on the 58 bus

BY JENNIFER KING

wrapped so tightly in my own suffering
          I hardly notice when little sister boards the bus
    her bottom lip's been   excommunicated from her fine
face
    small dark (thunder) cloud   behind bunched brows
     eyes flash where they should shine
        if I lift my love boweddown head a moment

I could see
             when she jerks her brother onto the bus
           shoves him into an available seat
    demands he be quiet   wait a minute
      I miss her drama   rewind my own
Can't look up   got to   flex my hand
    sore from holding a head/heart/back that wants me

gone
flexing   trying to ease an ache   I fail
    to see little sister's fish clench after she pays her(his)way
closed tight from giving.
    little sister throws herself onto the seat fixes a stony gaze
out the window   toward
        nothing knowing it's nothing
      while I compose an ending that has no future
me   too busy to see
the straight in little sister's back
        I miss her
resolution   to recognize nothing when she doesn't
see it
      I'm still trying to capture a haint

convince myself that unchecked dropping

                                is flying

   little sister smacks the sleep from her brother

signaling the end of the ride

          her arms block

his small attempt to get in front   try to move ahead of her

        wait a minute   youjustbetterwaitaminute

    little sister's leading the way

       she knows he doesn't know

            passing

               beneath my window

     mad   but going somewhere

                    out

in front

     where she belongs.

Fantasy

BY RALPH FENNO

At night the cranes stop lifting containers
they step into the water
and fish, long-legged as egrets,
they drink their fill
after all that work

ships still come in after midnight
and they wait until those
enormous cranes (some of the
biggest in the world)
get ready to lift the containers again